15

RN ZULU

# LEARN ZULU

C. L. SIBUSISO NYEMBEZI

REVISED AND ENLARGED EDITION

PIETERMARITZBURG
SHUTER AND SHOOTER

Shuter & Shooter (Pty) Ltd
Gray's Inn, 230 Church Street
Pietermaritzburg, South Africa 3201



First edition 1957
Fourth edition (revised and enlarged) 1972
*Eighth impression 1982*

ISBN 0 86985 021 0

Set in 10 on 12 pt Times Roman
Printed by The Natal Witness (Pty) Ltd, Pietermaritzburg
1360L

# PREFACE

This book is intended to help those who wish to learn Zulu. As a beginners' course, it excludes many of the more complicated constructions.

The book is based upon Prof. C. M. Doke's *Text Book of Zulu Grammar*, a book which all aspiring students of Zulu will find very useful.

Anyone wishing to attain fluency in, and mastery of, the language is advised to speak the language as often as opportunity presents itself. The help of a Zulu should be solicited in order to acquire correct pronunciation.

In this edition new material has been introduced which is designed to make this little book more useful to the beginner.

# CONTENTS

# CHAPTER 1

## SOME MAIN FEATURES OF ZULU

ZULU, the language of the Zulu people, is spoken throughout Zululand and Natal, the North-eastern Free State, the South-eastern Transvaal and the Witwatersrand area.

Zulu belongs to the Nguni group of South African Bantu languages. The Nguni group includes Xhosa and Swazi. Ndebele spoken in Matabeleland of Southern Rhodesia, Ndebele of the Transvaal and Ngoni spoken in Malawi are all dialectal forms of Zulu.

The following are some of the linguistic features of Zulu:-

1. Nouns are grouped into classes according to their prefixes. The prefixes are not indicative of sex. Zulu does not employ sex gender but class gender.

2. A word subordinate to a noun must show its agreement with that noun as to class and number. The element which brings about this agreement is called a concord.

3. Zulu syllables are open, i.e. they are either vowels or end in vowels. **m** does occur however, as a syllabic consonant without a vowel but it retains the length of a full syllable, e.g. *a-si-m-bo-na-nga* (six syllables).

4. Zulu has five vowels, viz. **a e i o u**.

5. Zulu is a tone language, i.e. words of different meaning but otherwise identical are differentiated by tone only.

6. There are many verbal derivatives and there is a high development of verb tenses.

7. Generally, the penultimate syllable of a Zulu word is lengthened.

8. Zulu employs click sounds.

## PRONUNCIATION

To acquire the correct pronunciation of the sounds in Zulu, it is recommended that wherever possible, the help of a Zulu should be enlisted.

### VOWELS

**a** is pronounced somewhat as in English "ark"; e.g. *idada* (duck).

**e** has two pronunciations: it is pronounced somewhat as in English "bed" or "bay" (depending on the following vowel); e.g. *bheka* (look), *ibhubesi* (lion).

**i** is pronounced somewhat as in English "ease"; e.g. *siza* (help).

**o** has two pronunciations: it is pronounced somewhat as in English "law" or "boat" (depending on the following vowel); e.g. *lola* (sharpen), *umgodi* (hole).

**u** is pronounced somewhat as in English "pool"; e.g. *umuzi* (village).

### SEMI-VOWELS

**y** is pronounced as in English "yes"; e.g. *uyise* (his/her/their father).

**w** is pronounced as in English "wall"; e.g. *iwele* (twin).

### CONSONANTS

**m** is pronounced as in English; e.g. *umama* (my/our mother).

**n** is pronounced as in English; e.g. *unina* (his/her/their mother).

**ny** is pronounced as in Vignette; e.g. *inyoni* (bird).

**ng** is pronounced as in English "finger"*; e.g. *ingane* (child).

**p** is pronounced somewhat as in English "speech"; e.g. *ipipi* (pipe for smoking).

**ph** is pronounced somewhat as "p" in English "pet" but more fully aspirated; never pronounced as in English "phone"; e.g. *pheka* (cook).

**t** is pronounced somewhat as in English; e.g. *itiye* (tea).

**th** is pronounced somewhat as "t" in English but more fully aspirated; never pronounced as in English "thing" or "this"; e.g. *thatha* (take).

**k** is pronounced somewhat as in English; e.g. *umakoti* (bride).

**k** is a sound between English "k" and "g"; e.g. *ukuza* (to come).

**kh** is pronounced somewhat as "c" in English but more fully aspirated; e.g. *ikhanda* (head).

**g** is pronounced more or less as in English "go"; never pronounced as in English "gem"; e.g. *ugogo* (grandmother).

**b** is pronounced with implosion; the movement of the muscles approaches more or less that when smoking a pipe; e.g. *ubaba* (my/our father).

**bh** is pronounced more or less as in English "bed"; e.g. *bhala* (write).

**d** is pronounced more or less as in English "duck"; e.g. *idada* (duck).

---

*In certain areas a difference is made with some Zulu words in which the pronunciation is that in English "sing"

**f** is pronounced more or less as in English "fun"; e.g. *ifu* (cloud).

**v** is pronounced as in English "van"; e.g. *vala* (close).

**s** is pronounced as in English "say"; never as in English "rose"; e.g. *isisu* (stomach).

**sh** is pronounced as in English "shall"; e.g. *ishumi* (ten).

**h** is pronounced as in English "hand"; e.g. *hamba* (go); in other words it is a voiced sound; e.g. *ihashi* (horse).

**l** is pronounced as in English "laugh"; e.g. *lala* (sleep).

**hl** is pronounced as in Welsh "ll" in "Llanelly"; e.g. *hlala* (sit).

**dl** is the voiced form of hl; e.g. *ukudla* (food).

**tsh** is pronounced somewhat as in English "chin"; e.g. *utshani* (grass).

**j** is pronounced as in English "Jack"; e.g. *uju* (honey).

Some of the consonants may appear in combination with **m** or **n**; e.g. **mb, mp, nt, nd, ns, nz,** etc.

**kl** To pronounce this sound:

(i) Raise the back of the tongue against the soft palate.

(ii) Keep the front part of the tongue down behind the lower teeth.

(iii) Force air through the closure caused by raising the back of the tongue against the soft palate. e.g. *klwebha* (scratch); *klaya* (split).

## CLICK SOUNDS

**c** To pronounce this sound:

(i) Place the tip of the tongue against the upper front teeth and gum.

(ii) Depress the centre of the tongue.

(iii) Release the tip of the tongue drawing it slightly backward. This is the click heard in English "tut-tut". e.g. *cula* (sing), *iculo* (song, hymn).

**q** To pronounce this sound:

(i) Press the upper part of the tongue-tip against the part between the teeth ridge and the hard palate.

(ii) Raise the back of the tongue so that it touches the soft palate.

(iii) Depress the centre of the tongue.

(iv) Release sharply downwards the tip of the tongue, e.g. *qala* (start, begin), *qeda* (finish).

**x** To pronounce this sound:

(i) Place the upper part of the tongue-tip against the part between the teeth ridge and the hard palate.

(ii) Raise the back of the tongue towards the soft palate.

(iii) Withdraw one side of the tongue from the upper teeth, e.g. *xoxa* (chat, converse); *ixoxo* (frog).

This sound is generally used in urging a horse.

| | | | |
|---|---|---|---|
| When aspirated these clicks are written | **ch** | **qh** | **xh** |
| Nasalised they are written .. .. | **nc** | **nq** | **nx** |
| With voicing .. .. .. .. | **gc** | **gq** | **gx** |
| Voiced forms with a nasal .. .. | **ngc** | **ngq** | **ngx** |

# CHAPTER 2

## COMMANDS

The following are some action words (verbs) of Zulu:

*funda* (read)
*sebenza* (work)
*lima* (plough)
*thunga* (sew)
*gijima* (run)
*geza* (wash)
*luma* (bite)
*cabanga* (think)
*bala* (count)
*biza* (call)
*khumbula* (remember)
*cula* (sing)
*bopha* (tie)
*phumula* (rest)
*khetha* (choose, select)
*sheshisa* (act quickly)
*thatha* (take)
*khombisa* (show)
*basa* (kindle fire)
*siza* (help)
*shanela* (sweep)
*hleka* (laugh)
*thenga* (buy)
*bulala* (kill)
*landa* (fetch)
*letha* (bring)
*khanyisa* (light)
*bamba* (catch)
*thwala* (carry)
*landela* (follow)
*donsa* (pull)
*hamba* (go)
*pheka* (cook)
*gibela* (ride)
*thanda* (like, love)
*phinda* (repeat)

These action words may be used, unchanged, as commands to a single person; e.g.:—

*funda!* (read![1])
*gijima!* (run![1])
*letha!* (bring![1])
*phinda!* (repeat![1])
*sebenza!* (work![1])
*phumula!* (rest![1])
*biza!* (call![1])
*cabanga!* (think![1])

[1]Singular

If the command is given to more than one, these action words take *-ni* in final position; e.g.:—

| | |
|---|---|
| *fundani!* (read![2]) | *sebenzani!* (work![2]) |
| *gijimani!* (run![2]) | *phumulani!* (rest![2]) |
| *lethani!* (bring![2]) | *bizani!* (call![2]) |
| *phindani!* (repeat![2]) | *cabangani!* (think![2]) |

Some of the action words have one syllable only. When used in commands, these words change as follows:—

| | | |
|---|---|---|
| *-ma* (stand, stop) | > | *yima!* (stand![1]) |
| *-dla* (eat) | > | *yidla!* (eat![1]) |
| *-zwa* (hear, feel) | > | *yizwa!* (hear! feel![1]) |
| *-za* (come) | > | *yiza!* (come![1]) |
| *-lwa* (fight) | > | *yilwa!* (fight![1]) |
| *-pha* (give) | > | *yipha!* (give![1]) |
| *-fa* (die) | > | *yifa!* (die![1]) |
| *-kha* (pluck. pick, draw water) | > | *yikha!* (pluck, pick, draw![1]) |
| *-sha* (burn) | > | *yisha!* (burn![1]) |
| *-mba* (dig) | > | *yimba!* (dig![1]) |

Although there are variants in the case of the one-syllable action words, these variants will not be given at this stage.

In the plural these commands also add *-ni* in final position:—

| | |
|---|---|
| *yimani!* (stand![2]) | *yidlani!* (eat![2]) |
| *yizwani!* (hear![2]) | *yizani!* (come![2]) |
| *yilwani!* (fight![2]) | *yiphani!* (give![2]) |
| *yifani!* (die![2]) | *yishani!* (burn![2]) |

---

[1]Singular [2]Plural

Zulu has action words which commence in a vowel. These action words may take *y-* initially when used as commands, e.g.:—

-*akha* (build) > *akha!* or *yakha!* (build![1])
-*enza* (make, do) > *enza!* or *yenza!* (make/do![1])
-*ala* (refuse) > *ala!* or *yala!* (refuse![1])
-*osa* (roast, grill, toast, fry) > *osa!* or *yosa!* (roast, etc.![1])
-*eqa* ( jump) > *eqa!* or *yeqa!* ( jump![1])

In the plural *-ni* is suffixed:—

*akhani/yakhani!* (build![2]) *enzani/yenzani!* (make ![2])
*alani/yalani!* (refuse![2]) *osani/yosani!* (roast, etc.![2])
*eqani/yeqani!* ( jump![2])

### Exercise 1

(*a*) Revise all the verbs given above.

(*b*) Use these verbs in commands, singular and plural.

(*c*) A few nouns are given below with which you may practise your commands. The noun *must follow* the verb;

N.B. Zulu does not have the indefinite and definite articles 'a' and 'the'. For instance *funda* means read or learn; *incwadi* means book, letter. A command may be expressed using these two words by simply juxtaposing them: *funda incwadi* (read book/letter). From your knowledge of English you will be able to determine which article to use in a given situation.

More examples:

*landa* (fetch) *iposi* (mail) — *landa iposi* (fetch mail)
*letha* (bring) *isibane* (lamp) — *letha isibane* (bring lamp)
*biza* (call) *umfana* (boy) — *biza umfana* (call boy)

---

[1]Singular [2]Plural

A proper name may be prefixed to the command, e.g. *James, funda incwadi* (James, read book/letter). *Frank, landa iposi*! (Frank, fetch mail!)

| | | |
|---|---|---|
| *incwadi* (book/letter) | *iposi* (mail) | *umlilo* (fire) |
| *amalahle* (coal) | *inyama* (meat) | *abantu* (people) |
| *amanzi* (water) | *ihashi* (horse) | *inja* (dog) |
| *indlu* (house/room) | *inqola* (wagon) | *amatshe* (stones) |
| *isibane* (lamp) | *itiye* (tea) | *inyoka* (snake) |
| *abazali* (parents) | *ubisi* (milk) | *izimvu* (sheep) |
| *umntwana* (child) | *ukudla* (food) | |

*izingubo* (dresses/clothes) *insimu* (field/cultivated land)
*iculo* (song/hymn/hymn book) *impahla* (parcel/goods)
*izitsha* (dishes/utensils)

(*d*) Translate into Zulu:—(N.B. In the English sentences articles have been used. Ignore them when translating into Zulu.)

1. Help[1] the parents. 2. Bring[2] the stones. 3. Fetch[1] the water. 4. Kill[2] the snake. 5. Wash[1] the dresses. 6. Show[2] the child. 7. Ride[1] the horse. 8. Sweep[2] the house. 9. Tie[1] the dog. 10. Hear[2] the parents. 11. Make[1] tea. 12. Build[2] the house. 13. Roast[1] the meat. 14. Give[2] the child. 15. Sing[2] the hymn.

(*e*) Translate into Zulu:-

1. Mary bring coal. 2. James, fetch the horse. 3. Jane, make (kindle) the fire. 4. John, kill[2] the snake. 5. Annie, work. 6. Fred, sing. 7. Jerry, run[2]. 8. Ethel, catch[2] the dog. 9. Norah, wash[2] the dresses. 10. Mary, call the child. 11. Frank, stand. 12. Jane, come[2]. 13. Annie, cook[2] food. 14. Annie, cook meat. 15. Jerry, take the lamp. 16. Norah,

---

[1]Singular [2]Plural

sing a song. 17. Ethel, rest[2]. 18. Frank, go[2]. 19. Mary, sweep[2]. 20 Annie, count[2] the sheep. 21. Gertrude, sew[2] the dresses. 22. James, take stones. 23. James, speak.

## Noun Prefixes

For easy reference a complete list of noun prefixes is given below.

| *Class* | *Singular* | *Plural* |
|---|---|---|
| 1 | **um-, umu-** | **aba-** |
| 2 | **um-, umu-** | **imi-** |
| 3 | **i-, ili-** | **ama-** |
| 4 | **is-, isi-** | **iz-, izi-** |
| 5 | **in-, im-** | **izin-, izim-** |
| 6 | **u-, ulu-** | **izin-, izim-** |
| 7 | **ub-, ubu-** | |
| 8 | **uk-, uku-, ukw-** | |

[1]Singular [2]Plural

# CHAPTER 3

## THE NOUN

STUDY the following nouns:—

| | |
|---|---|
| **umu-***ntu* (person) | **aba-***ntu* (people) |
| **um-***fazi* (married woman) | **aba-***fazi* (married women) |
| **um-***fana* (boy) | **aba-***fana* (boys) |
| **um-***zali* (parent) | **aba-***zali* (parents) |
| **um-***numzane* (headman) | **aba-***numzane* (headmen) |
| **um-***fundisi* (teacher/parson) | **aba-***fundisi* (teachers/ parsons) |
| **um-***ntwana* (child) | **aba-***ntwana* (children) |
| **um-***zala* (cousin) | **aba-***zala* (cousins) |
| **um-***ngane* (friend) | **aba-***ngane* (friends) |
| **um-***limi* (farmer) | **aba-***limi* (farmers) |
| **um-***shumayeli* (preacher) | **aba-***shumayeli* (preachers) |
| **um-***sizi* (helper) | **aba-***sizi* (helpers) |
| **um-***lungu* (whiteman) | **abe-***lungu* (whitemen) |
| **um-***akhi* (builder) | **aba-***khi* (builders) |
| **um-***bazi* (carver/carpenter) | **aba-***bazi* (carvers/carpenters) |
| **um-***dlali* (player) | **aba-***dlali* (players) |
| **um-***fundi* (reader/learner) | **aba-***fundi* (readers/learners) |
| **um-***holi* (leader) | **aba-***holi* (leaders) |
| **um-***hedeni* (heathen) | **aba-***hedeni* (heathens) |
| **um-***pheki* (cook) | **aba-***pheki* (cooks) |
| **um-***khandi* (repairer) | **aba-***khandi* (repairers) |
| **um-***hloli* (supervisor/ inspector) | **aba-***hloli* (supervisors/ inspectors) |
| **um-***fowethu* (my/our brother) | **aba-***fowethu* (my/our brothers) |

| | |
|---|---|
| **um**-*fowenu* (your brother) | **aba**-*fowenu* (your brothers) |
| **um**-*fowabo* (his/her/their brother) | **aba**-*fowabo* (his/her/their brothers) |

This is what we notice about these nouns:—

(i) They are all personal.

(ii) The difference between singular and plural is not at the end of the word but at the beginning of it.

(iii) The initial part of the noun in the singular is **um-** or **umu**; in the plural it is **aba-** or **abe-**. These initial elements are called noun prefixes.

(iv) **Umu-** is used only when the noun stem has one syllable.

However, not all nouns in Zulu employ the prefixes **um-**, **umu-**; **aba-**, **abe-**. Eight classes of nouns occur according to their prefixes. All the nouns listed above in this Chapter belong to Class 1.

Although in listing the nouns above a hyphen has been used to separate the prefix from the stem, ordinarily the hyphen is not used in writing.

It is common in Zulu to derive nouns from verbs, and many nouns appearing above are derived from verbs; e.g.:—

| | | |
|---|---|---|
| *umzali* (parent) | < | *zala* (beget) |
| *umfundisi* (teacher/parson) | < | *fundisa* (teach) |
| *umfundi* (reader/learner) | < | *funda* (read) |
| *umlimi* (farmer) | < | *lima* (cultivate) |
| *umshayeli* (driver) | < | *shayela* (drive) |
| *umsizi* (helper) | < | *siza* (help) |
| *umakhi* (builder) | < | *akha* (build) |
| *umbazi* (carver/carpenter) | < | *baza* (carve) |
| *umdlali* (player) | < | *dlala* (play) |
| *umholi* (leader) | < | *hola* (lead) |

*umhloli* (inspector/ supervisor) < *hlola* (inspect)
*umpheki* (cook) < *pheka* (cook)
*umshumayeli* (preacher) < *shumayela* (preach)
*umkhandi* (mender/repairer) < *khanda* (mend/repair)

## CONSTRUCTION OF A SIMPLE SENTENCE

The normal order in a sentence is subject-verb-object. Examine the following sentences:—

The boy likes the child — *Umfana* **u**-*thanda umntwana.*
The horse likes the child — *Ihashi* **li**-*thanda umntwana.*
The dog likes the child — *Inja* **i**-*thanda umntwana.*

The three English sentences are alike except that a different subject has been used in each. This change of subject does not cause any change in the remaining part of the sentence as long as the subject remains singular in number. In the corresponding Zulu sentences, however, **u-** is prefixed to the verb in the first sentence, **li-** in the second and **i-** in the third. Why is that? It is because in a Zulu sentence, relationship of words to the governing noun must always be indicated. The verb must show definite relationship with its subject. Qualifying words must show definite relationship with the words qualified. The means for bringing about this relationship are prefixal elements attached to the different parts of speech. Because of their function of bringing about concordance, i.e. agreement, in the sentence, these prefixal elements are called concords. The concords in a particular class generally have a common sound occurring in them all.

In the three Zulu sentences above, the three nouns used as subjects belong to different classes. That is why the concords used with the verb differ, for each concord agrees with its particular subject. If we were to switch round the concords in the sentences above, our sentences would be wrong.

The concord showing relationship between subject and verb is called a subjectival concord.

In the following sentences, the subject in each case is a Class 1 noun.

1. *Umuntu* **u***thanda umfana* (The person likes a boy).
   *Abantu* **ba***thanda umfana* (The people like a boy).
2. *Umfundi* **u***funda incwadi* (The reader reads/is reading a book).
   *Abafundi* **ba***funda incwadi* (The readers read a book).
3. *Umzali* **u***bona abantwana* (The parent sees children).
   *Abazali* **ba***bona abantwana* (The parents see children).
4. *Umfowethu* **u***landa ihashi* (My brother fetches a horse).
   *Abafowethu* **ba***landa ihashi* (My brothers fetch a horse).
5. *Umfazi* **u***shanela indlu* (The woman sweeps a house).
   *Abafazi* **ba***shanela indlu* (The women sweep a house).
6. *Umpheki* **u***pheka ukudla* (The cook cooks food).
   *Abapheki* **ba***pheka ukudla* (The cooks cook food).
7. *Umkhandi* **u***donsa inqola* (The repairer pulls a wagon).
   *Abakhandi* **ba***donsa inqola* (The repairers pull a wagon).
8. *Umlimi* **u***lima insimu* (The farmer ploughs the field).
   *Abalimi* **ba***lima insimu* (The farmers plough the field).
9. *Umfundisi* **u***funa abahedeni* (The parson wants heathen).
   *Abafundisi* **ba***funa abahedeni* (The parsons want heathen).
10. *Umfowenu* **u***landela umnumzane* (Your brother follows the headman).
    *Abafowenu* **ba***landela umnumzane* (Your brothers follow the headman).

11. *Umakhi* **u***thwala amatshe* (The builder carries stones).
*Abakhi* **ba***thwala amatshe* (The builders carry stones).
12. *Umlungu* **u***gibela ihashi* (The whiteman rides a horse).
*Abelungu* **ba***gibela ihashi* (The whitemen ride a horse) .
13. *Umntwana* **u***cula iculo* (The child sings a song).
*Abantwana* **ba***cula iculo* (The children sing a song).
14. *Umfana* **u***letha iposi* (The boy brings mail).
*Abafana* **ba***letha iposi* (The boys bring mail).
15. *Umshumayeli* **u***khanyisa isibane* (The preacher lights a lamp).
*Abashumayeli* **ba***khanyisa isibane* (The preachers light a lamp).

## EXERCISE 2

1. Translate into Zulu:-

| | | | | |
|---|---|---|---|---|
| The/A | person/ people | | the/a | child/ children |
| | woman/ women | likes/ like | | friend/ friends |
| | minister/ ministers | strikes/ strike | | cousin/ cousins |
| | farmer/ farmers | wants/ want | | heathen/ heathen |
| | parent/ parents | calls/ call | | player/ players |
| | headman/ headmen | helps/ help | | boy/ boys |
| | builder/ builders | shows/ show | | your brother/ brothers |
| | my brother/ brothers | gives/ give | | my brother/ brothers |
| | whiteman/ whitemen | | | his brother/ brothers |

2. READ (*FUNDA*):

(a) *Umntwana ubona umlungu. Umlungu ugibela ihashi. Umlungu uthanda ihashi. Umlungu ugibela ihashi, ulanda izimvu. Umlungu upha izimvu amanzi.*

(b) *Umfazi ubasa umlilo. Umfazi ufuna ukupheka* (to cook). *Umfazi ufuna ukupheka ukudla, futhi* (also, moreover) *ufuna ukupheka inyama. Umntwana ulanda amalahle.*

(c) *Umfundisi ubiza umntwana. Umntwana ubona umlimi. Umntwana ulandela umlimi. Umlimi ubulala inyoka.*

(d) *Umzala ukha amanzi. Umzala ufuna ukugeza* (to wash) *izingubo, futhi umzala ufuna ukugeza izitsha.*

(e) *Umfowethu usiza umakhi. Umakhi ufuna amatshe. Umakhi ulanda amatshe. Umakhi ufuna ukwakha* (to build) *indlu. Umakhi ukhetha amatshe. Umakhi ufuna futhi amanzi. Umakhi ulanda amanzi. Umakhi uthatha inqola, ulanda amatshe, futhi ulanda amanzi. Umakhi ukhombisa umfowabo amatshe. Umakhi uthanda ukusebenza* (to work).

(f) Read (a), (b), (c), (d) and (e) again but change singular subject into plural.

3. Revise section on Commands. If a noun precedes a command its initial vowel is dropped. Remember that the subjectival concord is not used in commands, e.g.:—

(a) *Mfazi, geza izingubo!* (Woman, wash clothes).
(b) *Mfowethu, landa iposi!* (My brother, fetch mail).
(c) *Mshumayeli, shumayela!* (Preacher, preach).
(d) *Bafana, bophani ihashi!* (Boys, tie up the horse).
(e) *Maggie, yenza itiye!* (Maggie, make tea).

(f) *John, lima ingadi!* (John, plough the garden—*ingadi*, garden).

(g) *Mshayeli, letha inqola!* (Driver, bring the wagon).

(h) *Mhloli, funda incwadi*! (Inspector, read the letter/book).

(i) *Makhi, bala amatshe!* (Builder, count the stones).

(j) *Lizzie, geza amafasitele!* (Lizzie, wash the windows—*amafasitele*, windows).

(k) *Bafowethu, yizani!* (Brothers, come).

(l) *Mzala, thenga amalahle!* (Cousin, buy coal).

4. Translate into Zulu: (a) Friend, bring the book. (b) Leader, choose the people. (c) My brother, rest. (d) Woman, be quick. (e) Preacher, sing a hymn. (f) Cousin, cook meat. (g) Whitemen, kill the snake. (h) Boy, light the lamp. (i) Parents, remember the children. (j) Heathen, follow the parson. (k) Brothers, catch the horse. (l) Helper, go. (m) Friend, take the food. (n) My brother, think. (o) Cousin, repeat. (p) Children, laugh. (q) Children, eat food. (r) People, come (s) Boys, stand. (t) Women, repeat the song. (u) Ministers, read the book.

5. Translate No. 4 again but change the number of the subject in every case, i.e. singular to plural and vice versa.

# CHAPTER 4

## THE NOUN (*Continued*)

### CLASS 1A

THERE are in Zulu nouns which are very much like Class 1 nouns in that the concords used are the same as for Class 1. The difference is in the prefix. The singular prefix is **u-** and the plural prefix **o-**. (Cf. Cl. 1 prefixes: **umu- aba-**).

Nouns occurring in this class may be grouped as follows:

(*a*) Proper names:—

| Singular | Plural | Singular | Plural |
|---|---|---|---|
| *uJames* (James) | *oJames* | *uJohn* (John) | *oJohn* |
| *uSipho* (Sipho) | *oSipho* | *uShaka* (Shaka) | *oShaka* |
| *uVusi* (Vusi) | *oVusi* | *uThoko* (Thoko) | *oThoko* |

The plural forms also have a collective or associative significance, e.g. *oJames* (i) more than one person of that name. (ii) James and those associated with him.

(*b*) Kinship Terms:—

| Singular | Plural |
|---|---|
| *ubaba* (my/our father) | *obaba* |
| *uyihlo*[1] (your father) | *oyihlo* |
| *uyise* (his/her/their father) | *oyise* |
| *umama* (my/our mother) | *omama* |
| *unyoko*[2] (your mother) | *onyoko* |

[1]Some people now resent this word and prefer *ubaba wakho* (sg.) *ubaba wenu* (pl.) (noun followed by possessive).

[2]Some people now prefer *umama wakho* (sg.), *umama wenu* (pl.).

| Singular | Plural |
|---|---|
| *unina* (his/her/their mother) | *onina* |
| *umalume* (my/our maternal uncle) | *omalume* |
| *ugogo* (grandmother) | *ogogo* |
| *ubabamkhulu* (my/our grandfather) | *obabamkhulu* |
| *uyihlomkhulu* (your grandfather) | *oyihlomkhulu* |
| *uyisemkhulu* (his, etc. grandfather) | *oyisemkhulu* |
| *udadewethu* (my/our sister) | *odadewethu* |
| *udadewenu* (your sister) | *odadewenu* |
| *udadewabo* (his/her/their sister) | *odadewabo* |
| *umkami* (my wife) | *omkami* |
| *umkakho* (your wife) | *omkakho* |
| *umkakhe* (his wife) | *omkakhe* |
| *umakoti* (bride) | *omakoti* |

(*c*) Foodstuffs (*See also page* 91):—

| Singular | Plural |
|---|---|
| *uanyanisi* (onion) | *oanyanisi* (varieties of) |
| *ubhontshisi* (beans) | *obhontshisi* (varieties of) |
| *uletisi* (lettuce) | *oletisi* (varieties of) |
| *ushizi* (cheese) | *oshizi* (kinds of) |
| *utamatisi* (tomatoes) | *otamatisi* (varieties of) |
| *ukhokho* (cocoa) | |
| *upelepele* (pepper) | *opelepele* (varieties of) |
| *usawoti* (salt) | |
| *ujamu* (jam) | *ojamu* (kinds of) |

*N.B.* These plural forms are hardly ever used.

(*d*) Miscellaneous (mainly imported nouns):

| Singular | Plural |
|---|---|
| *umakhelwane* (neighbour) | *omakhelwane* |
| *udokotela* (doctor) | *odokotela* |
| *unesi* (nurse) | *onesi* |
| *uthisha* (teacher) | *othisha* |
| *umentshisi* (matches) | *omentshisi* (kinds of) |

| Singular | Plural |
|---|---|
| *usikilidi* (cigarette) | *osikilidi* (kinds of) |
| *ugwayi* (tobacco) | *ogwayi* (varieties of) |
| *uphalafini* (paraffin) | |
| *uKhisimusi* (Christmas) | *oKhisimusi* |
| *ubani?* (who?) | *obani?* |
| *ujeke* (jug) | *ojeke* |
| *umese* (knife) | *omese* |
| *ukhiye* (key) | *okhiye* |
| *uthayela* (corrugated iron) | *othayela* |
| *uthayi* (neck-tie) | *othayi* |
| *ukhololo* (collar) | *okhololo* |
| *usofa* (sofa) | *osofa* |
| *ukotini* (cotton) | *okotini* |
| *upende* (paint) | *opende* |
| *umpompi* (tap) | *ompompi* |
| *ugesi* (electricity/electric lights) | *ogesi* |

Sentence examples:—

1. *UJames ubona inyoka* (James sees a snake).
   *OJames babona inyoka* (James and the others with him see a snake).
2. *USipho udonsa inqola* (Sipho pulls a wagon).
   *OSipho badonsa inqola* (Sipho and the others pull a wagon).
3. *Udadewenu uthwala amalahle* (Your sister carries coal).
   *Odadewenu bathwala amalahle* (Your sisters carry coal).
4. *Ugogo ukhumbula abantwana* (Grandmother remembers the children).
   *Ogogo bakhumbula abantwana* (The grandmothers/grandmother and the others remember the children).

5. *Umakoti ugeza izingubo* (The bride washes the clothes).

*Omakoti bageza izingubo* (The brides wash clothes).

6. *Umakhelwane uthenga ukotini* (The neighbour buys cotton).

*Omakhelwane bathenga ukotini* (The neighbours buy cotton).

7. *USipho ubona ubani? USipho ubona uJames.* (Whom does Sipho see? Sipho sees James.)

Learn the following verbs:—

*bonda* (stir, e.g. porridge)
*baba* (be bitter)
*banda* (be cold)
*bila* (boil)
*nakekela* (take care of)
*ncibilika* (melt)
*nonga* (flavour)
*phuma* (go out)
*phuza* (drink)
*bhema* (smoke, e.g. cigarette)
*bheka* (look/look after/look for)
*beka* (put, place)
*bola* (rot)
*nandisa* (make nice)
*ngena* (enter)
*nuka* (smell)
*qoqa* (collect)
*sefa* (sift)
*thela* (pour, e.g. water; also *thela itiye*, pour out tea).
*chathaza* (pour out part of, e.g. milk, sugar, etc.)
*caphuna* (scoop up, take part out of container, e.g. sugar, mealie meal; only used of solids).
*chitha* (throw out, e.g. water, refuse).

### Simple Sentence with no Adjunct

It is not always that we have an object or some other adjunct after the verb. When no adjunct appears, we insert *-ya-* between the subjectival concord and the verb, e.g.:—

(a) *Umama uyapheka* (Mother is cooking).
(b) *Abantwana bayadlala* (The children are playing).
(c) *Umkami uyathunga* (My wife is sewing).
(d) *Umzala uyahleka* (The cousin is laughing).

(e) *Umfowethu uyaphumula* (My brother is resting).
(f) *Usawoti uyababa* (Salt is bitter).
(g) *Umntwana uyacula* (The child is singing).
(h) *Umdlali uyagijima* (The player is running).
(i) *Abasizi bayasebenza* (The helpers are working).
(j) *Abangane bayahleka* (The friends are laughing).

### Negative Commands

To give a negative command, use *musa* followed by the verb with *uku-* prefixed (i.e. *musa* plus verb infinitive). e.g.
*musa ukufunda* (do not read) *musa ukuma* (do not stand)
*musa ukugijima* (do not run) *musa ukudla* (do not eat)
*musa ukusebenza* (do not work)
*musa ukulwa* (do not fight)
*musa ukuthwala* (do not carry)
*musa ukwakha* (do not build)
*musa ukwala* (do not refuse)
*musa ukosa* (do not roast)

In the plural *-ni* is added to *musa*; e.g.:—
*musani ukufunda* (do not read)
*musani ukuma* (do not stand)
*musani ukugijima* *musani ukudla*
*musani ukusebenza* *musani ukulwa*
*musani ukuthwala* *musani ukwakha*
*musani ukwala* *musani ukosa*

Notice how **uku-** becomes **ukw-** before a stem commencing in **-a**. This is also true of a stem commencing in **-e**. Before a stem commencing in **-o, uku-** becomes **uk-**.

In the negative the commands on p. 16 (3) would be:-
(a) *Mfazi, musa ukugeza izingubo.*
(b) *Mfowethu, musa ukulanda iposi.*
(c) *Mshumayeli, musa ukushumayela.*
(d) *Bafana, musani ukubopha ihashi.*
(e) *Maggie musa ukwenza itiye.*

(f) *John musa ukulima ingadi.*
(g) *Mshayeli musa ukuletha inqola.*
(h) *Mhloli musa ukufunda.*
(i) *Makhi musa ukubala amatshe.*
(j) *Lizzie musa ukugeza amafasitele.*
(k) *Bafowethu musani ukuza.*
(l) *Mzala musa ukuthenga amalahle.*

Note also that verbs in Zulu take the prefix **uku-** to convey the Infinitive; e.g.

| | |
|---|---|
| *ukufunda* (to read) | *ukusebenza* (to work) |
| *ukulima* (to plow) | *ukugijima* (to run) |
| *ukukhuluma* (to speak) | *ukudla* (to eat) |
| *ukubona* (to see) | *ukuma* (to stand/stop) |
| *ukulwa* (to fight) | *ukwakha* (to build) |
| *ukwenza* (to make/do) | *ukosa* (to roast/grill/fry) |

### Exercise 3

A. Learn the following subjectival concords:—

1st person—*ngi-* (I) singular; *si-* (we) plural

2nd person, *u-* [1] (you) singular; *ni-* (you) plural

Examples:—

*Ngibona abantu* (I see people).

*Sibona izimvu* (We see sheep).

*Ukhanyisa ugesi* (You switch on the electric lights).

*Nisiza ubaba* (You help father).

B. *FUNDA*:—

(i) *Umakhelwane uyathenga. Umakhelwane uthenga ubhontshisi. Ufuna ukutshala* (to plant). *Ufuna ukutshala ubhontshisi. Umlungu uyacaphuna. Ucaphuna ubhontshisi. Umlungu unika* (gives, i.e. hands over) *umakhelwane ubhontshisi. Umakhelwane uthatha*

[1] The subjectival concord 2nd person singular and Class 1 singular is *u-*. However there is a difference in tone. 2nd Person sg. *u-* has a low tone; 3rd person Class 1 sg. *u-* has a high tone.

*ubhontshisi. Umakhelwane uthanda ubhontshisi.*

(ii) *Umalume ufuna ugwayi futhi umalume ufuna umentshisi. Umalume uyathenga. Umalume uthenga ugwayi futhi umalume uthenga umentshisi. Umalume uthanda ukubhema* (to smoke). *Umalume ubhema ugwayi.*

(iii) *Ngibona ubani? Ngibona umama. Ngibona futhi udadewethu. Umama uyasebenza, uthunga izingubo. Umama uthanda ukuthunga* (to sew) *izingubo. Ngibona izingubo. Ngibona futhi ukotini. Udadewethu uyasebenza. Uyapheka. Udadewethu upheka iphalishi futhi upheka inyama. Udadewethu ufaka* (*faka*—put in) *usawoti, ufaka utamatisi, ufaka uanyanisi, ufaka upelepele; udadewethu unonga ukudla. Ubaba uthanda ukudla* (to eat) *iphalishi. Ubaba ufaka ushukela, futhi uthela ubisi. Ubaba futhi uthanda inyama.*

C. Translate into English: (a) *Jane, bonda iphalishi.* (b) *Caphuna ushukela.* (c) *Nonga inyama.* (d) *Sefa ufulawa.* (e) *Udadewethu uchitha amanzi.* (f) *Usawoti uyababa.* (g) *Umntwana uphuza ubisi.* (h) *Mzala, thela itiye.* (i) *Khanyisa ugesi.* (j) *Umlimi ufuna uphalafini.* (k) *Umfowethu uthanda ujamu, futhi uthanda ushizi.* (l) *Umakhi uqoqa amatshe.* (m) *Ngithanda ukhokho.* (n) *Unesi ufuna udokotela.* (o) *John, phuma! Landa amalahle. Ngifuna ukubasa* (to kindle) *umlilo.* (p) *Dadewethu, bheka abantwana.*

D. Translate into Zulu: (a) Uncle smokes cigarettes. (b) The children drink milk. (c) The woman buys beans and cocoa. (d) Throw out the water. (e) The boy follows the neighbour. (f) The white-man rides a horse. (g) The children are laughing. (h) My sister sweeps the house. (i) Be quick, I want tea. (j) The farmers are resting. (k) The parson hears a song. (l) The Inspector reads a letter. (m) The woman flavours the meat. (n) The boys are fighting. (o) My sister gives the child food.

E. Translate Exercise 2(4) making the commands negative.

F. Complete the following sentences by supplying the correct concord and translate into English: (a) Abaholi —funa ukubona abalimi. (b) Umhloli —biza abafana. (c) Abafundisi —khombisa abahedeni. (d) Abazali —funa ukulanda ushukela. (e) Umbazi —bala okhiye. (f) Uyisemkhulu —thanda ushizi. (g) Ugogo —yaphumula. (h) Abalimi —donsa amatshe. (i) Abelungu —funa ukulanda amafasitele. (j) Odadewethu —yacula. (k) Udokotela —yageza. (1) Onesi —siza odokotela. (m) Umakhelwane —funa ukuthenga amalahle. (n) Ubabamkhulu —yahleka. (o) Umkami —pheka iphalishi.

# CHAPTER 5

## THE USE OF NA- (AND, WITH)

BEFORE giving examples illustrating the use of *na-*, a few remarks are necessary on the behaviour of vowels. In Zulu, vowels are never found following one another in the same word. Sometimes words or parts of words have to be joined together, and in so doing two vowels may be juxtaposed. Then one of three things happens:—

(i) One of the vowels may be dropped or elided;
(ii) *y* or *w* (or occasionally *s* or *k* ) may be inserted to keep the vowels apart;
(iii) The vowels may merge or fuse and give rise to a new vowel.

The merging of vowels is called coalescence.

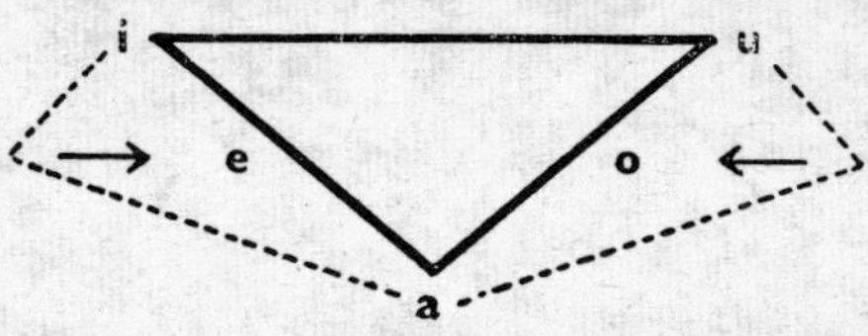


This diagram of Zulu vowels showing the three primary vowels *a, i, u,* and the secondary vowels *e, o,* illustrates the coalescence pattern. When coalescence takes place, it is always the primary vowel *a* which comes first, with the primary vowels *a, i* or *u* juxtaposed. The vowels which result from such coalescence are *a, e,* and *o* respectively. Thus $a + a > a$; $a + i > e$; $a + u > o$.

This explanation has been necessary because *na-* never stands by itself. It always forms one word group with the word to which it is prefixed. *Na-* ends in a vowel, and all nouns commence in vowels. Therefore prefixing *na-* to any noun, except Class 1a plural, will result in the juxtaposition and, usually, merging of vowels. However, in some negative constructions with *na-* there is no coalescence.

In Class 1a plural, the *-a* of *na-* may drop before the prefix *o-*, or the two vowels may be kept apart by using the semi-vowel *w*.

Examples:—

1. *Umuntu ubona uJames noSipho* (*na* + *uSipho*)—The person sees James and Sipho.

2. *Ngithanda ubaba nomama* (*na* + *umama*)—I love father and mother.

3. *Umfana ushaya ihashi nenja* (*na* + *inja*)—The boy hits the horse and the dog.

4. *Sifuna ukudla netiye* (*na* + *itiye*) (*funa*—want, look for)—We want food and tea.

5. *Abantu baphuza ubisi namanzi* (*na* + *amanzi*)—People drink milk and water.

6. *Ngifuna odadewethu nabafowethu* (*na* + *abafowethu*)—I want my sisters and my brothers.

7. *Umama uza namalahle* (*na* + *amalahle*)—Mother is coming with coal (i.e. bringing coal).

8. *Umfana ulwa nomzala* (*na* + *umzala*)—The boy is fighting with the cousin.

9. *Umfundisi udla nobaba* (*na* + *ubaba*)—The minister is eating with father.

10. *UJames uza neposi* (*na* + *iposi*)—James is coming with the mail.

11. *Umlungu usebenza nabakhi* (*na* + *abakhi*)—The Whiteman is working with the builders.

12. *UJane ugijima nesibane* (*na* + *isibane*)—Jane is running with the lamp.

13. *Ubaba ukhuluma nobani?* (*na* + *ubani?*) *Ubaba ukhuluma nomama* (*na* + *umama*)—With/to whom is father speaking? Father is speaking with/to mother.

14. *Umalume uza nobani?* (*na* + *ubani?*) *Umalume uza nomfundisi* (*na* + *umfundisi*)—With whom is uncle coming? Uncle is coming with the minister.

EXERCISE 4

Add *-ni?* to verb to ask question What? e.g.

*Ubonani* (*Ubona—ni?*)—What do you see? or What does he/she see?

*Uphekani* (*Upheka—ni?*)—What do you cook/are you cooking? or What does he/she cook? What is he/she cooking?

(1) FUNDA

A: *Ubona obani?*

B: *Ngibona abafowethu nawodadewethu. Ngithanda abafowethu nawodadewethu kakhulu* (very much). *Abafowethu nawodadewethu bathanda ukudlala.*

A: *Abafowenu nawodadewenu badlalani?*

B: *Abafowethu badlala ibhola* (ball, soccer) *kodwa* (but) *odadewethu bayagijima.*

A: *Uthandani?* (*u-* 2nd pers. sg.)

B: *Ngithanda ukudlala ibhola futhi ngithanda ukugijima.*

A: *Ubona obani futhi?*

B: *Ngibona futhi ubaba nomama. Ngithanda ubaba nomama kakhulu. Ubaba uyafunda.*

A: *Uyihlo ufundani?*

B: *Ubaba ufunda amaphepha nezincwadi* (*amaphepha*—papers; *izincwadi*—books/letters). *Ubaba uthanda kakhulu ukufunda amaphepha nezincwadi. Ubaba uthenga amaphepha nezincwadi. Umama uyasebenza.*

A: *Umama usebenzani?*

B: *Umama uyathunga.*

A: *Umama ukhuluma nobani?*

B: *Umama ukhuluma nobaba.*

A: *Umama uthungani?*

B: *Umama uthunga izingubo. Umama uthanda kakhulu ukuthunga futhi uthanda kakhulu ukupheka.*

A: *Umama uphekani?*

B: *Umama upheka inyama. Umama ufaka usawoti noanyanisi nopelepele notamatisi. Futhi umama upheka ubhontshisi nobhatata* (*ubhatata*—sweet potatoes—Class 1a.)

A: *Odadewenu basiza ubani?*

B: *Odadewethu basiza umama.*

2. Translate into English: (a) *Umama ucaphuna ushukela nosawoti; ufuna ukupha ugogo.* (b) *Udadewethu unonga ukudla; ufaka utamatisi noanyanisi nopelepele nosawoti.* (c) *Niphuzani? Siphuza itiye kodwa abantwana baphuza ubisi.* (d) *Abantwana bayagijima; bayadlala.* (e) *Umhloli uyabhema. Ubhemani? Ubhema usikilidi.* (f) *Umakhi uqoqani? Umakhi uqoqa amatshe; uthwala amatshe namanzi.* (g) *James, letha isibane nomentshisi.* (h) *Ngifuna ukulanda iposi nempahla.* (i) *Umzala uchitha amanzi; ugeza izitsha.* (j) *Thela itiye dadewethu!* (k) *Abafana bashaya ubani? Abafana bashaya umsizi.* (l) *Abashumayeli basebenzani? Abashumayeli bayashumayela.* (m) *Ulandani?* (2nd pers. sg.) *Ngilanda amalahle.*

3. Translate into Zulu: (a) My father wants your brother and your sister. (b) Buy tobacco and matches. (c) Whitemen like lettuce and cheese; children like jam. (d) The preacher is singing and the people are singing. (e) The neighbour works with the farmers. (f) What is the farmer buying? The farmer is buying sheep and a horse. (g) The woman kindles a fire but my sister washes clothes. (h) Father reads

books and papers but mother sews dresses. (i) Parents take care of the children. (j) We like to drink tea and milk but my sister likes to drink cocoa. (k) Whom is the doctor calling? The doctor is calling the nurse. (l) What is the boy fetching? The boy is fetching cigarettes and matches. (m) What does the builder want? The builder wants paint and paraffin. (n) With whom is James speaking? James is speaking with Norah.

# CHAPTER 6

## THE NOUN (*Continued*)

### CLASS 2

The following is a list of some nouns of Class 2:

| Singular | Plural |
|---|---|
| *umuzi* (kraal) | *imizi* |
| *umunwe* (finger) | *iminwe* |
| *umlenze* (leg) | *imilenze* |
| *umsebenzi* (work) | *imisebenzi* |
| *umsila* (tail) | *imisila* |
| *ummbila* (maize) | *imimbila* |
| *umbhede* (bed) | *imibhede* |
| *umfula* (river) | *imifula* |
| *umzimba* (body) | *imizimba* |
| *umlilo* (fire) | *imililo* |
| *umkhonto* (spear) | *imikhonto* |
| *umthunzi* (shade) | |
| *umgodi* (hole) | *imigodi* |
| *ummese* (knife) | *imimese* |
| *umnyaka* (year) | *iminyaka* |
| *umkhumbi* (ship) | *imikhumbi* |
| *umshini* (machine) | *imishini* |
| *umqwayiba* (biltong) | *imiqwayiba* |
| *umkhuhlane* (fever, common cold) | *imikhuhlane* |
| *umuthi* (tree, medicine) | *imithi* |
| *umnyango* (door, doorway) | *iminyango* |

| Singular | Plural |
|---|---|
| *umhlaba* (earth, country, world) | *imihlaba* |
| *umhlabathi* (soil, ground) | *imihlabathi* |
| *umoya* (wind, air) | *imimoya* |
| *umgwaqo* (road, street) | *imigwaqo* |
| *umbane* (lightning) | *imibane* |
| *umthetho* (law, rule, regulation) | *imithetho* |
| *umquba* (manure) | |
| *umsindo* (noise) | *imisindo* |
| *umusa* (kindness) | |

Many nouns in Zulu are derived from verbs, as we illustrated, on page 12, with examples of verb-derived personal nouns. A number of non-personal nouns also stem from verbs, and here are a few in Class 2:—

| | |
|---|---|
| *umshado* (wedding, marriage) | <*shada* (wed, marry) |
| *umshanelo* (broom) | <*shanela* (sweep) |
| *umbuzo* (question) | <*buza* (ask) |
| *umqamelo* (pillow) | <*qamela* (place head on pillow) |
| *umthungo* (sewing) | <*thunga* (sew) |
| *umdanso* (dance) | <*dansa* (dance) |
| *umdlalo* (game) | <*dlala* (play) |
| *umculo* (singing) | <*cula* (sing) |
| *umthandazo* (prayer) | <*thandaza* (pray) |
| *umthwalo* (load, burden) | <*thwala* (carry) |
| *umvuzo* (reward) | <*vuza* (reward) |
| *umfanekiso* (picture, illustration) | <*fanekisa* (liken) |
| *umhlangano* (meeting, assembly) | <*hlangana* (assemble, meet) |
| *umjuluko* (perspiration) | <*juluka* (perspire) |
| *umncintiswano* (competition) | <*ncintisana* (compete) |
| *umjaho* (a race meeting) | <*jaha* (race) |

*N.B.* (i) The singular prefix is *umu-*, *um-* (*umu-* is only used when the noun stem is monosyllabic.

(ii) The plural prefix is *imi-*. This prefix is heard as *imi-* when used with monosyllabic noun stems; otherwise it is often heard as *im-*. However, it is always written *imi-*.

(iii) The subjectival concords are *u-* and *i-* for singular and plural respectively.

Examples:—

1. *Umuthi ufuna umhlabathi namanzi* (A tree wants/needs soil and water).
   *Imithi ifuna umhlabathi namanzi* (Trees want/need soil and water).
2. *Umsebenzi uyasiza* (Work helps).
   *Imisebenzi iyasiza* (Work helps).
3. *Umkhumbi uthwala abantu* (A ship carries people).
   *Imikhumbi ithwala abantu* (Ships carry people).
4. *Umshini uyathunga* (A machine sews).
   *Imishini iyathunga* (Machines sew).
5. *Umthwalo uyasinda* (The load is heavy—*sinda*, heavy; recover; escape).
   *Imithwalo iyasinda* (The loads are heavy).

STATEMENT CONVERTED INTO QUESTION BY CHANGE OF TONE

In Zulu a statement may be converted into a question by change of tone only, e.g.

1. *Umfana ubona ubaba.* (The boy sees father).
   *Umfana ubona ubaba?* (Does the boy see father?)
2. *Umntwana uphuza ubisi.* (The child drinks milk.)
   *Umntwana uphuza ubisi?* (Does the child drink milk?)
3. *Umalume ubhema usikilidi.* (Uncle smokes cigarettes.)
   *Umalume ubhema usikilidi?* (Does uncle smoke cigarettes?)
4. *Udokotela ubiza unesi.* (The doctor calls the nurse.)
   *Udokotela ubiza unesi?* (Is the doctor calling the

nurse?)

*Na?* is often added to the question; e.g.

*Umfana ubona ubaba na?*

*Umntwana uphuza ubisi na?*

### Exercise 5

1. Complete the following sentences by supplying the correct form of the verb; e.g. *Umshumayeli* **uyashumayela.**

| | |
|---|---|
| (a) *Umakhi* .................. | (f) *Umbazi* .................. |
| (b) *Umdlali* .................. | (g) *Umpheki* .................. |
| (c) *Umkhandi* .................. | (h) *Umhloli* .................. |
| (d) *Umsizi* .................. | (i) *Umfundi* .................. |
| (e) *Umfundisi* .................. | (j) *Umholi* .................. |

2. *FUNDA: Khipha umlotha* (ash—Cl. 2). *Chitha umlotha. Landa amaphepha nezinkuni* (firewood) *namalahle. Thatha umentshisi. Basa umlilo. Geza amabhodwe* (pots). *Yikha amanzi. Thela amanzi. Pheka ukudla. Chathaza usawoti. Faka usawoti. Sika uanyanisi notamatisi. Faka uanyanisi notamatisi. Bonda iphalishi.*

3. *John, landa izinkomo. Umfowethu ufuna ukusenga* (to milk). *Ufuna ukusenga ngoba* (because) *umama ufuna ubisi. Umntwana uyakhala. Umntwana ufuna ubisi. Umntwana ufuna ukuphuza ubisi. Umntwana uphuza ubisi kakhulu. Umntwana uthanda ubisi na? Yebo umntwana uthanda ubisi. Umntwana uphuza ubisi namanzi.*

Answer the following questions in Zulu:

(a) *UJohn ulandani na?*
(b) *Umama ufunani na?*
(c) *Umntwana ukhala ngoba ufunani na?*
(d) *Umntwana uthanda ubisi na?*
(e) *Umntwana uphuzani na?*

4. *Sibona umuzi. Umuzi uyasha. Sibona futhi abantu. Abantu bayagijima. Abantu babona umlilo nentuthu* (smoke) *ngoba umuzi uyasha. Abantu bakha amanzi. Bathela amanzi.*

*Abantu bafuna ukucima* (to extinguish) *umlilo kodwa umlilo uyavutha. Umuzi uyasha.*

Answer these questions (*Phendula lemibuzo*):

(a) *Nibonani na?*
(b) *Abantu babonani na?*
(c) *Abantu benzani na?* (*ba* + *enza*).
(d) *Abantu bakhani na?*
(e) *Abantu bafuna ukucimani na?*

5.

A: *Nibona obani na?*
B: *Sibona odokotela nodadewethu.*
A: *Odokotela benzani na?*
B: *Odokotela bayakhuluma futhi bayabhema. Babhema ugwayi.*
A: *Odokotela bakhuluma nobani na?*
B: *Odokotela bakhuluma nobaba nomama.*
A: *Udadewenu wenzani na?*
B: *Udadewethu ubeka izitsha.*
A: *Udadewenu ubeka izitsha nani?* (*na* + *ni?*—And what else?).
B: *Udadewethu ubeka izitsha nesibane.*
A: *Nibona obani futhi na?*
B: *Sibona umlimi nabafana.*
A: *Abafana benzani na?*
B: *Abafana baqoqa izimvu.*
A: *Umlimi wenzani na?*
B: *Umlimi uyasebenza.*
A: *Umlimi usebenzani na?*
B: *Umlimi uyalima.*
A: *Umlimi ulimani na?*
B: *Umlimi ulima insimu* (plot of ground).
A: *Umlimi ulima nobani na?*
B: *Umlimi ulima nomfowethu.*

A: *Umfowenu usiza umlimi na?*

B: *Yebo umfowethu usiza umlimi. Umfowethu uqoqa umquba.*

A: *Umlimi uthanda ukubhema na?*

B: *Yebo umlimi uthanda ukubhema.*

A: *Umlimi uthanda ukubhemani na?*

B: *Umlimi uthanda ukubhema usikilidi.*

A: *Umlimi uthanda ukubhema nani na?*

B: *Umlimi uthanda ukubhema nokusebenza.*

# CHAPTER 7

## THE NEGATIVE

Study the following sentences:—

*Ngifuna uJane* (I want Jane).
*Angifuni uJane* (I do not want Jane).
*Sithanda ubhanana* (We like bananas).
*Asithandi ubhanana* (We do not like bananas).
*Ufuna umentshisi* (You (sg.) want matches).
*Awufuni umentshisi* (You do not want matches).
*Nidlala ibhola* (You (pl.) play/are playing soccer).
*Anidlali ibhola* (You do not play/are not playing soccer).
*Umfana uyacula* (The boy sings/is singing).
*Umfana akaculi* (The boy does not sing/is not singing).
*Abantu bayasebenza* (The people work/are working).
*Abantu abasebenzi* (The people do not work/are not working).
*Umuthi uyakhula* (The tree grows/is growing).
*Umuthi awukhuli* (The tree does not grow/is not growing).
*Imithi iyakhula* (The trees grow/are growing).
*Imithi ayikhuli* (The trees do not grow/are not growing).

In the negative forms we notice the following:—

(a) The final vowel of the verb changes to *-i*.

(b) *a-* is prefixed to the verb. (Some speakers use *ka-*; e.g. *kangifuni*).

(c) In Class 1 sg. and Class 1a sg. *aka-* is prefixed.

(d) *-ya-* is never used in the negative.

(e) Where the subjectival concord is a vowel only:

-*w*- comes between *a*- and *u*- (e.g. 2nd pers. sg.; Cl. 2 sg.).

-*y*- comes between *a*- and *i*- (e.g. Cl. 2 pl.).

-*w*- comes between *a*- and *a*- (e.g. Cl. 3 pl.).

Examples:—

1. *Umhloli akafundi incwadi; ufunda amaphepha* (The Inspector does not read/is not reading a book; he reads/is reading papers).

2. *Ubaba akasizi umshumayeli; usiza umakhelwane* (Father does not help/is not helping the preacher; he helps/is helping the neighbour).

3. *Umlimi akathengi izinkomo; uthenga izimvu namahashi* (The farmer does not buy/is not buying cattle; he buys/is buying sheep and horses) (*amahashi*—horses).

4. *Umfazi akapheki inyama; upheka ubhatata* (The woman does not cook/is not cooking meat; she cooks/is cooking sweet potatoes).

5. *Angithandi ukulima; ngithanda ukudlala* (I do not like to plough; I like to play).

6. *Abantwana abahleki* (The children do not laugh/are not laughing).

7. *Udadewethu akathandi ukuthunga; uthanda ukudansa* (My sister does not like to sew; she likes to dance).

8. *Umalume ufuna umquba; akafuni ummbila* (Uncle wants manure; he does not want maize.)

9. *Uthisha akabizi umhlangano* (The teacher does not call/is not calling a meeting).

*N.B.*—*-zwa* does not change to *-zwi* in the negative;
e.g. *angizwa* (I do not hear) *asizwa* (we do not hear).

### Exercise 6

1. Learn the following verbs:—

| | |
|---|---|
| *hluthulela* (lock) | *lungisa* (make ready) |
| *jikijela* (throw) | *gwinciza* (meander) |

*goba* (bend/twist)
*tshala* (plant)
*khula* (grow)
*vula* (open)
*lola* (sharpen)
*geleza* (flow)
*vala* (close)
*vunguza* (blow, of wind)

2. Learn the following:—

*ekuseni* (in the morning)
*emini* (in the daytime/at noon)
*ntambama* (in the afternoon)
*kusihlwa* (in the evening)
*ebusuku* (at night)
*manje* (now)
*namuhla* (today)
*kusasa* (tomorrow)
*ngomhlomunye* (day after tomorrow)
*izolo* (yesterday)
*kuthangi* (day before yesterday)

3. Complete the following sentences by giving the correct form of the verb in the negative:

(a) *Umfowethu* (*landa*) *iposi.* (b) *Umfazi* (*geza*) *izingubo.* (c) *ULizzie* (*letha*) *amalahle.* (d) *Abadlali* (*landela*) *umnumzane.* (e) *Odadewethu* (*shanela*). (f) *Abakhi* (*funa*) *usikilidi.* (g) (*Ngithenga*) *izimvu.* (h) (*Sibona*) *abakhi.* (i) *Umkhumbi* (*siza*) *abantu;* (*thwala*) *abantu.* (j) *Imithi* (*funa*) *umlilo.* (k) *Ubaba* (*gibela*) *ihashi.* (l) *Abashumayeli* (*gijima*). (m) *Udadewenu* (*thanda*) *umdanso.* (n) *Umnumzane* (*biza*) *umhlangano.* (o) *Umakhelwane* (*thatha*) *umthwalo.* (p) *Umlimi* (*tshala*) *namuhla.* (q) *Umalume* (*lola*) *umese* (r) *Abafana* (*vula*) *iminyango.* (s) *Umama* (*lungisa*) *ukudla.* (t) *Udokotela* (*khuluma*) *nobaba.*

4. Re-write the complete sentences under 3 above but change the number of the subject in each case (i.e. singular to plural or plural to singular).

5. *FUNDA*:—

*Ngithanda kakhulu ukufunda. Ngifunda amaphepha kodwa angithandi ukufunda izincwadi. Ngithanda ukufunda kusihlwa ngoba emini ngiyasebenza. Umfowethu uthanda ukufunda izincwadi, akathandi ukufunda ebusuku. Udadewethu akafuni ukufunda. Akafuni ukufunda amaphepha futhi akafuni ukufunda izincwadi. Udadewethu uthanda ukusebenza. Udadewethu uyapheka, ugeza izitsha, ugeza izingubo. Uthanda kakhulu ukupheka nokugeza izitsha nokugeza izingubo. Udadewethu akathandi ukuthunga kodwa umama uthanda kakhulu ukuthunga. Udadewethu uyashanela futhi. Ushanela ekuseni.*

*Umama uthanda ukusebenza. Ekuseni umama ubasa umlilo, upheka ukudla. Emini umama uthunga izingubo. Ntambama umama uyaphumula. Ekuseni umama upha ubaba iphalishi, noshizi netiye. Futhi ekuseni umama ugeza abantwana. Upha abantwana iphalishi nobisi. Abantwana abaphuzi itiye. Baphuza ubisi kuphela* (only).

*Ubaba akathandi ukusebenza. Uthanda ukubhema usikilidi nokufunda amaphepha nezincwadi. Ubaba ubhema njalo* (always). *Kodwa ubaba uyathanda ukugeza imoto* (car). *Ubaba uthanda imoto kakhulu. Ubaba ushayela imoto kodwa umama akashayeli, nabafowethu abashayeli nawodadewethu abashayeli. Umama akathandi ukushayela; uyesaba* (*esaba*—be afraid).

*Phendula lemibuzo:*

(a) *Ngithanda ukufundani na?*
(b) *Ngithanda ukufunda nini?* (*nini?*—when?)
(c) *Emini ngenzani na?* (*ngi* + *enzani*).
(d) *Umfowethu uthanda ukufundani na?*
(e) *Umfowethu uthanda ukufunda nini?*
(f) *Udadewethu akafuni ukufundani na?*
(g) *Udadewethu uthanda ukwenzani na?* (*uku* + *enzani*).
(h) *Udadewethu ushanela nini na?*
(i) *Umama uthanda ukwenzani na?*
(j) *Ekuseni umama wenzani na?*
(k) *Umama uthunga nini izingubo na?*
(l) *Umama uphumula nini na?*

(m) *Umama upha abantwana iphalishi nani na?*

(n) *Ubaba uthanda ukubhema nani na?*

(o) *Ubaba uthanda ukugezani na?*

(p) *Ubaba ushayelani na?*

(q) *Umama akathandi ukwenzani na?*

6. Translate into Zulu:—

(a) Mother does not want coal because the fire is burning. (b) Grandmother opens the doors in the morning because she likes air. My sister closes the doors in the evening. (c) The people are running because the kraal is burning. (d) We do not want to play soccer today because the wind is blowing. (e) My brother is throwing stones; he is hitting cattle. (f) I want to lock up because we are going. (g) The boys are digging a hole; they are not cutting trees. (h) Mother does not like to drive the car because the road meanders. (i) The neighbour is ploughing; he wants to plant maize and beans. He does not want to plant sweet potatoes. (j) Jane, prepare tea; your father wants tea. (k) Uncle sharpens a knife because he wants to cut meat. (1) The child is playing; he is closing the doors. (m) My brothers like dance very much but my sister does not like to dance. (n) Whitemen like biltong. (o) The preacher is not planting; he is reading a book. (p) Father is not calling the doctor; whom is he calling? (q) The trees are not rotting; they are growing. (r) Do you (sg.) remember? No, I do not remember. (s) The children are not laughing; they are crying.

# CHAPTER 8

## THE NOUN (*Continued*)

### Class 3

The following are a few nouns of Class 3:—

| Singular | Plural |
|---|---|
| *ibhotela* (butter) | |
| *izambane* (potato) | *amazambane* |
| *ithanga* (pumpkin) | *amathanga* |
| *iphalishi* (porridge) | *amaphalishi* |
| *igeja* (hoe/plough) | *amageja* |
| *ibhakede* (bucket) | *amabhakede* |
| *ibhantshi* (jacket) | *amabhantshi* |
| *ipipi* (smoking pipe) | *amapipi* |
| *ibhulukwe* (trousers) | *amabhulukwe* |
| *ikhandlela* (candle) | *amakhandlela* |
| *igundane* (mouse) | *amagundane* |
| *isaka* (sack/bag) | *amasaka* |
| *ifasitele* (window) | *amafasitele* |
| *iklabishi* (cabbage) | *amaklabishi* |
| *idolobha* (town) | *amadolobha* |
| *ibhuloho* (bridge) | *amabhuloho* |
| *izinyo* (tooth) | *amazinyo* |
| *isela* (thief) | *amasela* |
| *ikhofi* (coffee) | *amakhofi* |
| *ilahle* (piece of coal) | *amalahle* |
| *iculo* (song/hymn/hymn book) | *amaculo* |
| *iphepha* (paper/newspaper) | *amaphepho* |

| Singular | Plural |
| --- | --- |
| *ilanga* (sun, day) | *amalanga* |
| *ikhanda* (head) | *amakhanda* |
| *ithambo* (bone) | *amathambo* |
| *ihashi* (horse) | *amahashi* |
| *ibhubesi* (lion) | *amabhubesi* |
| *idada* (duck) | *amadada* |
| *ikati* (cat) | *amakati* |
| *ibhande* (belt) | *amabhande* |
| *iyembe* (shirt) | *amayembe* |
| *iqanda* (egg) | *amaqanda* |
| *ikhekhe* (cake) | *amakhekhe* |
| *ibhodwe* (pot) | *amabhodwe* |
| *ijazi* (overcoat) | *amajazi* |
| *itshe* (stone) | *amatshe* |
| *ifu* (cloud) | *amafu* |
| *isango* (gate) | *amasango* |
| *itafula* (table) | *amatafula* |
| *ijezi* (jersey) | *amajezi* |
| *itiye* (tea) | *amatiye* |
| *ihlathi* (forest) | *amahlathi* |
| *ibhola* (ball/soccer) | *amabhola* |

*N.B.* (i) The singular prefix is *i-* and the plural prefix is *ama-*.

(ii) The subjectival concords are *li-* and *a-* for the singular and plural respectively.

Although the full singular prefix is *ili-*, Zulu no longer uses this full form except with monosyllabic stems when it may be used; e.g. *ifu* or *ilifu* (cloud); *itshe* or *ilitshe* (stone); *izwi* or *ilizwi* (word/voice); *izwe* or *ilizwe* (country).

Class 3 Nouns with no corresponding singular forms:—

| | | |
| --- | --- | --- |
| *amanga* (falsehoods) | *amafutha* (fat/oil) | *amanzi* (water) |
| *amasi* (curdled milk) | *amafinyila* (mucus) | *amakhaza* (cold) |

*amandla* (strength) *amanyala* (filth) *amathe* (spittle) *amahloni* (timidity) *amazolo* (dew)

Examples:—

1. *Ihashi liza nobaba* (The horse is coming with father).
2. *Ikati lilwa nenja* (The cat is fighting with a dog).
3. *Amakati alwa nenja* (The cats are fighting with a dog).
4. *Amalahle ayavutha* (The coal is burning).
5. *Isela lifuna izingubo* (The thief wants clothes).
6. *Amasela afuna izingubo* (The thieves want clothes).
7. *Ikhandlela liyavutha* (The candle is burning).
8. *Amakhandlela ayavutha* (The candles are burning).
9. *Amanzi ayabila* (The water is boiling).

## DAYS OF THE WEEK (*IZINSUKU ZESONTO*)

*iSonto* (Sunday), *uMsombuluko* (Monday), *oLwesibili* (Tuesday), *oLwesithathu* (Wednesday), *oLwesine* (Thursday), *oLwesihlanu* (Friday), *uMgqibelo* (Saturday).

Observe the following expressions:—

*ngeSonto* (on Sunday) *ngoMsombuluko* (on Monday)
*ngoLwesibili* (on Tuesday) *ngoLwesithathu* (on Wednesday)
*ngoLwesine* (on Thursday) *ngoLwesihlanu* (on Friday)
*ngoMgqibelo* (on Saturday)

## MEANS OF TRAVEL (*IZINTO ZOKUHAMBA*)

| | |
|---|---|
| *imoto* (motor car) | *izimoto* (Class 5) |
| *isithuthuthu* (motor cycle) | *izithuthuthu* (4) |
| *ibhayisikili* (bicycle) | *amabhayisikili* (3) |
| *ibhasi* (bus) | *amabhasi* (3) |
| *ithilamu* (tram car) | *amathilamu* (3) |
| *inqola* (wagon) | *izinqola* (5) |
| *isitimela* (train) | *izitimela* (4) |
| *ibhanoyi* (aeroplane) | *amabhanoyi* (3) |

*umkhumbi* (ship) — *imikhumbi* (2)
*unyawo* (foot) — *izinyawo* (6)

These nouns are used with *nga-* to convey the idea of "by means of", (*nga-* is used with other nouns in this book to convey the same idea of instrument).

| | |
|---|---|
| *ngemoto* (by motor car) | *ngezimoto* |
| *ngesithuthuthu* (by motor cycle) | *ngezithuthuthu* |
| *ngebhayisikili* (by bicycle) | *ngamabhayisikili* |
| *ngebhasi* (by bus) | *ngamabhasi* |
| *ngethilamu* (by tram) | *ngamathilamu* |
| *ngenqola* (by wagon) | *ngezinqola* |
| *ngesitimela* (by train) | *ngezitimela* |
| *ngebhanoyi* (by aeroplane) | *ngamabhanoyi* |
| *ngomkhumbi* (by ship) | *ngemikhumbi* |
| | *ngezinyawo* (on foot) |

Note also the interrogative *ngani?*—by means of what? e.g.

1. *Umama usika ngani?*—Mother cuts with what? lit. by means of what?

*Umama usika ngomese*—Mother cuts with a knife, i.e. by means of a knife.

2. *Ubaba uhamba ngani?*—Father goes by means of what?

*Ubaba uhamba ngemoto*—Father is going by car.

## Exercise 7

1. Learn the following verbs:—

| | |
|---|---|
| *wela* (cross) | *gcoba* (smear/anoint) |
| *khanya* (shine) | *bhonga* (roar) |
| *vilapha* (be lazy) | *hlamba* (wash/swim) |
| *khuluma* (speak) | *klwebha* (scratch) |
| *cwecwa* (peel) | *deka* (set table) |
| *xega* (be loose) | *shisa* (hot/iron) |
| *cima* (put out/extinguish) | *baleka* (run away) |

*dabula* (tear)
*khahlela* (kick)
*khipha* (take out)
*gqoka* (put on/wear)
*songa* (wrap/fold)
*futha* (inflate/ache)
*bila* (boil)
*banda* (be cold)

2. Translate into English:—

(a) *Ekuseni odadewethu babasa umlilo, futhi bayapheka kodwa ubaba ugeza imoto. Emini odadewethu bageza amafasitele.* (b) *Umfana ulanda iphepha nobisi ekuseni ngoba ntambama ulanda izinkomo namahashi.* (c) *Umfowethu akathandi ukufunda amaphepha nezincwadi ebusuku; uthanda ukufunda emini.* (d) *Emini ilanga liyashisa kakhulu kodwa ntambama alishisi kakhulu; lishisa kancane* (a little). (e) *Abanumzane nabafana balola imikhonto; bafuna ukubulala ibhubesi.* (f) *Umama ulungisa ukudla; ufuna ukupha abantwana ngoba abantwana bafuna ukulala* (to sleep); *udadewethu akasizi umama ngoba uyavilapha.* (g) *Ubaba ushaya uSipho noThemba ngoba bayalwa.* (h) *Umalume ufuna ukukhipha izinyo ngoba liyaxega.* (i) *Ubaba ucobela ipipi ngoba ufuna ukubhema* (*cobela*—stuff pipe). (j) *Jane, letha itiye nobisi noshukela.* (k) *Abafana baxosha* (chase) *amasela ngoba amasela eba* (steal) *amadada.* (l) *Maggie, deka; ubaba ufuna ukudla manje.* (m) *Umama ushaya ikati ngoba ikati liklwebha umntwana.* (n) *Amanzi ayabanda.* (o) *Umlungu usonga ibhotela.* (p) *Udokotela ubiza ubani? Udoketela ubiza unesi.* (q) *Udadewethu usika uanyanisi nani na? Udadewethu usika uanyanisi notamatisi.*

3. Translate into Zulu:—

(a) My brother wants to cross the river but father does not want to. (b) The boys are kicking a ball but John is not playing. (c) Sipho does not like to work because he is lazy. (d) Father and mother are talking but my maternal uncle is working. (e) The children are singing songs. (f) The inspector calls the boys because he wants to speak to (with) the boys. (g) In the morning we work but at noon we do not work; we rest. (h) Her brothers are planting trees but my maternal uncle is planting maize. (i) Choose a hymn; we want to sing; we do not want to read. (j) The thieves are running away; they see a dog. (k) Today I do not want to put on an overcoat because the sun is hot. (l) Jane, wash the pots; mother wants to cook. (m) The water is flowing. (n) Open the windows and the doors; we want air. (o) Father likes to read and to smoke. He does not like to sing.

4. *FUNDA*:—

(a) *Sibona amabhubesi. Amabhubesi ahlala ehlathini* (in the forest). *Amabhubesi athanda inyama. Adla inyama namathambo. Futhi amabhubesi abulala abantu* (*bulala*—kill) *adla abantu.*

(b) *Umalume uyahamba. Umalume uhamba ngezinyawo. Umalume uthanda ukuhamba ngezinyawo. Akathandi ukuhamba ngenqola, futhi akathandi ukuhamba ngesithuthuthu. Umfowethu uthanda ukuhamba ngesithuthuthu. Uthanda ukugibela isithuthuthu kodwa udadewethu akathandi ukuhamba ngesithuthuthu. Akathandi ukugibela isithuthuthu. Uthanda ukugibela ihashi. Umfowethu uthanda futhi ukuhamba ngebhanoyi kodwa akathandi ukuhamba ngezinyawo. Umfowethu uyavilapha kakhulu.*

(c) *UJane ukhipha umlotha ngoba ufuna ukubasa. UJane uchitha umlotha. Usiza umama. UJane ufuna ukupheka futhi ufuna ukubhaka* (bake) *amakhekhe. Sithanda amakhekhe kakhulu. UJane ubhaka kahle* (well). *UMary akabhaki; ucwecwa amazambane nethanga. UMary ufuna ukupheka amazambane nenyama nethanga neklabishi.*

(d) *Ngiyagqoka. Ngigqoka ibhulukwe neyembe nebhantshi. Abafana bagqoka amabhulukwe namayembe namabhantshi. Ngibopha ibhulukwe ngebhande kodwa umfowethu akathandi ukubopha ibhulukwe ngebhande. Futhi ngigqoka amasokisi* (socks/stockings—3) *nezicathulo* (shoes). *Ebusika* (in winter) *ngigqoka ijezi nejazi.*

(e) *Sibona ikati. Ikati lihlala* (sit/stay/live) *nabantu. Ikati lithanda inyawa nobisi kodwa alithandi amathambo nephalishi namakhekhe. Futhi ikati alithandi amaqanda nebhotela. Ikati lithanda ukubamba* (to catch) *amagundane. Ikati lithanda kakhulu ukudla amagundane. Ikati lithanda ukudlala nabantwana. Ikati libamba amagundane ebusuku. Emini ikati lithanda ukulala.*

(f)

A: *Udadewenu ulandani na?*
B: *Udadewethu ulanda amanzi.*
A: *Udadewenu ulanda amanzi ngani na?*
B: *Udadewethu ulanda amanzi ngebhakede.*
A: *Udadewenu ufuna ukugezani namuhla na?*
B: *Udadewethu ufuna ukugeza izingubo.*
A: *Udadewenu ufuna ukugeza izingubo nani na?*
B: *Udadewethu ufuna ukugeza izingubo namafasitele.*
A: *Udadewenu ufuna ukugeza amafasitele nini na?*
B: *Udadewethu ufuna ukugeza amafasitele ntambama.*
A: *Udadewenu ufuna ukugeza izingubo nini na?*
B: *Udadewethu ufuna ukugeza izingubo emini.*
A: *Udadewenu ufuna nokupheka futhi na?*
B: *Yebo udadewethu ukha amanzi ngoba ufuna nokupheka.*
A: *Udadewenu uza nani na?*
B: *Udadewethu uza namanzi ngebhakede.*
A: *Udadewenu uyavilapha na?*
B: *Cha udadewethu akavilaphi.*

# CHAPTER 9

## THE NOUN (*Continued*)

### CLASS 4

THE following are some nouns of Class 4:—

| Singular | Plural |
|---|---|
| *isikole* (school) | *izikole* |
| *isihlabathi* (sand) | *izihlabathi* |
| *isinkwa* (bread) | *izinkwa* |
| *isilwane* (animal) | *izilwane* |
| *isilonda* (sore) | *izilonda* |
| *isitofu* (stove) | *izitofu* |
| *isibuko* (mirror) | *izibuko* |
| *isigqoko* (hat) | *izigqoko* |
| *isithelo* (fruit) | *izithelo* |
| *isibhamu* (gun) | *izibhamu* |
| *isikhathi* (time) | *izikhathi* |
| *isifo* (disease/illness) | *izifo* |
| *isibane* (lamp) | *izibane* |
| *isisefo* (sieve) | *izisefo* |
| *isiboshwa* (prisoner) | *iziboshwa* |
| *isitini* (brick) | *izitini* |
| *isifundo* (lesson) | *izifundo* |
| *isando* (hammer) | *izando* |
| *isipikili* (nail) | *izipikili* |
| *isikhukhukazi* (hen) | *izikhukhukazi* |
| *isihlalo* (seat/chair) | *izihlalo* |
| *isimungulu* (dumb person) | *izimungulu* |
| *isithulu* (deaf person) | *izithulu* |
| *isitulo* (stool/chair) | *izitulo* |

| Singular | Plural |
|---|---|
| *isicathulo* (shoe/boot) | *izicathulo* |
| *isikhwama* (bag/pocket) | *izikhwama* |
| *isalukazi* (old woman) | *izalukazi* |
| *isibaya* (cattle kraal) | *izibaya* |
| *isihambi* (stranger/traveller) | *izihambi* |
| *isisebenzi* (servant/worker) | *izisebenzi* |
| *isivalo* (lid/door) | *izivalo* |
| *isitolo* (store/shop) | *izitolo* |
| *isithombe* (picture/photograph) | *izithombe* |
| *isitsha* (vessel/dish) | *izitsha* |
| *isiteshi* (railway station) | *iziteshi* |
| *isihlahla* (tree/bush) | *izihlahla* |
| *isikhumba* (skin/hide) | *izikhumba* |
| *isihluthulelo* (key) | *izihluthulelo* |

The prefixes are *isi-* and *izi-* for the singular and plural respectively. However, nouns with stems commencing in vowels prefix *is-* and *iz-*. The subjectival concords are *si-* and *zi-* for singular and plural respectively.

Names of languages are included in this class, e.g.:—

| | |
|---|---|
| *isiZulu* (Zulu) | *isiXhosa* (Xhosa) |
| *isiSuthu* (Sotho) | *isiBhunu* (Afrikaans) |
| *isiNgisi* (English) | *isiJalimane* (German) |
| *isiNtaliyane* (Italian) | *isiPutukezi* (Portuguese) |
| *isiSwazi* (Swazi) | *isiFulentshi* (French) |
| *isiMpondo* (Pondo) | *isiThonga* (Tonga) |

Examples:—

1. *Isisebenzi asifuni ukusebenza ngoba siyagula* (The servant does not want to work because he is ill).

2. *Izilwane ziyabaleka, zibona ibhubesi* (The animals are running away; they see a lion).

3. *Umama uthenga isisefo ngoba ufuna ukusefa ufulawa; ufuna ukubhaka amakhekhe* (Mother buys a sieve

because she wants to sift flour; she wants to bake cakes.)

4. *Isalukazi sithatha isitulo; sifuna ukuhlala* (The old woman takes a chair; she wants to sit).

5. *Isihambi sifuna isinkwa nenyama* (The traveller wants bread and meat).

6. *Izibane ziyakhanyisa* (The lamps give light).

7. *Isifo sifuna umuthi* (Illness wants/needs medicine).

8. *Isihlahla siyasha* (The bush is burning).

9. *Iziboshwa zimba umgwaqo* (The convicts are digging the road).

10. *Isikhukhukazi sidla ummbila* (The hen eats mealies)

## Verbs with Suffix—ela

A suffix commonly added to verbs in Zulu is *-ela*. The verb then means "to do for" or "on behalf of"; e.g.

1. *Umama uthungela abantwana* (Mother sews for the children).

2. *Abalimi bathengela amahashi* (The farmers buy for the horses).

3. *Inkosi yakhela abantu* (The chief builds for the people).

4. *Umnumzane ukhulumela abantu* (The kraal head speaks for/on behalf of the people).

5. *Umalume ulimela ugogo* (Uncle ploughs for grandmother).

This type of verb may take more than one object, e.g.

1. *Umama uthungela abantwana izingubo* (Mother sews dresses for the children).

2. *Abalimi bathengela amahashi ummbila* (The farmers buy mealies for the horses).

3. *Inkosi yakhela abantu indlu* (The chief builds a house for the people).

4. *Umalume utshalela ugogo ummbila* (Uncle plants mealies for grandmother).

The negative of such verbs is formed in the manner already described on page 37. e.g.

1. *Umama akathungeli abantwana* (Mother does not sew for the children).

2. *Abalimi abathengeli amahashi.*

3. *Inkosi ayakheli abantu.*

4. *Umnumzane akakhulumeli abantu.*

To ask "Why?". Suffix *-ni* to verb ending in *-ela.* e.g.

1. *Umntwana ukhalelani?* (Why is the child crying? lit. The child is crying for what?)

2. *Ubaba uhambelani?* (Why is father going?)

3. *Odadewenu babalekelani?* (Why are your sisters running away?)

4. *Abantwana baculelani?* (Why are the children singing?)

5. *UThoko ulandelani amanzi?* (Why is Thoko fetching water?)

6. *Umama ubaselani?* (Why is mother making fire?)

7. *Umfowenu ukhulumelani?* (Why is your brother speaking?)

8. *Umfazi ushanelelani?* (Why is the woman sweeping?)

9. *Umfana uphumelani?* (Why is the boy going out?)

10. *Abantu badlelani?* (Why are the people eating?)

To ask "why . . . not?" note that the verb is used in its normal negative form (i.e. omitting "-elani") and is then followed by *ngani.*

1. *Umntwana udlelani* (Why is the child eating) but
*Umntwana akadli ngani?* (Why is the child not eating?)

2. *Abafana babalekelani?* (Why are the boys running away?) but
*Abafana ababaleki ngani?* (Why are the boys not running away?)

3. *Ubaba uhambelani?* (Why is father going?) but
*Ubaba akahambi ngani?* (Why is father not going?)
4. *Odadewethu baculelani?* but
*Odadewethu abaculi ngani?*
5. *UJames uthengelani?* but
*UJames akathengi ngani?*

## Exercise 8

1. Learn the following verbs:—

*khala* (cry)
*thengisa* (sell)
*thuma* (send)
*layisha* (load)
*dubula* (shoot)
*gawula* (fell tree)
*cela* (ask for/beg)
*thandaza* (pray)
*cimeza* (close eyes)
*khwehlela* (cough)
*khumula* (undo/untie/undress)
*bethela* (nail)
*vuka* (wake up)
*buya* (return)
*ngenisa* (bring in)
*zalela* (lay eggs)
*qhaqhazela* (shiver)
*hola* (earn, lead)
*vuma* (agree)
*casha* (hide)
*khohlisa* (deceive)

2. *Humusha ngesiNgisi* (Translate into English):—

(a) *Umlimi uthengisani na? Umlimi uthengisa amahashi nezimvu kodwa akathengisi izikhumba. Udadewenu uthengisani na? Udadewethu uthengisa izingubo.* (b) *Sipho, letha isando. Ufunelani isando na? Ngifuna ukubethela izipikili.* (c) *Isikhukhukazi sizalela amaqanda kodwa iqhude* (cock—3) *alizaleli.* (d) *John, ngenisa isihlalo; ubaba ufuna ukuhlala.* (e) *Abafana abalimi ngani namuhla? Abafana abalimi ngoba bagawula imithi ehlathini.* (f) *Amakholwa* (Christians—3) *ayacula futhi ayathandaza kodwa abahedeni abaculi amaculo futhi abathandazi.* (g) *Umfundisi ushayelani abantwana na? Umfundisi ushaya abantwana ngoba abantwana bakhohlisa abazali.* (h) *Udokotela unika umama umuthi ngoba umama uyagula; uyakhwehlela.* (i) *Umakhi uthe-*

*ngani? Umakhi uthenga izitini nothayela ngoba ufuna ukwakha indlu; umakhi uthwala izitini nothayela ngenqola.* (j) *Umlimi ubulala izilwane ngesibhamu; isibhamu sidubula izilwane.* (k) *Ngifuna isihluthulelo; ngifuna ukuhluthulela indlu ntambama ngoba siyahamba.* (l) *Ubabamkhulu uvuka ekuseni kakhulu* (very early). (m) *Umalume ukhuluma isiNgisi nesiBhunu nesiXhosa kodwa ubaba ukhuluma isiNgisi kuphela.* (n) *Umntwana uyakhala. Umntwana ukhalelani na? Umntwana uyakhala ngoba ufuna unina; unina uyasebenza; uthengisa izinkwa namakhekhe.* (o) *Isihambi sicela amanzi; sifuna ukuphuza.* (p) *Umfowenu akasebenzi ngani namuhla? Umfowethu akasebenzi ngoba uyagula. Umfowethu ukhumula ibhantshi neyembe nebhulukwe nezicathulo namasokisi ngoba ufuna ukulala.* (q) *Umakhi ulanda inqola; ufuna ukuthwala isihlabathi nezitini namatshe namanzi.* (r) *Umfowethu uyathanda ukusebenza ngoba uyahola; akasebenzi ngoMgqibelo nangeSonto.* (s) *Isimungulu asikhulumi.* (t) *INdiya lithengisa izikhumba nezithelo.* (u) *Abafana bayabaleka; bayacasha. Babalekelani na? Babaleka ngoba bayesaba. Besaba umnumzane.* (v) *Udadewethu akenzi itiye ngoba amanzi akabili, ayabanda.* (w) *Umlimi uthenga igeja namasaka.*

3. Translate into Zulu (*Humusha ngesiZulu*):—

(a) Why are the boys running away?
(b) Why is Norah cooking?
(c) Why is James fetching mail?
(d) Why is the headman calling the boys?
(e) Why is the carpenter resting?
(f) Why is the woman bringing coal?
(g) Why is the inspector working?
(h) Why is the preacher preaching?
(i) Why is the farmer ploughing?

4. In 3 above substitute "why . . . not?" for "why?" and translate into Zulu.

# CHAPTER 10

## Future Tense

To indicate an action which will take place in the future, *-zo-* is inserted between the subjectival concord and the verb stem; e.g.:—

| | |
|---|---|
| *ngiyafunda* (I am reading) | *ngizofunda* (I shall read) |
| *siyasebenza* | *sizosebenza* |
| *niyadlala* | *nizodlala* |
| *ubaba uyalima* | *ubaba uzolima* |
| *amabhubesi ayabaleka* | *amabhubesi azobaleka* |
| *isihambi siyacula* | *isihambi sizocula* |

*-zo-* is used of action which is regarded by the speaker as imminent. If the action is not regarded as imminent, then *-yo-* is used; e.g.:

*ngizofunda* (I shall read—in the immediate future).
*ngiyofunda* (I shall read—in the remote future).

To illustrate the psychological approach to the matter of tense the following example is given:

*Ngizohamba namuhla ntambama* (I shall go today in the afternoon); *-zo-* is used here because to this speaker the afternoon of today is something immediate.

*Ngiyohamba namuhla ntambama* (I shall go today in the afternoon). To this speaker the afternoon of today is something remote.

Observe also the following:—

*ngizohamba kusasa* - *ngiyohamba kusasa*

*ngizohamba ngomhlomunye* - *ngiyohamba ngomhlomunye*
*ngizohamba ngesonto elizayo* - *ngiyohamba ngesonto elizayo*
*ngizohamba ngenyanga ezayo* - *ngiyohamba ngenyanga ezayo*
*ngizohamba ngomnyaka ozayo* - *ngiyohamba ngomnyaka ozayo*

(*Ngomhlomunye*—day after tomorrow; *ngesonto elizayo* —next week; *ngenyanga ezayo*—next month; *ngomnyaka ozayo*—next year).

### FUTURE NEGATIVE

In the negative *-zo-* gives place to *-zu-* and *-yo-* to *-yu-*. Notice that in the future tense, the last vowel of the verb does not change to *-i* in the negative.

*ngizofunda* (I shall read) — *angizufunda* (I shall not read)
*sizosebenza* — *asizusebenza*
*nizodlala* — *anizudlala*
*ubaba uzolima* — *ubaba akazulima*
*umama uzothunga* — *umama akazuthunga*

### THE USE OF *njenga-* (like, just as)

*Njenga-* behaves like *na-* (see page 27). If the word following commences in a vowel there is coalescence. e.g.

*njenga* + *umuntu* > *njengomuntu* (like a person).
*njenga* + *ihashi* > *njengehashi* (like a horse).
*njenga* + *abantu* > *njengabantu* (like people).
*njenga* + *udokotela* > *njengodokotela* (like a doctor)
*njenga* + *isiboshwa* > *njengesiboshwa* (like a convict).
*njenga* + *amagundane* > *njengamagundane* (like mice)

1. *UThoko uthunga njengonina* (Thoko sews like her mother.

2. *Umfowenu usebenza njengevila* (Your brother works like a lazy person).

3. *UJames ukhuluma njengomntwana* (James speaks like a child).

4. *UNorah upheka njengodadewethu* (Norah cooks like my sister).

5. *Ubaba ushumayela njengomfundisi* (Father preaches like a minister).

## Exercise 9

1. Learn the following:—

*ukuphuma kwelanga* (the rising of the sun/at sunrise)
*ukushona kwelanga* (the setting of the sun/at sunset)
*ukuphuma kwenyanga* (at the rising of the moon)
*ukushona kwenyanga* (at the setting of the moon)
*ekuqaleni kwesonto* (at the beginning of the week)
*ekuqaleni kwenyanga* (at the beginning of the month)
*ekuqaleni konyaka* (at the beginning of the year)
*ekupheleni kwesonto* (at the end of the week)
*ekupheleni kwenyanga* (at the end of the month)
*ekupheleni konyaka* (at the end of the year)
*lonyaka* (this year)
*unyaka odlule* (last year)
*unyaka ozayo* (next year)
*lenyanga* (this month)
*inyanga edlule* (last month)
*inyanga ezayo* (next month)
*lelisonto* (this week/Sunday)
*isonto eledlule* (last week/Sunday).
*isonto elizayo* (next week/Sunday)
*ngalelisonto* (during this week/Sunday)
*ngalenyanga* (during this month)
*ngalonyaka* (during this year)
*ngesonto eledlule* (during last week/Sunday)
*ngenyanga edlule* (during last month)
*ngonyaka odlule* (during last year)
*ngesonto elizayo* (during next week/Sunday)
*ngenyanga ezayo* (during next month)
*ngonyaka ozayo* (during next year)

2. *Humusha ngesiNgisi* (Translate into English):—

(a) *Ngonyaka ozayo ngizofunda uStd.* 6. (b) *Abafana bazodlala ibhola ngesonto elizayo.* (c) *Umama uzobuya ukushona kwelanga.* (d) *Asizuhamba namuhla; sizohamba kusasa kusihlwa.* (e) *Izisebenzi ziyahola njalo ekupheleni kwenyanga kodwa zifuna ukuhola ekupheleni kwesonto.* (f) *Ubaba uzoshaya abantwana. Ubaba uzoshayelani abantwana? Ubaba uzoshaya abantwana ngoba abantwana bajikijela amafasitele ngamatshe.* (g) *Umbazi uzobaza izitulo namatafula kodwa akazubaza iminyango.* (h) *Umalume akahambi ngani manje? Umalume akahambi manje ngoba isitimela sizofika ukushona kwelanga.* (i) *Udadewethu akazugeza amafasitele namuhla; uzogeza izingubo kuphela.* (j) *Ngonyaka ozayo sizofunda isiBhunu; ngalonyaka sifunda isiNgisi nesiZulu.* (k) *Ngizogqoka ijezi kodwa angizugqoka ijazi. Ijazi liyasinda.* (l) *Asizuthenga amakhandlela ngoba sikhanyisa ugesi.* (m) *Udadewethu uzoshada ngesonto elizayo.* (n) *Umhloli uzobiza umhlangano.* (o) *Umfana uyajabula ngoba uzothola umvuzo.* (p) *Umfowethu ugcoba isilonda ngamafutha.* (q) *Umzala uzothenga izithombe; akazuthenga amabhakede.* (r) *Udadewenu usebenza njengobani? Udadewethu usebenza njengomama.* (s) *Ibhokisi* (box—3) *liyasinda. Lisinda njengetshe.* (t) *Umntwana ukhalelani? Umntwana ukhala ngoba ufuna ukudla.*

3. *FUNDA:*

*Kusasa ekuseni sizohamba nomama nodadewethu nabafowethu. Sifuna ukuthenga. Umama uzothenga izicathulo namasokisi, futhi umama uzothenga izithombe. Umama akazuthenga ijazi nesigqoko. Udadewethu uzothenga ijazi nesigqoko. Akazuthenga izicathulo namasokisi. Umfowethu uzothenga ibhulukwe neyembe nebhantshi nebhande. Umfowenu uthengelani ibhande? Umfowethu uthenga ibhande ngoba ubopha ibhulukwe ngebhande njengobaba. Mina ngi-*

*zothenga isigqoko kuphela. Mina angibophi ibhulukwe ngebhande. Sizobuya emini. Sizohamba ngebhasi noma ngethilamu. Asithandi ukuhamba ngezinyawo ngoba ilanga liyashisa.*

*Ubaba akahambi. Ubaba akahambi ngani? Ubaba akahambi ngoba akafuni ukuthenga. Uzosala* (remain). *Ubaba uzobaza izitulo namatafula, futhi ubaba uzobheka umuzi. Ubaba uthengisa izitulo namatafula. Ubaba ubaza kahle kakhulu futhi uyathanda ukubaza. Ubaza emini kuphela; ebusuku akabazi. Ebusuku ufunda iphepha.*

*NgoLwesihlanu ubaba uzoya esitolo* (to the store). *Uzothenga amapulangwe* (planks—3) *nezipikili. Ubaba uzolayisha amapulangwe ngenqola noma* (or) *ngelori. Ubaba usika amapulangwe ngesaha* (*isaha*-saw—3), *ubethela izipikili ngesando.*

*NgeSonto sizoya esontweni* (to church) *nobaba nomama nodadewethu nabafowethu kodwa ugogo akazuya esontweni; uzosala. Esontweni siyacula futhi siyathandaza. Udadewethu ucula kahle kakhulu. Ucula njengomama. Esontweni futhi silalela umshumayeli. Umshumayeli ufunda iBhayibheli* (Bible—3) *futhi uyashumayela.*

*Ngalelisonto ugogo akazuya esontweni kodwa ugogo uthanda kakhulu ukuya esontweni. Ugogo akazuya ngani esontweni ngalelisonto? Ugogo akazuya esontweni ngoba uyagula. Njalo ngamaSonto ugogo uya esontweni. Ugogo uphatha* (carry) *iculo neBhayibheli nobaba nomama baphatha amaculo namaBhayibheli. Umalume akathandi ukuya esontweni. Uthanda ukudlala ithenisi nebhola ngeSonto.*

*Siya esontweni ngemoto; asihambi ngezinyawo.*

# CHAPTER 11

## THE NOUN (*Continued*)

### Class 5

The following is a list of some nouns of Class 5:—

| Singular | Plural |
|---|---|
| *imbuzi* (goat) | *izimbuzi* |
| *inkabi* (ox) | *izinkabi* |
| *indlovu* (elephant) | *izindlovu* |
| *inyoka* (snake) | *izinyoka* |
| *inyoni* (bird) | *izinyoni* |
| *intaba* (mountain) | *izintaba* |
| *indlu* (house/room) | *izindlu* |
| *incwadi* (book/letter) | *izincwadi* |
| *imvu* (sheep) | *izimvu* |
| *inja* (dog) | *izinja* |
| *ingulube* (pig) | *izingulube* |
| *inhlanzi* (fish) | *izinhlanzi* |
| *inkukhu* (fowl) | *izinkukhu* |
| *imbewu* (seed) | *izimbewu* |
| *ingadi* (garden) | *izingadi* |
| *intombi* (maiden) | *izintombi* |
| *insimbi* (iron/bell) | *izinsimbi* |
| *inyama* (meat) | |
| *ingubo* (dress/blanket) | *izingubo* |
| *imbali* (flower) | *izimbali* |
| *imali* (money) | *izimali* |

| Singular | Plural |
|---|---|
| *impuphu* (mealie meal) | |
| *insipho* (soap) | |
| *ingane* (child) | *izingane* |
| *inhlabathi* (soil) | |
| *indlela* (road/path/way) | *izindlela* |
| *inkomo* (cow/beast) | *izinkomo* |
| *insizwa* (young man) | *izinsizwa* |
| *into* (thing) | *izinto* |
| *intambo* (rope/string) | *izintambo* |
| *imbobo* (hole) | *izimbobo* |
| *imvula* (rain) | *izimvula* |
| *indwangu* (cloth) | *izindwangu* |
| *intuthu* (smoke) | |
| *induku* (stick) | *izinduku* |
| *inyosi* (bee) | *izinyosi* |

The singular prefix is *i-* plus a variable nasal written *m* or *n* thus *im-*, *in-*. The plural prefix is *izi-* plus a variable nasal; *izim-*, *izin-*. This variable nasal is capable of bringing about sound changes only two of which will be mentioned at this stage:

(i) When it combines with the implosive *b*, this sound becomes explosive.

(ii) When it combines with an aspirated consonant, the aspiration is lost.

These changes are clearly illustrated in Class 6 (see pages 67-68).

The subjectival concords are *i-* and *zi-* for singular and plural respectively.

Nouns of Class 5 with plurals in Class 3:—

Some nouns with singular forms in Class 5 have their plurals in Class 3. The singular forms use Class 5 singular concords and the plural forms use Class 3 plural concords, e.g.:—

| | |
|---|---|
| *inkosi* (chief/king) | *amakhosi* |
| *inkosikazi* (queen/married woman) | *amakhosikazi* |
| *inkosana* (heir/king's son) | *amakhosana* |
| *inkosazana* (king's daughter/ eldest daughter) | *amakhosazana* |
| *indoda* (man) | *amadoda* |
| *indodana* (son) | *amadodana* |
| *indodakazi* (daughter) | *amadodakazi* |
| *intombazane* (girl) | *amantombazane* |
| *insimu* (cultivated land) | *amasimu* |

Notice the reappearance of aspiration in the plural forms of the first four nouns in the absence of nasal influence.

## *IMALI* (MONEY)

| | | | |
|---|---|---|---|
| ½ cent | *ihafusenti* (3) | cent | *isenti* (3) |
| 10c coin | *usheleni* (1a) | 5c coin | *uzuka* (1a) |
| 50c coin | *osheleni abahlanu isihlanu* (4) | 20c coin | *osheleni ababili* |
| | | rand | *irandi* (3) |

*amahafusenti*
*amasenti*
*amarandi*
} These employ the same concord; e.g.

| | |
|---|---|
| 2 half cents | *amahafusenti amabili; amahafusenti angu*—2 |
| 2 cents | *amasenti amabili; amasenti angu*—2 |
| 2 rand | *amarandi amabili; amarandi angu*—2 |
| 3 cents | *amasenti amathathu; amasenti angu*—3 |
| 4 cents | *amasenti amane; amasenti angu*—4 |
| 5 cents | *amasenti amahlanu; amasenti angu*—5 |
| 6 cents | *amasenti ayisithupha; amasenti angu*—6 |
| 7 cents | *amasenti ayisikhombisa; amasenti angu*—7 |
| 8 cents | *amasenti ayisishiyagalombili; amasenti angu*—8 |

1 cents *amasenti ayisishiyagalolunye; amasenti angu*—9
90 cents *amasenti ayishumi; amasenti angu*—10

*ozuka*
*osheleni* } These employ the same concord; e.g.

*ozuka ababili; ozuka abangu*—2
*osheleni ababili; osheleni abangu*—2
*ozuka abathathu, abane, abahlanu, abayisithupha, abayisikhombisa, abayisishiyagalombili, abayisishiyagalolunye, abayishumi*; *abangu*—3, 4, 5, etc.

Because the Zulu forms tend to be cumbersome, especially with large numbers, it is common to use the alternative forms with the prefix *ngu-*.

Further examples:—

| | |
|---|---|
| 15 cents | *amasenti angu*—15 |
| 20 cents | *amasenti angu*—20 |
| 35 cents | *amasenti angu*—35 |
| 100 cents | *amasenti angu*—100 |
| 150 cents | *amasenti angu*—150 |
| 15 rand, etc. | *amarandi angu*—15, etc. |
| 18 five cents | *ozuka abangu*—18 |
| 43 five cents | *ozuka abangu*—43 |
| 95 five cents | *ozuka abangu*—95 |
| 176 five cents | *ozuka abangu*—176 |
| 18 shillings etc | *osheleni abangu*—18 etc. |

The following words will be found useful in connection with money:—

*ushintshi* (1a) change
*isikweleti* (4) debt
*indali* (5) sale
*isheke* (3) cheque
*irisiti* (3) receipt
*imali ebomvu* (lit. red money, i.e. gold coins)
*imali emhlophe* (lit. white money, i.e. silver coins)

*imali engamaphepha* (lit. paper money, i.e. bank notes)
*ukudula* (to be expensive) *-dulile* (expensive)
*ukushibha* (to be cheap) *-shibhile* (cheap)
*ukubiza* (to call, i.e. to cost)

### Exercise 10

1. Learn the following verbs:—

*gunda* (shear/cut hair)
*doba* (fish)
*fukama* (brood)
*lunguza* (peep)
*gwaza* (stab)
*hlinza* (flay)
*fuya* (rear stock)
*shisa* (iron)
*ncela* (suck)
*netha* (get wet/be soaked with rain)
*diliza* (demolish; unload)
*nqamuka* (snap/break)
*qhakaza* (bloom)
*jabula* (be happy)
*holela* (pay wages)
*ndiza* (fly)
*bekela* (patch)
*gaya* (grind)
*ayina* (iron)
*ncenga* (beg/plead)
*thunqa* (smoke)
*anda* (increase)
*ngcolisa* (make dirty)

2. *Humusha ngesiNgisi:* (a) *Izimbuzi zidlani? Izimbuzi zidla imithi kodwa amahashi aphuza amanzi.* (b) *Inja iyakhonkotha. Ikhonkothani? Ibona izinkomo nezimbongolo. Inja izoxosha izinkomo nezimbongolo. Izinkomo nezimbongolo zesaba inja.* (c) *NgoMgqibelo sizodoba izinhlanzi ngoba sithanda izinhlanzi; asizulanda umquba. Sizodoba nomalume ngoba umalume akasebenzi ngoMgqibelo. Umalume uthanda ukudoba njengobaba.* (d) *Umlungu ugayani? Umlungu ugaya ummbila. Umlungu ugaya ngani? Umlungu ugaya ngomshini. Ugayelani? Ugaya ngoba ufuna impuphu.* (e) *Ilanga liyashisa namuhla; amafutha ayancibilika.* (f) *Umlungu uholela izisebenzi ekupheleni kwenyanga; izisebenzi aziholi ekupheleni kwesonto. Izisebenzi ziholani? Zihola imali.* (g) *Udadewethu ubasa umlilo. Ubasela umama. Sibona intuthu iyathunqa.*

*Ugogo akabasi ngani? Ugogo akabasi ngoba uyagula.* (h) *Izinja ziyakhonkotha, izimvu ziyadla, izinkomo ziyaphuza, izinyoni ziyandiza.* (i) *Kusasa ntambama ubaba uzohlaba* (*hlaba*—slaughter; pierce) *inkomo nemvu. Ubaba uthengisa inyama. Akazuhlabela inkosi.* (j) *Izikhukhukazi ziyafukama; zizochamusela* (*chamusela*—hatch) *ngesonto elizayo.* (k) *Umlimi akagundi ngani izimvu? Umlimi uzogunda izimvu ngenyanga ezayo. Umlimi uthengisa uvolo* (wool—1a). *Umfowethu uzosiza umlimi kodwa umfowethu akaholi.* (l) *Umntwana uyajabula ngoba ubona unina. Unina uzopha umntwana amaswidi namakhekhe.* (m) *Umama uzogezani ekuseni? Umama uzogeza izingubo ekuseni kodwa udadewethu uzoayina* (*uzoshisa*). *Udadewethu uayina njengomama.* (n) *Ubaba uncengelani umlimi? Ubaba uncenga umlimi ngoba ufuna ukuthenga ihashi kodwa umlimi akathengisi.* (o) *Ugogo ukhipha abantwana ngoba abantwana bangcolisa indlu.* (p) *Imvula iyana* (*na*—rain); *abantwana bazonetha.* (q) *Umalume uthengela abantwana amaswidi. Umalume akathengi ngani isinkwa? Umalume akathengi isinkwa ngoba abantwana abafuni isinkwa. Bafuna amaswidi.*

3. *FUNDA:*

(a) *Izicathulo zibiza amarandi amahlanu* (Shoes cost R5.00).
(b) *Ngizothenga izicathulo ngamarandi angu*—5 (I shall buy shoes for R5.00).
(c) *Iphepha libiza uzuka* (A newspaper costs five cents).
(d) *Ngizothenga iphepha ngozuka* (I shall buy a newspaper for five cents).
(e) *Iyembe libiza amarandi amathathu namasenti angu*—25 (A shirt costs R3.25).
(f) *Ngizothenga iyembe ngamarandi amathathu namasenti angu*—25 (I shall buy a shirt for R3.25).
(g) *Isinkwa sibiza amasenti angu*—9 (Bread costs 9c).

(h) *Ngizothenga isinkwa ngamasenti angu*—9 (I shall buy bread for 9c).
(i) *Ijazi liyadula. Libiza amarandi angu*—28 *namasenti angu*—75 (A coat is expensive. It costs R28.75).
(j) *Ngizothenga ijazi ngamarandi angu*—28 *namasenti angu*—75 (I shall buy a coat for R28.75).
(k) *Amasokisi ashibhile. Abiza amasenti angu*—35 (Socks are cheap. They cost 35c).
(l) *Ngizothenga amasokisi ngamasenti angu*—35 (I shall buy socks for 35c).

# CHAPTER 12

## THE NOUN (*Continued*)

### CLASS 6

THE following is a list of a few nouns of Class 6:—

| Singular | Plural |
|---|---|
| *uphoňdo* (horn) | *izimpondo* |
| *uthi* (stick) | *izinti* |
| *ubonda* (wall) | |
| *ulwandle* (sea) | *izilwandle* |
| *ubisi* (milk) | |
| *udaka* (mud) | |
| *uxolo* (peace) | |
| *uhlamvu* (grain) | *izinhlamvu* |
| *uhambo* (journey) | (*izinkambo*) |
| *uphaphe* (feather) | *izimpaphe* |
| *ufa* (crack) | *izimfa* |
| *ukhezo* (spoon) | *izinkezo* |
| *uthuli* (dust) | *izintuli* |
| *uju* (honey) | |
| *uthando* (love) | |
| *ufudu* (tortoise) | *izimfudu* |
| *uhleko* (laughter) | |
| *uhlupho* (trouble) | |
| *ulaka* (temper) | |
| *usizo* (help) | |
| *uphiko* (wing) | *izimpiko* |

| Singular | Plural |
|---|---|
| *uphawu* (mark/brand) | *izimpawu* |
| *usizi* (sorrow/sadness) | *izinsizi* |
| *udonga* (wall/ravine) | *izindonga* |
| *ukhuni* (piece of firewood) | *izinkuni* |
| *ulimi* (tongue/language) | *izilimi* |
| *uhla* (row/list/column) | *izinhla* |
| *ucingo* (fence/telegram/ telephone) | *izingcingo* |
| *ukhetho* (election) | |
| *usiba* (feather) | *izinsiba* |
| *ukhamba* (clay pot) | *izinkamba* |
| *ucezu* (piece/slice) | *izingcezu* |
| *ukhula* (weed/weeds) | |

The prefixes are *u-* in the singular and *izim-*, *izin-* in the plural. The plural prefix has a variable nasal as in Class 5. The subjectival concords are *lu-* and *zi-* for singular and plural respectively.

Notice the loss of aspiration when the plurals of nouns such as *uthi*, *ukhuni*, *ukhezo*, etc. are formed.

Examples:—

1. *Uphondo luyanuka; luyasha* (The horn is smelling; it is burning).
2. *Izimpondo ziyanuka; ziyasha* (The horns are smelling; they are burning).
3. *Uphaphe luhamba nomoya* (The feather is going with the wind).
4. *Izimpaphe zihamba nomoya* (The feathers are going with the wind).
5. *Umakhi ulungisa ubonda ngoba ubonda luyawa* (The builder is repairing the wall because the wall is falling; *wa*—fall).
6. *Ufudu lufuna amanzi* (The tortoise wants water).

7. *Izimfudu zifuna amanzi* (The tortoises want water).
8. *Ukhula lubulala ummbila namabele* (The weeds kill mealies and kaffir-corn).
9. *Ukhula luyanda* (The weeds are increasing).

## Exercise 11

1. Learn the following verbs:—

*thukuthela* (become angry)
*nqonqotha* (knock)
*qhekeka* (crack)
*dilika* (fall down/collapse)
*qhelisa* (move aside, push back)
*qala* (start/commence)
*xova* (mix dough/mud)
*canda* (chop wood)
*opha* (bleed)
*casuka* (get annoyed)
*nuka* (smell)
*thintitha* (remove dust)
*qhela* (move aside/stand back)
*qeda* (finish)
*qhuga* (limp)
*dabuka* (get torn/be sorry)
*buka* (look at)

2. *Humusha ngesiNgisi:* (a) *Umakhi ubuka udonga; udonga luyaqhekeka. Umakhi uzolungisa udonga ngoba indlu izodilika.* (b) *Abantwana bayadlala; baxova udaka. Abantwana bazongcolisa izingubo ngodaka.* (c) *Umalume uzoqeda ukulima amasimu kusasa.* (d) *Izisebenzi ziqala umsebenzi ngo-7 ekuseni.* (e) *Umfana usebenzani? Umfana ucanda izinkuni namuhla; kusasa uzolanda amalahle ngenqola.* (f) *Sipho, qhelisa ijazi, ubaba ufuna ukuhlala.* (g) *Umfowethu uvula umnyango ngoba uzwa umuntu uyanqonqotha.* (h) *Umalume uzothukuthela ngoba umntwana udabula amaphepha nezincwadi.* (i) *Umzala akazudlala ithenisi kusasa ngoba uyaqhuga.* (j) *Ubabamkhulu uyagula kodwa uzosinda ngoba uphuza umuthi.* (k) *Intombazane ithintitha amatafula nezitulo nezindonga; isusa* (remove) *uthuli.* (l) *UThemba uyakhala ngoba ubona igazi; uyopha* (*igazi*-blood-3). (m) *Musa ukudonsa kakhulu, intambo izodabuka.* (n) *Qhela, ngifuna*

*ukuhlala.* (o) *Umama ulahla* (*lahla*—throw away) *inyama ngoba iyanuka; inyama ibola masinyane* (quickly) *ngoba ilanga liyashisa.* (p) *Ntambama ngizogunda izinwele futhi ngifuna ukugeza umzimba.* (q) *Abantu bathanda izinyosi ngoba izinyosi zenza uju.* (r) *Ngizoshaya ucingo kusasa ekuseni* (*ukushaya ucingo*—to send a telegram). (s) *Umlimi ufuna ukufuya amakati ngoba amagundane aqeda ummbila namabele.* (t) *Umfana ukhuluma njengobani? Umfana ukhuluma njengoyise.* (u) *Udadewenu uhambelani? Udadewethu uhamba ngoba uyavilapha. Akafuni ukusebenza. Akafuni ukugeza izingubo. Akafuni ukukha amanzi.* (v) *Uyise akabuyi ngani namuhla? Uyise akabuyi namuhla ngoba uyasebenza ngoMgqibelo. Uzobuya kusasa.*

3. Supply the correct concords in the following sentences:—

(a) *Abantwana -funa ukubona izinkomo nezimvu.* (b) *Amahashi -phuza amanzi kodwa izimbuzi -dla ummbila.* (c) *Umfowethu -sebenzi namuhla ngoba -yaqhuga; -zosebenza kusasa.* (d) *Umama -funa ukupheka inyama ngoba inyama -zobola.* (e) *Kusasa sizolima futhi -zotshala.* (f) *Isihamb -thenga isinkwa noshukela; -thengi ufulawa.* (g) *Izinyon. -yandiza; -funa amabele.* (h) *Ubisi -yabila.* (i) *Amadoda -zolanda amatshe ngenqola kodwa umakhi -funi amatshe; funa izitini.* (j) *Imithi -yakhula; -thanda amanzi kakhulu.* k) *Inja -yakhonkotha; -bona amahashi nezimbongolo.* l) *Udadewethu -xova isinkwa; -zobhaka isinkwa ntambama.* (m) *Abantu -thanda ukubona umshado.*

4. *Humusha ngesiNgisi:* (a) *Ubaba uzothenga izinkomo namahashi ngamarandi angu*—400. *Izinkomo ziyadula namahashi ayadula.* (b) *Iyembe libiza malini?* (*malini*—money what i.e. how much?) *Iyembe libiza amarandi amane namasenti amahlanu.* (c) *Ubaba uzothenga izincwadi ngamarandi ayishumi namasenti angu*—60. (d) *Amalahle abiza amasenti*

*angu*—45 *isaka. Izinkuni zibiza amasenti angu*—25 *isaka. Amalahle ayadula.* (e) *Ngizothengela umalume isigqoko ngamarandi amane namasenti angu*—57. (f) *Umama uzo—thenga ushukela ngerandi namasenti angu*—15. (g) *Izimoto ziyadula. Umnumzane uthenga imoto ngamarandi angu*—2800. (h) *Umntwana uzothenga amakhekhe ngamasenti angu*—7. *Akafuni ukuthenga isinkwa.*

5. *Humusha ngesiZulu:* (a) Mother is buying a dress for R3.65. (b) I shall not buy shoes for R6.75. I shall buy shoes for R4.50. (c) How much does bread cost? It costs 9 cents. (d) Coal is expensive but wood is cheap. I shall buy coal for 45 cents. (e) A hat costs R6.75. A pair of trousers costs R12.00. Socks cost 95 cents. (f) The teacher will buy books for R13.65. (g) Mother wants a coat. She wants to buy a coat for R30.87. (h) I shall buy stamps for 10 cents tomorrow.

# CHAPTER 13

## THE NOUN (*Continued*)

### Class 7

The following are some nouns of Class 7:—

| | |
|---|---|
| *ubuso* (face) | *ubuhlungu* (pain) |
| *ubuhlalu* (beads) | *ubusuku* (night) |
| *ubuhle* (beauty) | *ubuthongo* (sleep) |
| *ubunzima* (hardship) | *uboya* (wool/hair) |
| *utshani* (grass) | *ubusika* (winter) |
| *ubukhulu* (bigness/greatness) | *ububi* (evil) |
| *ubuqotho* (honesty) | *utshwala* (beer) |
| *ubudala* (age) | |

The prefix of this class is *ubu-* but *ub-* with stems commencing in a vowel. The subjectival concord is *bu-*.

*N.B.*—(i) This class is non-indicative of number, i.e. nouns in this class may be used in the singular or plural without change of form or tone.

(ii) In *utshani, utshwala* the prefix *ubu-* has been camouflaged by a consonantal change.

(iii) Many abstract nouns are found in this class.

Abstract nouns may be formed from nouns of other classes by prefixing *ubu-* to the noun stem, e.g.:—

| | |
|---|---|
| *ubufundisi* (ministry) | <*umfundisi* (parson)—1 |
| *ubumanzi* (dampness) | <*amanzi* (water)—3 |
| *ubukhosi* (kingship) | <*inkosi* (king)—5 |
| *ubugebenga* (gangsterism) | <*isigebenga* (gangster)—4 |

| | |
|---|---|
| *ubusela* (thieving propensity) | <*isela* (thief)—3 |
| *ubuwula* (stupidity) | <*isiwula* (fool)—4 |
| *ubutha* (enmity) | <*isitha* (enemy—4) |
| *ubuvila* (laziness) | <*ivila* (lazy person)—3 |
| *ubukholwa* (Christianity) | <*ikholwa* (Christian, lit. believer)—3 |
| *ubudoda* (manhood) | <*indoda* (man)—5 |
| *ubulwane* (savagery) | <*isilwane* (animal)—4 |

Examples:—

1. *Izilwane ziyabaleka ngoba utshani buyasha nemithi iyasha* (The animals are running away because the grass is burning and the trees are burning).

2. *Uboya buzohamba ngesitimela nommbila uzohamba ngesitimela* (The wool will go by train and the mealies will go by train).

3. *Inkosi ayithandi ubusela* (The king does not like thieving).

4. *UNkulunkulu uzonda ububi* (God hates evil—*uNkulunkulu*-God-la).

## *IZITHO ZOMZIMBA* (PARTS OF THE BODY)

Only the singular forms are given. The class of the noun is indicated in brackets:—

| | |
|---|---|
| *umzimba*—body (2) | *ikhanda* —head(3) |
| *ubuchopho*—brain (7) | *unwele*—hair(6) |
| *ubuso*—face (7) | *ibunzi*—forehead(3) |
| *iso, ihlo*—eye; *amehlo* (3) | *ishiya*—eyebrow (3) |
| *ukhophe*—eyelash (6) | *indlebe*—ear (5) |
| *impumulo*—nose (5) | *ikhala*—nose, nostril (3) |
| *isihlathi*—cheek (4) | *umlomo*—mouth (2) |
| *udebe*—lip (6) | *ulimi*—tongue (6) |
| *izinyo*—tooth (3) | *umhlathi*—jaw (2) |
| *amadevu*—moustache (3) | *isilevu*—chin (4) |
| *intshebe*—beard (5) | *intamo*—neck (5) |

*ihlombe*—shoulder (3)
*umkhono*—arm, forearm (2)
*isihlakala*—wrist (4)
*umunwe*—finger (2)
*isithupha*—thumb (4)
*unkomba*—forefinger (la)
*umminzo*—gullet (2)
*isifuba*—chest (4)
*inhliziyo*—heart (5)
*isibindi*—liver (4)
*inso*—kidney (5)
*ithumbu*—intestine (3)
*umhlane*—back, of animal or person (2)
*isinqe*—buttock (4)
*ithanga*—thigh (3)
*idolo*—knee (3)
*iqakala*—ankle (3)
*unyawo*—foot (6)
*ingalo*—arm (5)
*indololwane*—elbow (5)
*isandla*—hand (4)
*uzipho*—fingernail (6)
*ucikicane*—small finger (la)
*umphimbo*—throat (2)
*uqhoqhoqho*—windpipe (la)
*iphaphu*—lung (3)
*ubambo*—rib *izimbambo* (6)
*inyongo*—bile, gall-bladder (5)
*isisu*—stomach (4)
*isinye*—bladder (4)
*iqolo*—small of back (3)
*ukhalo*—waist (6)
*umlenze*—leg (2)
*umbala*—shin-bone (2)
*isithende*—heel (4)
*uzwane*—toe (6)

The following verbs may be found useful with parts of the body:—

*cabanga* think)
*cimeza* (close eyes)
*hlafuna* (chew)
*finya* (blow nostril)
*khothama* (bow, bend)
*shefa* (shave)
*phefumula* (breathe)
*khamisa* (open mouth)
*cwayiza* (blink)
*gwinya* (swallow)
*khotha* (lick)
*xubha* (rinse mouth)
*guqa* (kneel)
*enyela* (get sprained)

## Exercise 12

1. Learn the following verbs:—

*linga* (try)
*dlula* (pass)
*zonda* (hate)
*cosha* (pick up)

| | |
|---|---|
| *ozela* (drowse) | *fihla* (hide) |
| *qhuba* (drive/continue) | *phatha* (hold/carry) |
| *phela* (get finished) | *phendula* (answer/turn) |
| *phika* (deny) | *thi* (say) |
| *themba* (trust/hope) | *cinga* (search/look for) |

2. *FUNDA:* (a) *Udokotela uthi khamisa. Ufuna ukubona ulimi nomphimbo.* (b) *Umntwana uyacimeza. Ucimezelani? Ufuna ukulala.* (c) *Umalume ucela umuthi. Umalume ucelelani umuthi? Umalume ucela umuthi ngoba umkakhe uyakhwehlela kakhulu ebusuku; akalali.* (d) *Letha iduku* (handkerchief—3); *ngifuna ukufinya.* (e)*Ubaba uyashefa njalo ekuseni. Akashefi ebusuku.* (f) *Umntwana ulinga ukuvula iminyango namafasitele.* (g) *Amantombazane abona isibuko nezithombe.* (h) *Umalume uthini? Umalume ubuza umbuzo; phendula.* (i) *Udadewenu ucoshelani amalahle nezinkuni? Udadewethu ucosha amalahle nezinkuni ngoba ufuna ukubasa umlilo.* (j) *Abantwana abaculi ngani? Abantwana abaculi ngoba bayozela; bafuna ukulala.* (k) *Umama uzothengani? Umama uzothenga ushukela. Umama uzothengelani ushukela? Umama uzothenga ushukela ngoba ushukela uzophela kusasa.* (l) *Umfana uqhuba izinkomo. Izinkomo zifunani? Izinkomo zifuna amanzi.* (m) *Isitimela sizodlula kusasa ekuseni.* (n) *Ngizophatha ijazi nesigqoko ngoba izulu liyana.* (o) *Umntwana ufuna ukuncela.* (p) *Malini ijazi? Ijazi libiza amarandi angu—32.* (q) *Udadewenu ucula njengobani? Udadewethu ucula njengoNorah.*

# CHAPTER 14

## THE NOUN (*Continued*)

### CLASS 8

*ukudla* (food/eating/to eat)
*ukukhanya* (light/to shine)
*ukuphela* (end/ending/to end)
*ukuvuma* (consent/to agree)
*ukufa* (death/to die)
*ukugula* (illness/to be ill)
*ukuthola* (finding/to find)
*ukufika* (arriving/to arrive)
*ukubuka* (looking at/to look at)
*ukulalela* (listening/to listen)
*ukudabuka* (sorrow/to be sorry)
*ukuphinda* (repeating/to repeat)
*ukuphupha* (dreaming/to dream)
*ukuthinta* (touching/to touch)
*ukufundisa* (teaching/to teach)
*ukuphila* (health/to be in health)
*ukuhlakanipha* (wisdom/to be wise)
*ukushisa* (heat/to be hot)
*ukukhala* (cry/to cry)
*ukuthi* (saying/to say)
*ukubuza* (asking/to ask)
*ukuthula* (quietness/to be quiet)
*ukubanda* (cold/to be cold)
*ukulamba* (hunger/to be hungry)
*ukushanela* (sweeping/to sweep)
*ukudabuka* (getting torn/to get torn)
*ukuphosa* (throwing/to throw)
*ukuphuza* (drinking/to drink)
*ukufihla* (hiding/to hide)
*ukusukuma* (standing up/to stand up)

*ukuhlabelela* (singing/to sing) *ukuhlafuna* (chewing/to chew).

The prefix is *uku-* and the subjectival concord is *ku-*.

*N.B.* (i) This class is non-indicative of number.

(ii) This is a class of verbal nouns.

When the prefix *uku-* is used with vowel commencing verb stems, the second *-u* becomes *w* before *a-* and *e-* and drops before *o-*, e.g.:—

| | |
|---|---|
| *ukwakha* (building/to build) | *ukwazi* (knowledge/to know) |
| *ukwaba* (dividing/to divide) | *ukwalusa* (herding/to herd) |
| *ukwala* (refusing/to refuse) | *ukwaphula* (breaking/to break) |
| *ukwenza* (doing/to do/to make) | *ukweba* (stealing/to steal) |
| *ukwehla* (climbing down/to climb down) | *ukwesaba* (fear/to fear) |
| *ukona* (wrong-doing/to do wrong) | *ukosa* (grilling, etc./to grill, etc.) |
| *ukondla* (supporting, as family/to support, e.g. family) | *ukopha* (bleeding/to bleed) |

## Vowel Commencing Verbs

When using vowel commencing verbs, observe the following:—

1. When there is no adjunct, insert *-ya-* between the subjectival concord and the verb stem but *-ya-* > *-y-;* e.g.:

*ngi-ya-akha* > *ngiyakha* (I am building)
*ba-ya-akha* > *bayakha* (They are building)
*ngi-ya-esaba* > *ngiyesaba* (I am afraid)
*ngi-ya-osa* > *ngiyosa* (I am frying)
*ba-ya-osa* > *bayosa* (they are frying)

2. When there is an adjunct, i.e. when something comes after the verb: (i) *-ya-* is not used;

(ii) When the subjectival concord has a consonant (except Cl. 6 sg. and Cl. 8) its vowel is dropped.

| | | |
|---|---|---|
| *ngi-akha indlu* | > | *ngakha indlu* (I build a house) |
| *ba-akha indlu* | > | *bakha indlu* (They build a house) |
| *ngi-enza itiye* | > | *ngenza itiye* (I make tea) |
| *ba-enza itiye* | > | *benza itiye* (They make tea) |
| *ngi-osa inyama* | > | *ngosa inyama* (I fry meat) |
| *ba-osa inyama* | > | *bosa inyama* (They fry meat) |

(iii) The *-u-* of the subjectival concord in Cl. 6 sg. and Cl. 8 becomes *w* before *a-* and *e-* but drops before *o-*.

Cl. 6:

| | | |
|---|---|---|
| *lu-akha indlu* | > | *lwakha indlu* (it builds a house) |
| *lu-enza itiye* | > | *lwenza itiye* (it makes tea) |
| *lu-osa inyama* | > | *losa inyama* (it fries meat) |

Cl. 8:

| | | |
|---|---|---|
| *ku-akha indlu* | > | *kwakha indlu* (it builds a house) |
| *ku-enza itiye* | > | *kwenza itiye* (it makes tea) |
| *ku-osa inyama* | > | *kosa inyama* (it fries meat) |

(iv) When the subjectival concord is a vowel only:

Subj. concord *u*, becomes *w* before *a-*, *e-*, *o-*

Subj. concord *i-* becomes *y* before *a-*, *e-*, *o-*

Subj. concord *a-* drops in every case.

*u-* > *w*: 2nd pers. sg.:

| | | |
|---|---|---|
| *u-akha* | > | *wakha indlu* (you build a house) |
| *u-enza* | > | *wenza itiye* (you make tea) |
| *u-osa* | > | *wosa inyama* (you fry meat) |

Cl. 1 sg.:

| | | |
|---|---|---|
| *Umuntu u-akha* | > | *wakha indlu* (The person builds a house). |
| *Umuntu u-enza* | > | *wenza itiye* (The person makes tea). |
| *Umuntu u-osa* | > | *wosa inyama* (The person fries meat). |

*I* > *y*: Cl. 5 sg.:

| | | |
|---|---|---|
| *inkosi i-akha* | > | *yakha indlu* (The chief builds a house). |

*Inkosi i-enza* > *yenza itiye* (The chief makes tea).
*Inkosi i-osa* > *yosa inyama* (The chief fries meat).

*a* drops: Cl. 3 pl.

*Amadoda a-akha* > *akha indlu* (The men build a house).
*Amadoda a-enza* > *enza itiye* (The men make tea).
*Amadoda a-osa* > *osa inyama* (The men fry meat).

Negative:—

| | | |
|---|---|---|
| *ngakha, ngiyakha* | > | *angakhi* |
| *bakha, bayakha* | > | *abakhi* |
| *ngesaba, ngiyesaba* | > | *angesabi* |
| *ngosa, ngiyosa* | > | *angosi* |
| *bosa, bayosa* | > | *abosi* |
| *lwakha, luyakha* | > | *alwakhi* |
| *lwenza, luyenza* | > | *alwenzi* |
| *losa, luyosa* | > | *alosi* |
| *kwakha, kuyakha* | > | *akwakhi* |
| *kwenza, kuyenza* | > | *akwenzi* |
| *kosa, kuyosa* | > | *akosi* |
| *ngazi, ngiyazi* | > | *angazi* |
| *sazi, siyazi* | > | *asazi* |
| *wazi, uyazi* | > | *awazi* |
| 2nd. pers. sg. | | |
| *nazi, niyazi* | > | *anazi* |
| 3rd. pers. Cl. 1 sg. | | |
| *wazi, uyazi* | > | *akazi* |

Examples:

1. *Umakhi wakha indlu ngamatshe. Akakhi isibaya* (The builder is building a house with stones. He is not building a cattle kraal).
2. *Odadewenu bosani na? Odadewethu bosa amaqanda Abosi amasositshi* (What are your sisters frying/

roasting/grilling? My/our sisters are frying eggs. They are not frying sausages).

3. *Unesi ufuna ukwenza itiye. Akenzi ikhofi* (The nurse wants to make tea. She is not making coffee).
4. *Siyosa. Sosa inyama. Asosi amaqanda* (We are frying/roasting/grilling. We are frying/roasting/grilling meat. We are not frying eggs).
5. *Ubaba uyazi kodwa abafundisi abazi* (Father knows but the ministers do not know).
6. *Amadoda ayesaba. Esaba inkosi. Akesabi umfundisi* (The men are afraid. They fear the chief. They are not afraid of the minister).
7. *Intombazana yenza iphalishi. Ayenzi itiye* (The girl is making porridge. She is not making tea).
8. *Ngosa ummbila. Angosi inyama. Ngosela ubaba* (I am roasting mealies. I am not roasting meat. I am roasting for Father).
9. *Wenza itiye na? Cha angenzi itiye./Yebo ngenza itiye. Ngenzela umama* (Are you making tea? No, I am not making tea./Yes, I am making tea. I am making (it) for mother).
10. *Abantwana besaba izinja. Abesabi amakati* (The children fear dogs. They do not fear cats).
11. *Uhlanya lwephula amafasitele* (The mad man is breaking windows).
12. *Umfana wona umsebenzi* (The boy is spoiling the work).

# CHAPTER 15

## THE USE OF NA- (*HAVE*)

THE English "have" is expressed in Zulu by using *na-*. *Na-* comes in between the subjectival concord of the governing noun and the noun or pronoun indicating that which is "had". In the positive forms vowel coalescence takes place when *na-* is prefixed to nouns. Examples:—

1. *Ngi-na-umntwana* > *Nginomntwana* (I have a child).
2. *Si-na-inja* > *Sinenja* (We have a dog).
3. *Ubaba u-na-izincwadi* > *unezincwadi* (Father has books).
4. *Umfula u-na-amatshe* > *unamatshe* (The river has stones).
5. *Ihashi li-na-umsila* > *linomsila* (The horse has a tail).
6. *Ulwandle lu-na-izinhlanzi* > *lunezinhlanzi* (The sea has fish).

In the negative *a-* or *ka-* (*aka-* in Cl. 1 sg.) is prefixed to the positive forms. No coalescence, however, takes place as the initial vowel of the noun to which *na-* is prefixed is dropped in every case.

1. *A-ngi-na-umntwana* > *Anginamntwana* (I have no child).
2. *A-si-na-inja* > *Asinanja* (We have no dog).
3. *Ubaba aka-na-izincwadi* > *akanazincwadi* (Father has no books).
4. *Umfula a-w-u-na-amatshe* > *awunamatshe* (The river has no stones).

5. *Ihashi a-li-na-umsila* > *alinamsila* (The horse has no tail).

6. *Ulwandle a-lu-na-izinhlanzi* > *alunazinhlanzi* (The sea has no fish).

## EXERCISE 13

1. *Humusha ngesiNgisi:* (a) *Umlimi unamahashi nezinkomo nezimvu nezinkukhu namageja, futhi umlimi unenqola.* (b) *Umuntu unekhanda namehlo nezandla nezinyawo kodwa umuntu akanazimpaphe.* (c) *Umhloli akazufika kusasa ngoba unomkhuhlane; uyakhwehlela kakhulu.* (d) *Umakhi akazulanda izitini nothayela ngenqola ngoba unelori; futhi akanazinkabi.* (e) *UJane akenzi itiye ngoba akanashukela; uzothenga ushukela kusasa ngerandi.* (f) *Imithi iyafa ngoba ayinamanzi; ilanga liyashisa, imvula ayini. Abantu bayathandaza, bacela imvula.* (g) *Indodana yakha indlu ngoba uyise akanandlu; uyise akanamali ngoba akasebenzi.* (h) *Ijazi libiza amarandi angu—25; umzala uzothenga ijazi ngoba unemali.* (i) *Inkomo inezimpondo nembuzi inezimpondo kodwa amahashi akanazimpondo.* (j) *Abantwana banezicathulo namasokisi kodwa abanazigqoko.* (k) *USipho akafundi ngoba akanazincwadi; uzofunda ngonyaka ozayo.* (l) *Umama akazubasa namuhla ngoba akanamalahle; amalahle azofika kusasa ekuseni ngenqola.* (m) *Inkosi inamadodana kodwa ayinamadodakazi. Inkosi ayijabuli ngoba ayinamadodakazi.* (n) *Umlimi akazutshala kusasa ngoba akanambewu.* (o) *Isikhukhukazi sinamaqanda kodwa iqhude alinamaqanda.* (p) *Ubaba unesibhamu; udubula izilwane nezinyoni ngesibhamu.* (q) *Izinkukhu ziyanda ngoba ziyazalela.*

2. *Humusha ngesiZulu:* (a) Do not beat the dog because it will run away. (b) A person chews with (by means of) teeth. (c) Why are the children crying? The children are crying because they want sweets and cakes. (d) What does

the boy say? He says he wants trousers and a shirt. Father will buy trousers and a shirt for the boy. (e) Uncle will not arrive tomorrow; he will arrive the day after tomorrow. Why will uncle not arrive tomorrow? He will not arrive tomorrow because he is working. (f) The parson teaches the heathen the Bible. (g) We do not like thieves because thieves steal. (h) The child is crying because he is afraid. What is he afraid of? (i) The boy is driving the cattle; they want water and grass. (j) The white man does not go by train. Why does he not go by train? He does not go by train because he has a car. (k) The carpenter will buy a hammer and nails. (l) The chief will pass in the afternoon. (m) The people are trying to make a road. (n) The Inspector is asking a question. Why does he not answer? (o) Why are the women kneeling? The women are kneeling because they are praying. (p) A person breathes by means of nostrils. (q) The girl is opening her mouth because she is drinking medicine. The girl does not like medicine. (r) The farmer sells horses, cattle, sheep and wool. (s) Children drink milk, women drink water and men drink beer. (t) On Sunday Christians go to church. Ministers preach on Sunday. (u) Why do the men beat the thief? The men beat the thief because they do not like thieving. (v) The woman will finish the work in the afternoon. (w) Why does uncle ask for forgiveness? Uncle is asking for forgiveness because he likes peace. (x) Don't tear the books. (y) We eat porridge with spoons. (z) We shall remove the weeds next week.

# CHAPTER 16

## THE PAST TENSE

THERE are several ways of expressing past action in Zulu. The past continuous is taken first.

### IMMEDIATE PAST CONTINUOUS

*bengifunda* (I have been reading).
*bengisebenza* (I have been working).
*besidlala ibhola* (We have been playing soccer).
*bewubhala* (You have been writing).
*benicula* (You (pl.) have been singing).

The following table illustrates this tense for all persons and classes:—

| | Singular | Plural |
|---|---|---|
| 1st Pers.: | | |
| | *bengifunda* | *besifunda* |
| 2nd Pers.: | | |
| | *bewufunda* | *benifunda* |
| 3rd Pers.: | | |
| 1. | (*umuntu*) *ubefunda* | *bebefunda* |
| 2. | (*umuthi*) *bewukhula* | *beyikhula* |
| 3. | (*ihashi*) *beligijima* | *abegijima* |
| 4. | (*isihambi*) *besiphumula* | *beziphumula* |
| 5. | (*inja*) *beyikhonkotha* | *bezikhonkotha* |
| 6. | (*ukhuni*) *belusha* | *bezisha* |
| 7. | (*utshani*) *bebusha* | |
| 8. | (*ukudla*) *bekusha* | |

*N.B.* (i) *be-* is prefixed to the present tense form without *-ya-*. (ii) In 2nd pers. sing., Cl. 2 sing. and pl. and Cl. 5 sing. *w* comes in between *e* and *u*, and *y* between *e* and *i*. (iii) In Cl. 1 sing. and Cl. 3 pl. a concord precedes *be-*. (Although variants occur in some cases, e.g. 2nd pers. sg., the variants are not given at this stage).

NEGATIVE

| | Singular | Plural |
|---|---|---|
| 1st Pers.: | | |
| | *bengingafundi* | *besingafundi* |
| 2nd Pers.: | | |
| | *bewungafundi* | *beningafundi* |
| 3rd Pers.: | | |
| Cl. 1 | *ubengafundi* | *bebengafundi* |
| Cl. 2 | *bewungakhuli* | *beyingakhuli* |
| Cl. 3 | *belingagijimi* | *abengagijimi* |
| Cl. 4 | *besingaphumuli* | *bezingaphumuli* |
| Cl. 5 | *beyingakhonkothi* | *bezingakhonkothi* |
| Cl. 6 | *belungashi* | *bezingashi* |
| Cl. 7 | *bebungashi* | |
| Cl. 8 | *bekungashi* | |

The negative is formed by inserting the negative element *-nga-* and changing the final *-a* to *-i*.

REMOTE PAST CONTINUOUS

| | Singular | Plural |
|---|---|---|
| 1st Pers.: | | |
| | *ngangifunda* | *sasifunda* |
| 2nd Pers.: | | |
| | *wawufunda* | *nanifunda* |
| 3rd Pers.: | | |
| Cl. 1 | *wayefunda* | *babefunda* |
| Cl. 2 | *wawukhula* | *yayikhula* |

| Singular | | Plural |
|---|---|---|
| Cl. 3 *laligijima* | | *ayegijima* |
| Cl. 4 *sasiphumula* | | *zaziphumula* |
| Cl. 5 *yayikhonkotha* | | *zazikhonkotha* |
| Cl. 6 *lwalusha* | | *zazisha* |
| Cl. 7 | *babusha* | |
| Cl. 8 | *kwakusha* | |

e.g.:

*bengifunda*—I have been reading.
*ngangifunda*—I was reading (sometime ago).
*bengibhala*—I have been writing.
*ngangibhala*—I was writing.

NEGATIVE

| Singular | | Plural |
|---|---|---|
| 1st Pers.: | | |
| *nganginga fundi* | | *sasingafundi* |
| 2nd Pers.: | | |
| *wawungafundi* | | *naningafundi* |
| 3rd Pers.: | | |
| Cl. 1 *wayengafundi* | | *babengafundi* |
| Cl. 2 *wawungakhuli* | | *yayingakhuli* |
| Cl. 3 *lalingagijimi* | | *ayengagijimi* |
| Cl. 4 *sasingaphumuli* | | *zazingaphumuli* |
| Cl. 5 *yayingakhonkothi* | | *zazingakhonkothi* |
| Cl. 6 *lwalungashi* | | *zazingashi* |
| Cl. 7 | *babungashi* | |
| Cl. 8 | *kwakungashi* | |

*N.B.* In the negative, the element *-nga-* is infixed to the positive forms and the final *-a* becomes *-i*.

The remote past employs past subjectival concords. These are:—

| Singular | | Plural |
|---|---|---|
| 1st Pers. : | | |
| *nga-* | | *sa-* |
| 2nd Pers.: | | |
| *wa-* | | *na-* |
| 3rd Pers.: | | |
| Cl. 1 *wa-* | | *ba-* |
| Cl. 2 *wa-* | | *ya-* |
| Cl. 3 *la-* | | *a-* |
| Cl. 4 *sa-* | | *za-* |
| Cl. 5 *ya-* | | *za-* |
| Cl. 6 *lwa-* | | *za-* |
| Cl. 7 | *ba-* | |
| Cl. 8 | *kwa-* | |

Examples:—

1. *Umfowethu ubelima ekuseni* (My brother has been ploughing in the morning).

2. *Amadoda abexosha amabhubesi* (The men have been chasing lions).

3. *Abakhi bebefuna amanzi namatshe nesihlabathi* (The builders have been wanting water and stones and sand).

4. *Bengithenga izicathulo namasokisi* (I have been buying shoes and socks/stockings).

5. *Udadewethu ubekhanyisa izibane* (My sister has been lighting lamps).

6. *USipho wayefunda* (Sipho was learning, i.e. attending school).

7. *Amadoda ayebaleka* (The men were running away).

8. *Ihashi lalidla ummbila* (The horse was eating mealies).

9. *Izinja zazixosha izinkomo* (The dogs were chasing cattle).

10. *Amadada ayendiza* (The ducks were flying).

In the negative the above sentences would be:—

1. *Umfowethu ubengalimi ekuseni.*
2. *Amadoda abengaxoshi amabhubesi.*
3. *Abakhi bebengafuni amanzi namatshe nesihlabathi.*
4. *Bengingathengi izicathulo namasokisi.*
5. *Udadewethu ubengakhanyisi izibane.*
6. *USipho wayengafundi.*
7. *Amadoda ayengabaleki.*
8. *Ihashi lalingadli ummbila.*
9. *Izinja zazingaxoshi izinkomo.*
10. *Amadada ayengandizi.*

## Exercise 14

1. *Humusha ngesiNgisi:* (a) *Izolo bengisebenza. Ekuseni bengimba imigodi ngoba ubaba ubefuna ukutshala imithi. Emini bengisika utshani ngoba amahashi adla utshani. Ntambama bengingasebenzi, bengiphumula. Ebusuku bengixoxa* (*xoxa*—converse) *ngoba angifundi izincwadi futhi angifundi amaphepha. Anginamaphepha futhi anginazincwadi.* (b) *Umama ubenzani? Umama ubethunga izingubo futhi ubepheka. Umama unomshini futhi unesitofu. Ubengagezi izingubo futhi ubenga-ayini.* (c) *Amahashi abedla utshani nommbila futhi abephuza amanzi kodwa abengalimi; ubaba ubelima ngezinkomo. Ubaba unezinkomo namahashi.* (d) *Ebusuku izinja bezikhonkotha ngoba bezibona amasela. Amasela abelinga ukweba izinkukhu namagalikuni* (turkeys—3). (e) *Ngonyaka odlule ngangifunda, ngangingasebenzi, kodwa ngalonyaka angifundi, ngiyasebenza.* (f) *Udadewethu wayesebenza eGoli* (in Johannesburg) *kodwa manje akasebenzi: usiza umama.* (g) *Ekuseni bengicosha amalahle ngoba bengifuna ukubasa umlilo. Bengifuna ukupheka ukudla nokubhaka isinkwa namakhekhe.* (h) *Ubaba ubebulala inyoka ngesibhamu. Ubaba unesibhamu; akabulali inyoka ngenduku.*

*Umama wesaba inyoka kakhulu.* (i) *Umalume wayenzani ngoMsombuluko ekuseni? Umalume wayekhombisa izihambi indlela.* (j) *Izinkabi zazidonsani ngoLwesithathu? Zazidonsa imoto; zazingadonsi inqola.* (k) *Besibala izimvu nezimbuzi izolo ntambama; ubaba unezimvu nezimbuzi nezinkomo nezingulube.* (l) *Besihleka ngoba besijabula; besidla amaswidi namakhekhe.* (m) *Kusihlwa ugogo ubekhanyisa amakhandlela; asikhanyisi ugesi.* (n) *Kuthangi besidlala ithenisi kodwa ngomhlomunye sizodlala ibhola.* (o) *Umntwana ubelandela unina ekuseni; ubengalandeli ugogo.* (p) *Umalume ubethenga amabhulashi* (brushes—3) *nopende ngoba uzopenda izindonga neminyango namafasitele.* (q) *Umfana ubengasebenzi kodwa uyaphika; uthi ubesebenza.* (r) *Amadoda esula umjuluko. Amadoda ayajuluka ngoba abesebenza.*

2. *Humusha ngesiZulu:* (a) In the morning we were digging holes; father wants to plant trees. (b) We were tying the horses because the horses wanted to run away. (c) In the evening I was reading books and newspapers. (d) Yesterday the builder was loading bricks and planks; tomorrow he will fetch sand. (e) The dogs were barking; they were chasing away thieves. (f) In the morning my sister was washing clothes; in the afternoon she will iron. (g) The girl was making tea; she was not sweeping and she was not baking bread. At noon she will set the table. (h) Yesterday the parson was preaching. (i) The men are drinking beer now; in the morning they were drinking tea; men do not like tea. (j) The thief was hiding money. (k) The man is beating the boys because the boys were throwing stones; they were hitting windows with stones. (l) The children are looking at the animals; children like to look at animals. (m) Grandmother has been ill but now she is not ill. (n) The boys were driving cattle; the cattle

wanted water. (o) I was sleepy but now I am not sleepy. (p) The child is licking the spoon because he likes honey very much; mother has been giving the child honey. (q) He is rinsing the mouth because he has been eating. (r) Sipho will look after the sheep and goats because Mandla s going away. (s) I have been cleaning my teeth.

3. *FUNDA!*

(a) *Izolo ekuseni umntwana ubekhalelani? Umntwana ubekhala ngoba ubefuna unina. Umntwana ubefuna ukuncela* (to suck). *Unina ubengafuni ukuncelisa* (suckle) *umntwana ngoba ubesebenza. Ubegeza izingubo ngamanzi nensipho. Uyise ubengagezi izingubo. Ekuseni uyise ubegeza imoto. Emini ubefunda amaphepha nezincwadi. Uyise uthanda ukufunda amaphepha nezincwadi. OJane bebengakhali, bebengagezi izingubo, bebengafundi izincwadi namaphepha, bebengagezi imoto. OJane bebedlala ibhola.*

(b) *Amahashi abedla utshani nezinkomo bezidla utshani. Amahashi abengalimi nezinkomo bezingalimi. Izinkomo bezilima kuthangi. Umlimi uthanda ukulima ngezinkabi. Akathandi ukulima ngamahashi. Umlimi akathandi ngani ukulima ngamahashi? Angazi. Inja beyingadli utshani. Izinja azidli utshani. Izinja zithanda inyama namathambo.*

(c) *Udokotela ubepopola* (examine) *isiguli. Isiguli besifike ebusuku. Isiguli besigula. Besishisa futhi besikhwehlela* (*khwehlela*—cough). *Unesi ubesiza udokotela kodwa unesi ubengapopoli. Unesi ubenza imithi. Udokotela unika iziguli imithi. Iziguli zinika udokotela imali.*

(d) *Umfowethu wayengafundi nabafowabo babengafundi. Umfowethu wayesebenza nabafowabo babesebenza. Udadewethu wayengasebenzi nawodadewabo babengasebenzi. Udadewethu wayefunda nawodadewabo babefunda. Udadewethu wayethanda ukufunda nawodadewabo babethanda ukufunda.*

*Ufukmethu wayengafuni ukufunda nabafowabo babengafuni owufunda. Udadewethu wayefunda amaphepha nezincwadi. Nawodadewabo babefunda amaphepha nezincwadi.*

(e) *Izinja zazikhonkothelani ngoMsombuluko ebusuku? Izinja zazikhonkotha ngoba zazibona izinkomo namahashi. Izinja zazixosha izinkomo namahashi. Izinja zazingakhonkothi amasela na? Cha, izinja zazingakhonkothi amasela. Izinkomo zazenzani? Izinkomo zazidla ummbila namahashi ayedla ummbila. Izolo ebusuku izinja bezingakhonkothi.*

4. Learn the following:—

*Ukudla* (Food)

| | |
|---|---|
| *ukolo*—wheat (la) | *ibele*—kaffir-corn (3) |
| *ikhabe*—sweet melon (3) | *iheleyisi* —mealie-rice (3 |
| *isitambu*—samp (4) | *ulaza*—cream (6) |
| *ukhali*—curry-powder (la) | *umqwayiba*—biltong (2) |
| *idombolo*—dumpling (3) | *uphuthini*—pudding (la) |
| *isaqathe*—carrot | *isobho*—soup/gravy (3) |
| *isitshulu*—stew (4) | *ujeli*—jelly (la) |
| *ukhasitadi*—custard (la) | *upoloni*—polony (la) |
| *inyama yenkomo*—beef | *inyama yemvu*—mutton |
| *inyama yengulube*—pork | *ubhakeni*—bacon (la) |

*Izithelo* (Fruit)

| | |
|---|---|
| *isithelo*—fruit (4) | *ipentshisi*—peach (3) |
| *ihabhula*—apple (3) | *iwolintshi, iorintshi*——orange (3) |
| *ilamula*—lemon (3) | *ubhanana*—banana (la) |
| *uphopho, upopo*—paw paw (la) | *ibhilikosi*—apricot (3) |
| *ipulamu*—plum (3) | *ugwava*—guava (la) |
| *inantshi*—naartjie (3) | *ikhiwane*—fig (3) |
| *umango*—mango (la) | *ikwipili*—quince (3) |
| *igilebhisi*—grape (3) | *uganandela*—granadilla (la) |
| *ihananadi*—pomegranate (3) | *uphayinaphu*—pine-apple |

*ukwatapheya*—avocado pear (la)

(la)

*umalikwata*—loquat (la)

Verbs:—

*ukuphaka* (to dish out food)
*ukumboza* (to cover, e.g. with lid, cloth, etc.)
*ukuhluba* (to peel)
*ukugcoba* (to smear, to anoint, e.g. butter)
*ukuqoba* (to chop to pieces, e.g. meat)
*ukwekhama* (to squeeze, e.g. lemon, orange)

# CHAPTER 17

## TO INDICATE PLACE AT, TO, FROM, IN, ETC.

ZULU has no prepositions. To indicate place at, to, from, in, etc. Zulu has special locative forms derived from nouns and pronouns, e.g.:—

*Ngihlala eGoli* (I live in Johannesburg)
*Ngivela eGoli* (I come from Johannesburg)
*Ngiya eGoli* (I am going to Johannesburg)

A. Place names of foreign origin:—

Prefix *e-* to form locative: e.g.:

*eCape Town*—to, from, in, etc. Cape Town
*eBloemfontein*—to, from, in, etc. Bloemfontein
*eSprings*—to, from, in, etc. Springs
*eJohannesburg*—to, from, in, etc. Johannesburg
*eWelkom*—to, from, in, etc. Welkom
*ePretoria*—to, from, in, etc. Pretoria

Johannesburg is commonly referred to as *eGoli*, Pretoria as *ePitoli*, and Bloemfontein as *eBlomfanteni*.

Examples:—

(a) *Umlungu ufuna ukuyaphi? Umlungu ufuna ukuya eWelkom ngoLwesithathu* (Where does the whiteman want to go?—lit. The whiteman wants to go where?—The whiteman wants to go to Welkom on Wednesday) *phi?*—where?

(b) *Udadewenu uhlalaphi? Udadewethu uhlala eSprings* (Where does your sister live? My sister lives at Springs).

(c) *Abaholi bavelaphi? Abaholi bavela eBlomfanteni* (Where do the leaders come from? The leaders come from Bloemfontein).

(d) *Ngiyazi eFilidi* (I know (at) Vryheid).

(e) *Siya ePitoli; sifuna ukubona umncintiswano* (We are going to Pretoria; we want to see the competition).

B. Nouns indicating rivers, mountains, towns:—

(i) Nouns indicating rivers, mountains, towns form the locative by prefixing *e-*, in place of the initial vowel of the noun. Nouns of Class 6 sing. prefix *o-*, e.g.:—

*uMnambithi* (Klip River, Ladysmith) > *eMnambithi*

*uMtshezi* (Estcourt) > *eMtshezi*

*uMgungundlovu* (Pietermaritzburg) > *eMgungundlovu*

*uKhahlamba* (Drakensberg) > *oKhahlamba*

*uThukela* (Tugela River) > *oThukela*

*uMsunduze* (uMsunduze River) > *eMsunduze*

(ii) Some place names, especially names of mountains, take *kwa-* in the locative. This construction is mainly found with place names which seem to be derived from names of persons, e.g.:—

*uJonono* (Jonono Mt.) > *kwaJonono*

*uCeza* (Ceza Mt.) > *kwaCeza*

*uHlazakazi* (Hlazakazi Mt.) > *kwaHlazakazi*

*uZulu* (the Zulu people) > *kwaZulu* (in, from, to, etc. Zululand, i.e. the land of Zulu).

Examples:—

(a) *Ngihlala kwaZulu* (I live in Zululand).

(b) *Abantwana bahlamba eMsunduze* (The children swim at uMsunduze River).

(c) *Ubaba uzothengisa izinkomo eMnambithi* (Father will sell cattle at Ladysmith).

C. Use of *ku-* in forming locatives:—

(i) With nouns of Class 1 sing. and plural: Drop the

initial vowel of the noun and prefix *ku*:

| | |
|---|---|
| *umfundisi* > *kumfundisi* | *abafundisi* > *kubafundisi* |
| *umuntu* > *kumuntu* | *abantu* > *kubantu* |
| *umzali* > *kumzali* | *abazali* > *kubazali* |

(ii) With nouns of Class 1a sing. and plural: In the sing. drop the initial vowel of the noun and prefix *ku-;* in the plural prefix *k-:*

| | |
|---|---|
| *ugogo* > *kugogo* | *ogogo* > *kogogo* |
| *umalume* > *kumalume* | *omalume* > *komalume* |
| *unogwaja* > *kunogwaja* | *onogwaja* > *konogwaja* |

(iii) With personal nouns of Class 3 plural: Prefix *ku-* in place of the initial vowel of the noun:

| | |
|---|---|
| *amadoda* > *kumadoda* | *amadodana* > *kumadodana* |
| *amadodakazi* > *kumadodakazi* | *amakhosi* > *kumakhosi* |
| *amakhosikazi* > *kumakhosikazi* | *amantombazane* > *kumantombazane* |

(iv) With Class 3 plural nouns which are names of races and tribes:

| | |
|---|---|
| *amaSwazi* > *kumaSwazi* | *amaXhosa* > *kumaXhosa* |
| *amaBhunu* > *kumaBhunu* | *amaNgisi* > *kumaNgisi* |
| *amaMpondo* > *kumaMpondo* | *amaJalimane* > *kumaJalimane* |

In (iii) and (iv) the construction with *ku* is a variant. The alternative construction is described below under D.

Examples:—

(a) *Ubaba uzoyaphi kusasa? Ubaba uzoya kumfundisi kusasa* (Where will father go tomorrow? Father will go to the parson tomorrow).

(b) *Abafana bavela kugogo* (The boys come from grandmother).

(c) *Sizolanda imali kumakhi* (We shall fetch money from the builder).

(d) *Umlimi uzothenga izimvu kumaMpondo* (The farmer

will buy sheep from the Pondos).

D. Locatives formed from nouns of Classes 2-8:—

(i) Prefix *e-* in place of the initial vowel of the noun except in Class 6 sing. In Class 6 sing. prefix *o-*.

(ii) The following suffixal changes operate:

*-a* and *-e* give place to *-eni*
*-i* gives place to *-ini*
*-o* gives place to *-weni*
*-u* gives place to *-wini*

Examples:—

| | | | |
|---|---|---|---|
| *intaba* | > *entabeni* | *ikhala* | > *ekhaleni* |
| *isandla* | > *esandleni* | *indlebe* | > *endlebeni* |
| *umlenze* | > *emlenzeni* | *umbhede* | > *embhedeni* |
| *umuthi* | > *emuthini* | *imbuzi* | > *embuzini* |
| *ihashi* | > *ehashini* | *idolo* | > *edolweni* |
| *isango* | > *esangweni* | *umdlalo* | > *emdlalweni* |
| *izulu* | > *ezulwini* (sky/ heaven) | *ubuhlalu* | > *ebuhlalwini* |

Class 6 singular:

| | | | |
|---|---|---|---|
| *ukhamba* | > *okhambeni* | *ukhezo* | > *okhezweni* |
| *ubisi* | > *obisini* | *uphondo* | > *ophondweni* |

Observe the locatives of the following nouns:—

| | | | |
|---|---|---|---|
| *indlu* | > *endlini* | *imvu* | > *emvini* |
| *inkomo* | > *enkomeni* | *insimu* | > *ensimini* |
| *indlovu* | > *endlovini* | | |

E. Nouns in which there is no suffixal change. There are several nouns in which there is no suffixal change, e.g.:—

| | |
|---|---|
| *iMpumalanga* (East) | > *eMpumalanga* |
| *iNtshonalanga* (West) | > *eNtshonalanga* |
| *iNyakatho* (North) | > *eNyakatho* |
| *iNingizimu* (South) | > *eNingizimu* |
| *imini* (mid-day/daytime) | > *emini* |
| *ihlobo* (summer) | > *ehlobo* |

| | |
|---|---|
| *ubusika* (winter) | > *ebusika* |
| *ikwindla* (autumn) | > *ekwindla* |
| *intwasahlobo* (spring) | > *entwasahlobo* |
| *iziko* (fireplace) | > *eziko* |
| *umsamo* (back of hut inside) | > *emsamo* |
| *umnyango* (door/doorway) | > *emnyango* |
| *ihlombe* (shoulder) | > *ehlombe* |
| *iqolo* (small of back) | > *eqolo* |
| *umhlane* (back of person/animal) | > *emhlane* |
| *isitolo* (shop) | > *esitolo* |
| *inkantolo* (Magistrate's Court) | > *enkantolo* |
| *ubusuku* (night) | > *ebusuku* |
| *ikhaya* (home) | > *ekhaya* |
| *ikhanda* (head) | > *ekhanda* |
| *isibhedlela* (hospital) | > *esibhedlela* |
| *ulwandle* (sea) | > *olwandle, elwandle* |

F. Sound changes in the formation of locatives:—

With some nouns, there is a change of sound when forming locatives. Generally, this will happen if the last syllable of the noun has a bilabial consonant (i.e. pronounced with both lips), and the following vowel is either *-o* or *-u*. The bilabial consonant changes into a palatal sound.

In Zulu, bilabial consonants may not be followed by *w*. In some cases *w* is dropped, but in the formation of locatives it gives place to a palatal sound. The following are the changes which occur: (i) **p** > **tsh, mp** > **ntsh, bh** > **j**: these three changes do not occur very frequently.

(ii) **ph** > **sh, b** > **tsh, m** > **ny, mb** > **nj**: these four changes occur more frequently, e.g.:—

| | | |
|---|---|---|
| **ph** > **sh:** | *ubuchopho* (brain) | > *ebuchosheni* |
| | *iphaphu* (lung) | > *ephashini* |
| | *impuphu* (mealie meal) | > *empushini* |

| | | |
|---|---|---|
| **b > tsh:** | *ingubo* (dress) | > *engutsheni* |
| | *imbobo* (hole) | > *embotsheni* |
| | *imvubu* (sjambok/ hippo) | > *emvutshini* |
| **m > ny:** | *umlomo* (mouth) | > *emlonyeni* |
| | *intamo* (neck) | > *entanyeni* |
| | *isibhamu* (gun) | > *esibhanyini* |
| **mb > nj:** | *ithambo* (bone) | > *ethanjeni* |
| | *intambo* (string/cord) | > *entanjeni* |
| | *ithumbu* (intestine/ hose pipe) | > *ethunjini* |

Examples:—

(a) *Isiguli sizwa ubuhlungu emaphashini* (The patient feels pain in the lungs).

(b) *Umama uvala imbobo engutsheni* (Mother is mending a hole in the dress).

(c) *Ngifaka ukhezo emlonyeni* (I put a spoon into the mouth).

(d) *Inja iya ethanjeni* (The dog is going to the bone).

(e) *Udadewethu uthela amanzi empushini* (My sister pours water into the mealie-meal).

G. Examples of other locatives:—

*phandle* (outside)
*phansi* (down)
*phakathi* (inside)
*emuva* (behind)
*eduze* (near)
*phezulu* (on top/above)
*phesheya* (across)
*phambili* (in front; forward)
*kude* (far)

Concords and other word-forming elements (formatives) may be prefixed to locatives, e.g.:

(a) *Umuntu uphandle* (The person is outside).

(b) *Inyoni iphezulu* (The bird is on top/above).

(c) *Amadoda akude* (The men are far away).

(d) *Ngiphambili* (I am in front).

(e) *Nisemuva* (You are behind).
(f) *Sisesontweni* (We are in Church).
(g) *Njengaphandle* (like outside).
(h) *phakathi naphandle* (inside and outside).

With locatives commencing in a vowel *-s-* comes in between the locative and the element prefixed to it; e.g.:

(a) *Abantu basendlini* (*ba-s-endlini*) (The people are in the house).

(b) *Izitolo zisedolobheni* (*zi-s-edolobheni*) (Shops are in town).

(c) *Amahashi aseduze* (*a-s-eduze*) (The horses are nearby).

(d) *Ngizoya esitolo nasePosini* (*na-s-ePosini*) (I shall go to the shop and to the Post Office).

(e) *njengasesontweni* (like in church)
(f) *emfuleni naselwandle* (in the river and in the sea)

EXERCISE 15

1. *Funda: Kusasa ngizovuka ekuseni kakhulu. Ngizoya esiteshini* (*isiteshi*—railway station, 4). *Ngizohamba ngemoto. Ubaba unemoto. Esiteshini ngizohlangabeza* (meet) *ubaba. Ubaba uvela eThekwini. Ubaba uzofika ngesitimela. Bengicabanga ukuthi uzofika namuhla kodwa umama uthi akazufika namuhla; uzofika kusasa ekuseni. Ubaba uyasebenza eThekwini; uthengisa esitolo. Ubaba uyathanda ukuthengisa esitolo. Ngonyaka odlule wayesebenza eGoli, eRissik Street.*

2. *Funda:*

X: *Uhlalaphi?*
Y: *Ngihlala eGoli.*
X: *Uhlalaphi eGoli?*
Y: *Ngihlala eParktown.*
X: *Uhlala nobani* (with whom?) *eParktown?* (*ubani?*—ho? -la)

Y: *Ngihlala nobaba nomama nabafowethu nawodadewethu. Ugogo nobabamkhulu abahlali eGoli; bahlala ePietersburg.*

X: *Nibonani eGoli?*

Y: *EGoli sibona izimoto nezithuthuthu namalori namabhasi namathilamu nezitimela namabhanoyi.*

X: *EGoli niyafunda na?*

Y: *Yebo* (yes) *siyafunda. Sifunda esikoleni eParktown.*

X: *Ngonyaka odlule bewufundaphi?*

Y: *Ngonyaka odlule bengifunda ePietersburg, kodwa odadewethu nabafowethu bebefunda eParktown. Ngonyaka odlule bengihlala nogogo nobabamkhulu.*

X: *Nifundani eParktown?*

Y: *Ngifunda uStd. VIII kodwa abafowethu bafunda uStd. X.*

X: *Abafowenu bazofundaphi ngonyaka ozayo?*

Y: *Abafowethu bafuna ukuya eWitwatersrand University.*

X: *Odadewenu bazoyaphi ngonyaka ozayo? Bazoya eWitwatersrand University?*

Y: *Cha* (no) *abazuya eWitwatersrand University. Bafuna ukuya esibhedlela. Bafuna ukufunda ukubheka iziguli.*

X: *Ngonyaka ozayo wena* (you) *uzoyaphi?*

Y: *Ngonyaka ozayo ngizofunda uStd. IX.*

X: *Uyathanda ukuya eWitwatersrand University?*

Y: *Yebo, ngiyathanda. Mhlawumbe* (perhaps) *ngelinye ilanga ngiyofunda eWitwatersrand University* (*ngelinye ilanga*—one day).

These inflected nouns may still be found in a position in which they govern concord. The verb (or other predicate) in agreement takes the concord *ku-;* e.g.

1. *Entabeni kuhlala izilwane* (On the mountain live animals).
2. *Elwandle kukhona izinhlanzi* (In the sea are fishes).
3. *Ekhaya kuzolima ubaba* (At home father will plough).

4. *Esibhedlela kulala iziguli* (In the hospital sleep patients).

5. *Endlini kucula abantwana* (In the house children are singing).

Adverbs with prefix *pha-:*

*phakathi* (within, in the middle)
*phandle* (outside)
*phansi* (down, beneath)
*phesheya* (across)
*phambili* (before, in front of); contracted form *phambi*
*phezulu* (up, above; contracted form *phezu*

All may be followed by *kwa-;* e.g.

*phakathi kobusuku*—in the middle of the night.
*phakathi kwehlathi*—in the middle of the forest.
*phansi kwetafula*—under the table
*phansi kombhede*—under the bed
*phezu kwetafula*—on top of the table
*phezu kwentaba*—on top of the hill
*phesheya komfula*—across the river
*phesheya kolwandle*—across the sea
*phambi kwendlu*—in front of the house
*phambi kwami*—in front of me

*Phakathi* is also commonly followed by *na-;* e.g. *phakathi nendaba*—in the middle of the story; *phakathi nehlathi*—in the middle of the forest.

Adverbs commencing in *pha-* are often used with prefix *nga-;* e.g.

*ngaphansi kwetafula*—on the under side of the table; under the table
*ngaphandle komuzi*—outside the kraal
*ngaphambi kwami*—in front of me
*ngaphandle kwami*—outside of me i.e. except me
*ngaphakathi kwesibaya*—inside the cattle kraal

*ngapheshey a komfula*—on the other side of the river

Other adverbs commonly used in Zulu are:—

*lapha* (here); *lapho* (there) *laphaya* (there yonder)

1. *Thina sihlala lapha* (We live here).
2. *Indoda ilima lapho* (The man is ploughing there).
3. *Abantwana badlala laphaya* (The children play there yonder).

*eduze* (near) followed by *kwa-* or *na-;*

1. *Sibone izinkomo eduze komuzi* (We saw cattle near the kraal).
2. *Imvu beyidla eduze kwesibaya* (The sheep was grazing near the cattle kraal).
3. *Usebenza eduze nasekhaya* (He works near home).

*kude* (far) followed by *na-;*

1. *Ngithanda ukuhlala kude nedolobha* (I like to live far from town).
2. *Silima kude nomfula* (We plough far from the river).
3. *Ihlathi likude nomuzi* (The forest is far from the kraal).

*emuva* (after, behind) followed by *kwa-;*

1. *Ubaba uzofika emuva kwedina* (Father will come after lunch).
2. *Sizobuya emuva kwamalanga amabili* (We shall return after two days).
3. *Abafana badlala emuva kwendlu* (The boys are playing behind the house).

*ecaleni, eceleni* (at the side of, near) followed by *kwa-;*

1. *Bebedlala eceleni kwendlela* (They were playing by the roadside).
2. *Hlala lapha eceleni kwami* (Sit here next to me).
3. *Wakhe eceleni komfula* (He has built near the river)

# CHAPTER 18

## THE ADJECTIVE

ZULU employs certain words which qualify nouns and pronouns. These words are called qualificatives. The adjective is one of the qualificatives of Zulu.

Study the following phrases:—

| | Singular | Plural |
|---|---|---|
| Cl. 1 | *umfana* **om**-*khulu* (a big boy) | *abafana* **aba**-*khulu* |
| Cl. 2 | *umuthi* **om**-*khulu* (a big tree) | *imithi* **emi**-*khulu* |
| Cl. 3 | *idada* **eli**-*khulu* (a big duck) | *amadada* **ama**-*khulu* |
| Cl. 4 | *isitsha* **esi**-*khulu* (a big dish) | *izitsha* **ezi**-*khulu* |
| Cl. 5 | *inja* **en**-*kulu* (a big dog) | *izinja* **ezin**-*kulu* |
| Cl. 6 | *unyawo* **olu**-*khulu* (a big foot) | *izinyawo* **ezin**-*kulu* |
| Cl. 7 | *ubuso* **obu**-*khulu* (a big face) | |
| Cl. 8 | *ukukhanya* **oku**-*khulu* (a great light) | |

-*khulu* is an adjectival stem. To it are prefixed adjectival concords. It is these concords which show agreement with the noun or pronoun qualified.

*N.B.* (i)—In Cl. 1 sg. and Cl. 2 sg. the adjectival concord is *omu-* if the adjectival stem is monosyllabic; e.g. *umuntu omude* (a tall person); *umuthi omude* (a tall tree).

(ii) In Cl. 5 sg. and plural and in Cl. 6 plural the concord has a variable nasal (cf. noun prefixes). Some Zulu speakers also introduce a nasal in the Cl. 4 plural adjectival concord.

(iii) Note that *kh* becomes *k* in Cl. 5 singular and plural, i.e. there is deaspiration. (see also pp. 61; 67-68.)

The following is a list of the adjectival stems:

*-khulu* (big/great)
*-ncane* (small/young)
*-ningi* (much/many)
*-bi* (bad/ugly/evil)
*-hle* (pretty/beautiful)
*-sha* (new)
*-bili* (two)
*-thathu* (three)
*-ne* (four)
*-hlanu* (five)
*-dala* (old)
*-fishane* (short)
*-nye* (some/other)
*-ngaki?* (how many?)
*-de* (tall/long)

Examples:

(a) *Umlungu uhamba nomfana omfishane* (The whiteman is walking with a short boy).

(b) *Izinkabi ezinkulu zidonsa inqola* (The big oxen are pulling the wagon).

(c) *Umhloli ufuna abafana ababili namantombazane amathathu* (The Inspector wants two boys and three girls).

(d) *Izinja bezidla inyama eningi namathambo amaningi izolo* (The dogs were eating a lot of meat and many bones yesterday).

(e) *Udadewethu uthanda izicathulo ezintsha* (My sister likes new shoes).

(f) *Umalume ufuna ukuthenga izincwadi ezimbili* (Uncle wants to buy two books).

From adjectival stems we may derive abstract nouns by prefixing the Class 7 prefix *ubu-*, e.g.:

*ubukhulu* (greatness)
*ubudala* (age/oldness)
*ubuncane* (smallness)
*ubuningi* (majority)
*ububi* (evil)
*ubude* (height/length)
*ubuhle* (beauty)
*ubufishane* (shortness/brevity)

### Exercise 16

*FUNDA: Edolobheni sibonani? Edolobheni sibona izimoto eziningi. Sibona izimoto ezinkulu nezimoto ezi-*

*ncane; sibona izimoto ezinhle nezimoto ezimbi; sibona izimoto ezinde nezimoto ezimfishane; sibona izimoto ezintsha nezimoto ezindala. Abelungu abaningi banezimoto kodwa abantu abaningi abanazimoto.*

*Izimoto zihambaphi? Izimoto zigijima emigwaqweni. Edolobheni kukhona* (it is present/there is) *imigwaqo eminingi, izitaladi* (streets—4) *eziningi. Edolobheni kukhona imigwaqo emide nemigwaqo emifishane; kukhona imigwaqo emihle nemigwaqo emibi; kukhona imigwaqo emikhulu nemigwaqo emincane. Emigwaqweni eminye kukhona amatshe nemigodi. Abashayeli abathandi amatshe nemigodi emigwaqweni ngoba amatshe alimaza* (damage/hurt/injure) *izimoto, nemigodi ilimaza izimoto. Amatshe adabula amasondo. Emadolobheni amakhulu imigwaqo eminingi inetiyela* (*itiyela*—coal tar—3).

*Emadolobheni amanye kukhona imifula. Imigwaqo eminye iwela imifula, kodwa izimoto azingeni phakathi emanzini ngoba kukhona amabhuloho. Amabhuloho ayasiza kakhulu. Kukhona amabhuloho amancane namabhuloho amakhulu.*

*Edolobheni sibona futhi izitolo eziningi. Kukhona izitolo ezinkulu nezitolo ezincane; kukhona izitolo ezinhle nezitolo ezimbi. Izitolo ezinye zithengisa izingubo, ezinye zithengisa ukudla. Esitolo sithenga ushukela nobhontshisi namazambane nofulawa nerayisi nojamu nopelepele nokhali netiye nekhofi nokhokho. Sithenga futhi izitsha, izindishi, amapuleti, imimese, izimfologo, ojeke, izinkezo namathispuni. Sithenga futhi ugwayi nomentshisi nophalafini namakhandlela* (*indishi*, dish—5; *ipuleti*, plate—3; *imfologo*, fork—5).

*Izitolo ezinye zithengisa izithelo. Zithengisa amapentshisi namahabhula namawolintshi namalamula nobhanana. Sithola futhi uphopho namabhilikosi namapulamu nogwava namakhiwane namagilebhisi nophayinaphu noganandela nezithelo ezinye.*

*Kukhona futhi amasilaha* (*isilaha*, butchery—3). *Emasilaheni sithenga inyama. Sithola inyama yenkomo nenyama yemvu nenyama yengulube. Emasilaheni sithola futhi izinkukhu namaqanda nebhotela nopoloni namasositshi,* (*isositshi*, sausage—3) *noshizi nenhlanzi.*

*Izitolo ezinye zithengisa izicathulo, ezinye zithengisa izigqoko, ezinye zithengisa utshwala, ezinye zithengisa amapulangwe nezinsimbi, ezinye zithengisa izitsha. Izitolo ezinye zithengisa amapiyane* (*upiyane*, piano—6) *namagramafoni* (gramophones—3) *namawayilense,* (wireless sets—3). *Edolobheni izinto ezinye zibiza imali eningi, ziyadula, kodwa ezinye zibiza imali encane, zishibhile. Edolobheni kukhona futhi amahotela* (*ihotela*, hotel—3).

*Edolobheni abantwana bathanda ukudlala emaPaki* (*iPaki*, Park—3) *kodwa abanye abantwana bathanda ukuya ebhayisikobho* (*ibhayisikobho*, bioscope—3).

*Emapulazini* (in the country; *ipulazi*, farm—3) *abantu balondoloza* (*londoloza*, keep) *imali ezindlini kodwa edolobheni abantu balondoloza imali ebhange* (*ibhange*, bank—3). *Kukhona amabhange amaningi. Kukhona iStandard neBarclays namanye. Ubaba uthanda ukulondoloza imali eBarclays. Amasela ayesaba ukweba imali ebhange.*

*Emadolobheni amakhulu kukhona abantu abaningi, izinhlobo* (*uhlobo*, type—6) *eziningi. Kukhona abantu nabelungu namaNdiya namaKhaladi namaShayina nezinhlobo ezinye. Futhi emadolobheni amakhulu sizwa izilimi eziningi. Sizwa isiNgisi nesiBhunu nesiZulu nesiSuthu nesiShangane nesiXhosa nezilimi ezinye eziningi.*

*Emadolobheni abantu nabelungu basebenza imisebenzi eminingi. Abanye basebenza ezitolo, abanye basebenza emawovisi* (*iwovisi*, office—3) *abanye basebenza emakhishini* (*ikhishi*, kitchen—3) *abanye basebenza imisebenzi eminye.*

*Ekuseni abantu nabelungu baya emsebenzi Abanye bahamba ngezimoto, abanye bahamba ngezitimela, abanye bahamba ngezinyawo, abanye bahamba ngamabhayisikili, abanye bahamba ngezithuthuthu, abanye bahamba ngamabhasi, abanye bahamba ngamathilamu. Abanba baqala umsebenzi ngo-7 ekuseni, abanye baqala ngo-8, abanye baqala ngo-8.30. Ntambama abanye bayeka* (leave off, stop) *ukusebenza ngo-4, abanye ngo-4.30, abanye ngo-5.*

*Emadolobheni amakhulu abantu abanye, bahola ekupheleni kwesonto, abanye bahola ekupheleni kwenyanga. Emadolobheni amancane abantu abaningi bahola ekupheleni kwenyanga.*

*Ebusuku ogesi bakhanyisa imigwaqo emadolobheni.*

# CHAPTER 19

## ADJECTIVES USED AS PREDICATIVES

QUITE often we use adjectives as predicatives, e.g.
*Umfana omkhulu* (a big boy)
*Umfana mkhulu* (The boy is big)
*Idada elihle* (a pretty duck)
*Idada lihle* (The duck is pretty)

To get these predicatives from adjectives we elide the initial vowel of the adjectival concord. In Class 5 sg. *i-* replaces *e-*.

1. *umfana omkhulu* (a big boy) > *umfana mkhulu*
2. *umuthi omuhle* (a pretty tree) > *umuthi muhle*
3. *ihashi elincane* (a small horse) > *ihashi lincane*
4. *isitsha esihle* (a pretty vessel) > *isitsha sihle*
5. *inja enkulu* (a big dog) > *inja inkulu*
6. *ukhamba oluncane* (a small claypot) > *ukhanba luncane*

*FUNDA: Edolobheni sibonani? Edolobheni sibona izimoto. Edolobheni izimoto ziningi. Izimoto edolobheni zinkulu, ezinye zincane. Izimoto ezinye zinhle, ezinye zimbi. Izimoto ezinye zinde, ezinye zimfishane. Izimoto ezinye zintsha, ezinye zindala. Edolobheni abelungu baningi nezimoto ziningi.*

*Edolobheni imigwaqo miningi. Imigwaqo eminye mide, eminye mifishane. Imigwaqo eminye mihle, eminye mibi. Imigwaqo eminye mikhulu, eminye mincane.*

*Edolobheni izitolo ziningi. Izitolo ezinye zinkulu kodwa ezinye zincane. Izitolo ezinye zinhle kodwa ezinye zimbi.*

*Izitolo ezinye zintsha ezinye zindala.*

Negative: Examples:

| | | |
|---|---|---|
| *umfana mkhulu* | > | *umfana akamkhulu* (the boy is not big) |
| *abafana bakhulu* | > | *abafana ababakhulu* |
| *umuthi mude* | > | *umuthi awumude* |
| *imithi mide* | > | *imithi ayimide* |
| *ihashi lincane* | > | *ihashi alilincane* |
| *amahashi mancane* | > | *amahashi akamancane* |
| *isitsha sihle* | > | *isitsha asisihle* |
| *izitsha zihle* | > | *izitsha azizihle* |
| *inja inkulu* | > | *inja ayinkulu* |
| *izinja zinkulu* | > | *izinja azizinkulu* |
| *uthi lude* | > | *uthi alulude* |
| *izinti zinde* | > | *izinti azizinde* |
| *utshani buhle* | > | *utshani abubuhle* |
| *ukufa kuningi* | > | *ukufa akukuningi* |

In Class 1 sg. and Cl. 3 pl. prefix *aka-*. Otherwise the pattern is *a* + sub. concord + predicative; e.g.

| | | |
|---|---|---|
| Cl. 1 pl. | *a — ba — bakhulu* | |
| Cl. 3 sg. | *a — li — lincane* | |
| Cl. 5 pl. | *a — zi — zinkulu* | |
| Cl. 2 pl. | *a (y) i — mide* | (y between *a* and *i*) |
| Cl. 2 sg. | *a (w) u — mude* | (w between *a* and *u*) |
| Cl. 5 sg. | *a (y) i (y) inkulu*<br>*a (y) i — nkulu* | (y between *a* and *i* and between *i* and *i* or one *i* is dropped) |

## Exercise 17

1. *Humusha ngesiNgisi:* (a) *Ubaba uya edolobheni. Idolobha likhulu nezindlu ziningi.* (b) *EJohannesburg nase-Pretoria abantu baningi nezimoto ziningi nemigwaqo miningi futhi mihle.* (c) *Umfowethu mkhulu kodwa umfowenu aka-mkhulu; mncane. Umfowethu ugqoka ibhulukwe elikhulu*

*kodwa umfowenu ugqoka ibhulukwe elincane.* (d) *Umama akafuni amanzi ngoba amanzi akamancane. Amanzi maningi.* (e) *Ubaba uthengelani amalahle na? Ubaba uthenga amalahle ngoba amalahle mancane. Akathengi ngani izinkuni? Akathengi izinkuni ngoba izinkuni zikhona futhi ziningi.* (f) *UJames akagqoki ngani ibhantshi na? UJames akagqoki ibhantshi ngoba likhulu.* (g) *UJohn usebenza njengoJames kodwa mncane; uJames mkhulu.* (h) *Abafana phandle bane noma bahlanu na? Abafana bane kodwa amantombazane mahlanu.* (i) *Udadewenu mude noma mfishane na? Udadewethu akamfishane; mude.* (j) *Abelungu esitolo babili noma bathathu? Abelungu esitolo bathathu; abababili.* (k) *Esibhedlela odokotela baningi nonesi baningi neziguli ziningi. Esibhedlela imibhede miningi.* (l) *Umalume ubethenga ihashi elincane kodwa ubaba ubengafuni ihashi elincane. Ubefuna ihashi elikhulu. Libize amarandi angu—45.*

2. *Humusha ngesiZulu:* (a) Is your brother tall? Yes my brother is tall but my sister is short. (b) In the big forest are many trees and many birds. (c) At school are many boys and many girls. (d) Are there four or five boys outside? There are four; there are not five. (e) My sister is pretty but your sister is ugly. (f) An ox is big but a dog is small. (g) The jacket is new but the trousers are old. Why did father buy old trousers? I don't know. (h) We see trees and grass. The trees are tall but the grass is short. (i) How many shops are there? There are four shops. (j) There are many cars but the road is long.

# CHAPTER 20

## THE POSSESSIVE

A POSSESSIVE is also a word which qualifies a noun or a pronoun. In a Zulu possessive construction, the noun indicating the thing possessed comes first in word order and is followed by the noun or pronoun indicating the possessor. The construction resembles the English construction "the . . . . of . . . ." (e.g. the dog of the man). Zulu does not have a construction like English: "the man's dog".

A possessive is made up of two parts, an initial part, the concord, and the stem to which the concord is prefixed. The concord always agrees with the thing possessed although it is prefixed to the part indicating the possessor.

The following is a list of possessive concords:

| | Sing. | Plural | | Sing. | Plural |
|---|---|---|---|---|---|
| Cl. 1 | *wa-* | *ba-* | Cl. 5 | *ya-* | *za-* |
| Cl. 2 | *wa-* | *ya-* | Cl. 6 | *lwa-* | *za-* |
| Cl. 3 | *la-* | *a-* | Cl. 7 | *ba-* | |
| Cl. 4 | *sa-* | *za-* | Cl. 8 | *kwa-* | |

When possessive concords are prefixed to nouns, vowel coalescence takes place: (i.e., $a+a>a$; $a+i>e$; $a+u>o$).

Examples:—

*umntwana womfundisi* (*wa+umfundisi*) the child of the minister.

*abantwana bomfundisi* (*ba+umfundisi*) children of the minister.

*ihashi lenkosi* (*la*+*inkosi*) a horse of the king.
*amahashi enkosi* (*a*+*inkosi*) horses of the king.
*ukudla kwabantwana* (*kwa*+*abantwana*) food of the children.
*izincwadi zabahloli* (*za*+*abahloli*) books of the Inspectors.

The noun or pronoun signifying the possessor may not be used but may be represented by a possessive pronominal stem. There are also possessive pronominal stems for 1st and 2nd persons.

1st Person

| | Singular | Plural |
|---|---|---|
| | -*mi* (of me, i.e. my) | -*ithu* (of us, i.e. our) |

2nd Person

| | | |
|---|---|---|
| | -*kho* (of you, i.e. your) | -*inu* (of you, i.e. your). |

3rd Person

| | | |
|---|---|---|
| Cl. 1 | -*khe* (of him/her, i.e. his/her) | -*bo* (of them, i.e. their) |
| Cl. 2 | -*wo* (of it) | -*yo* (of them) |
| Cl. 3 | -*lo* (of it) | -*wo* (of them) |
| Cl. 4 | -*so* (of it) | -*zo* (of them) |
| Cl. 5 | -*yo* (of it) | -*zo* (of them) |
| Cl. 6 | -*lo* (of it) | -*zo* (of them) |
| Cl. 7 | -*bo* (of it) | |
| Cl. 8 | -*kho* (of it) | |

Examples:

| | |
|---|---|
| *ihashi lami* (my horse) | *ihashi lethu* (*la*+*ithu*) |
| *ihashi lakho* (your horse) | *ihashi lenu* (la+inu) |
| *izinkomo zakhe* (his/her cattle) | *izinkomo zabo* |
| *amanzi awo* (*umfula*) (its (river) water) | *amanzi ayo* |
| *utshani balo* (*ihashi*) (its (horse) grass) | *utshani bawo* |
| *umsila wayo* (*inja*) its (dog) tail) | *imisila yazo* |

When the noun indicating the possessor is Class 1a sing., the construction is as follows:

(i) Drop prefix *u-;*

(ii) According to the class and number of the noun indicating the possessee, prefix the following concords to the noun indicating the possessor.

| | Sing. | Plural | | Sing. | Plural |
|---|---|---|---|---|---|
| Cl. 1 | *ka-* | *baka-* | Cl. 5 | *ka-* | *zika-* |
| Cl. 2 | *ka-* | *ka-* | Cl. 6 | *luka-* | *zika-* |
| Cl. 3 | *lika-* | *ka-* | Cl. 7 | *buka-* | |
| Cl. 4 | *sika-* | *zika-* | Cl. 8 | *kuka-* | |

Examples:—

1. *umntwana kababa* (father's child) *abantwana bakababa*
2. *umuthi kamalume* (uncle's medicine) *imithi kamalume*
3. *ihashi likaJane* (Jane's horse) *amahashi kaJane*
4. *isihlalo sikaTom* (Tom's chair) *izihlalo zikaTom*
5. *inja kaSipho* (Sipho's dog) *izinja zikaSipho*
6. *ukhezo lukayise* (his father's spoon) *izinkezo zikayise*
7. *ubuhlalu bukamama* (mother's beads)
8. *ukuhlakanipha kukadadewethu* (my sister's wisdom)

In Zulu the possessive does not always indicate direct ownership. It may be descriptive in function, e.g.:—

1. *indlu yamatshe* (a house of stones, i.e. built of stone)
2. *ukhezo lomuthi* (a spoon of wood, i.e. made of wood)
3. *ibhodwe lobisi* (a pot of milk, i.e. for boiling/keeping milk)
4. *indlu yesikole* (a house of school, i.e. school house)
5. *umntwana wesikole* (a child of school, i.e. school child)
6. *insimbi kagesi* (an iron of electricity, i.e. electric iron)
7. *isitimela samalahle* (a train of coal, i.e. steam engine)
8. *isaka likashukela* (a bag of sugar, i.e. a sugar bag or bagful of sugar)

9. *umuntu wesilisa* (a person of the masculine sex i.e. a male person)
10. *umuntu wesifazane* (a female person)

### Exercise 18

A. Read and Translate:—

1. *Landa izicathulo zami ezindala kumkhandi edolobheni.* 2. *Umnumzane uthengisa amahashi akhe amabili; unamahashi amaningi amahle kodwa akanazimbongolo.* 3. *Nginezinja eziningi ezinhle. Ngizothengisa izinja zami ezinye.* 4. *Bengifuna ibhulukwe lami; bengingafuni ibhantshi.* 5. *Umshumayeli ubona abantwana bakhe emgwaqweni; bavela esontweni. Umshumayeli unabantwana ababili, umfana nentombazane.* 6. *Ngizothenga iketanga* (chain—3) *lenja ngoba inja yami iluma abantu. Ngithanda inja yami ngoba ixosha amasela emini nasebusuku. Iketanga lenja alibizi imali eningi; lishibhile.* 7. *Abantwana bathanda abazali babo, nabazali bathanda abantwana babo.* 8. *Bengithatha isigqoko sami nenduku yami endlini; nginesigqoko esihle kodwa sibiza imali eningi.* 9. *Umfowethu uzokhipha amazinyo akhe amabili ngoba ayaxega; uzoya kudokotela wamazinyo eBrakpan.* 10. *Umlimi uzolanda ikalishi* (horse cart—3) *lakhe kumkhandi kusasa. Umlimi uzodonsa ikalishi ngamahashi akhe. Umkhandi ubelungisa amasondo alo.* 11. *Izinja ziza ngoba zizwa iphunga* (smell—3) *lenyama. Izinja zithanda inyama kakhulu.* 12. *Besipholisha* (*pholisha*—polish) *izicathulo zethu. Sinezicathulo ezinhle ezintsha. Izicathulo zethu ziyadula.* 13. *Ngifuna ukuthenga ibhodlela* (bottle—3) *lomuthi ekhemisi* (chemist—3) *ngoba ngiyakhwehlela; ebusuku ngiyajuluka.* 14. *Umakhi uzolayisha ifulaha* (load—3) *lesihlabathi nefulaha lamapulangwe ngenqola yakhe; unenqola enkulu.* 15. *Ezinkomponi* (*inkomponi*—mine—5) *abelungu bakhipha igolide* (gold—3) *elininingi.*

16. *Ekuseni bengithenga ithikithi* (ticket—3) *lesitimela; ntambama ngiya eThekwini.* 17. *Umama uthanda amanzi kampompi kodwa ubaba uthanda amanzi ethange* (*ithange*—water tank—3). 18. *Amabhasi athwala izisebenzi ekuseni nantambama; eGoli kukhona amabhasi amakhulu.* 19. *Ubaba ulungisa izincwadi zakhe; unezincwadi eziningi, ezinkulu nezincane. Unezincwadi zesiNgisi nezincwadi zesiBhunu.* 20. *Ubabamkhulu ubopha izimvu zakhe nezimbuzi zakhe; ubabamkhulu akathandi izingulube.* 21. *Abafana bangenisa izinkomo esibayeni.* 22. *Udokotela unika isiguli umuthi wekhanda nomkhuhlane. Isiguli sizophuza umuthi ekuseni nasemini nakusihlwa.* 23. *Udadewethu ufuna ukotini; ufuna ukuthunga ingubo yakhe. Uzothenga ukotini esitolo sezingubo.* 24. *Njalo kusihlwa ubaba ubhema ipipi lakhe kodwa emini ubhema usikilidi.* 25. *Abazali abahle banakekela abantwana babo; abantwana abahle bahlonipha* (respect) *abazali babo.* 26. *Ngizotshala izimbali engadini yami kusasa. Ngifuna ukutshala izinhlobo eziningi; izimbali zizobhalasa* (bloom) *ehlobo.* 27. *Izinkomo nezimvu zifuna ukungena esibayeni kodwa kukhona inja esangweni lesibaya.* 28. *Phuza itiye lakho; lizophola.* 29. *Chitha amanzi amabi.* 30. *Qoqa izimpahla zakho.* 31. *Bengilayisha amatafula nezitulo elorini.* 32. *Intombazane ilungisa umbhede wayo.* 33. *Ehlobo sibona izinhlobonhlobo zezimbali ezinhle kakhulu; ekhaya sinengadi enhle yezimbali.* 34. *Kusasa siya emshadweni kadadewethu ePitoli; udadewethu uzoshada nensizwa yasePitoli.* 35. *Izulu belina ebusuku; amanzi ayageleza emfuleni.* 36. *Ehlobo umbane ubulala abantu abaningi nezilwane eziningi; futhi umbane ushisa imizi.*

B. *FUNDA: Isikole sethu sisedolobheni. Sifunda esikoleni esihle kakhulu, esikhulu. Kukhona abantwana abaningi, abafana namantombazane. Kukhona futhi othisha abaningi. Ekuseni isikole singena ngo-8. Sihamba ekhaya ngo*-7.30 *ngemoto kababa. Siyaphumula ngo*-11 *nango*-1 *emini. Ntambama siphuma ngo*-3. *Ntambama siya ekhaya ngethilamu noma ngebhasi. Ebhasini sikhipha uzuka kodwa ethilamini sikhipha izindibilishi ezine.*

*Esikoleni kukhona izindlu eziningi. Ezindlini kukhona amatafula nezitulo namadesk namakhabethe* (*ikhabethe*—cupboard—3). *Kukhona futhi amablack-board amakhulu. Uthisha unetafula lakhe nesitulo sakhe. Ezindongeni kukhona izithombe namashadi* (charts—3) *neminye imifanekiso.*

*Nginesikhwama sami sezincwadi, nabafowethu nodadewethu banezikhwama zabo zezincwadi. Ezikhwameni sifaka izincwadi zethu namarula* (rulers—3) *ethu namapeni* (pens—3) *ethu namapenseli* (pencils—3) *ethu. Sifaka futhi ezikhwameni zethu isinkwa sethu namawolintshi ethu noma amahabhula ethu noma ezinye izithelo.*

*Esikoleni sifunda izifundo eziningi. Sithanda othisha bethu kakhulu ngoba bafundisa kahle. Ngesinye isikhathi siyacula. Sidlala imidlalo eminingi esikoleni. Sidlala ibhola nethenisi nerugby necricket. Amantombazane athanda ukudlala inet ball nethenisi. Sithanda isikole sethu kakhulu.*

C. *FUNDA: Umnumzane unabantwana abakhulu kuphela. Abafana bakhe bakhulu namantombazane akhe makhulu. Abantwana bomnumzane ababancane. Abafana bathathu, amantombazane mabili. Umfana omkhulu uneminyaka engu*-25. *Umfana omunye uneminyaka engu*-20. *Umfana omncane uneminyaka engu*-16. *Intombazane enkulu ineminyaka engu*-23. *Intombazane encane ineminyaka engu*-18.

*Umuzi womnumzane mkhulu; awumncane. Imithi miningi. Emzini womnumzane kukhona izinkukhu nezingulube nezimbuzi nezinkomo namahashi. Izinkukhu ziningi nezimbuzi ziningi nezinkomo ziningi kodwa amahashi akamaningi nezingulube azizininigi. Izinkomo zomnumzane zilala esibayeni, nezimbuzi zilala esibayeni sazo nezingulube zilala esibayeni sazo. Emzini womnumzane kukhona amaqanda amaningi nobisi oluningi namasi amaningi.*

*Umnumzane unenja enhle. Inja yakhe inkulu futhi inolaka. Abantu bayesaba ukungena emzini womnumzane. Besaba inja yakhe. Ebusuku nasemini ibheka umuzi womnumzane.*

*Inkosikazi yomnumzane inhle. Yinde futhi inkulu. Ebusweni iyakhanya* (light in complexion). *Inezinwele ezinhle ezinde. Amazinyo ayo mahle namehlo ayo mahle. Abantu bathanda inkosikazi yomnumzane ngoba inomusa.*

# CHAPTER 21

## PAST TENSE

### Immediate Past Tense

We have already observed how the past continuous tense is formed. We now illustrate another type of past indicating completed action. In place of the final *-a* of the verb suffix *-e* where there is an adjunct and *-ile* where there is no adjunct. This form generally signifies an immediate past tense.

Examples:—

1. *Umalume ubophe inja* (Uncle has tied the dog).
2. *Abakhi balande amatshe* (The builders have fetched stones).
3. *Abalimi balime izolo* (The farmers ploughed yesterday).
4. *Izinsizwa ziphuze utshwala ekuseni* (The young men drank beer in the morning).
5. *Inkosi ibize abantu bayo* (The king has called his people).
6. *Umfundisi ukhulumile* (The parson has spoken).
7. *Abantu bahambile* (The people have gone away).
8. *Amahashi abalekile* (The horses have run away).
9. *Umfazi ubasile* (The woman has kindled fire).
10. *Umuzi ushile* (The kraal has been burnt down).

Study the following negative forms:—

| | |
|---|---|
| *ubophe, ubophile* | > *akabophanga* (*aka-bopha-nga*) |
| *balande, balandile* | > *abalandanga* (*a-balanda-nga*) |
| *balime, balimile* | > *abalimanga* (*a-balima-nga*) |
| *ziphuze, ziphuzile* | > *aziphuzanga* (*a-ziphuza-nga*) |
| *ibize, ibizile* | > *ayibizanga* (*a-y-ibiza-nga*) |

*ukhulume, ukhulumile* > *akakhulumanga* (*aka-khuluma-nga*)
*bahambe, bahambile* > *abahambanga* (*a-bahamba-nga*)
*abaleke, abalekile* > *akabalekanga* (*aka-baleka-nga*)
*ubase, ubasile* > *akabasanga* (*aka-basa-nga*)

Examples:—

(a) *Umalume akabophanga inja* (Uncle did not tie the dog).

(b) *Abakhi abalandanga amatshe* (The builders did not fetch stones).

(c) *Abalimi abalimanga izolo* (The farmers did not plough yesterday).

(d) *Izinsizwa aziphuzanga utshwala ekuseni* (The young men did not drink beer in the morning).

(e) *Inkosi ayibizanga abantu bayo* (The king did not call his people).

(f) *Umfundisi akakhulumanga* (The parson did not speak).

There is, however, another way of expressing the negative in which *-ile* does not change; e.g.:

*Abantu abalimile* (People have not ploughed).
*Umfazi akabasile* (The woman has not made a fire).
*Amahashi akabalekile* (The horses have not run away).
*Izinsizwa aziphuzile utshwala* (The young men have not drunk beer).

### Remote Past Tense

This requires the use of past subjectival concords (see page 87).

Examples:—

1. *Ngathenga izimvu kumlimi* (I bought sheep from the farmer).
2. *Sabona izimoto eziningi ePitoli* (We saw many cars in Pretoria).
3. *Nabaleka* (You ran away).

4. *Umfundisi washumayela esontweni* (The parson preached in church).
5. *Abantu batshalu ummbila* (The people planted mealies).
6. *Inja yakhonkotha* (The dog barked).

In the negative the above sentences would read:—

1. *Angithenganga izimvu kumlimi.*
2. *Asibonanga izimoto eziningi ePitoli.*
3. *Anibalekanga.*
4. *Umfundisi akashumayelanga esontweni.*
5. *Abantu abatshalanga ummbila.*
6. *Inja ayikhonkothanga.*

Zulu has verbs where the use of *-e* or *-ile* does not indicate past time, e.g.:—

1. *Ngilambile* (I am hungry).
2. *Umfowethu uhlakaniphile* (My brother is wise).
3. *Umfana umile* (The boy is standing).
4. *Inyoka icashile* (The snake is hiding).
5. *Ngomile* (I am thirsty).
6. *Inkomo izacile* (The beast is lean).
7. *Ihashi linonile* (The horse is fat).

All these verbs indicate a state entered into and persisting. The negative is formed by prefixing *a-* (*aka-* in Cl. 1 sing. and Cl. 3 plural).

1. *Angilambile.*
2. *Umfowethu akahlakaniphile.*
3. *Umfana akamile.*
4. *Inyoka ayicashile.*
5. *Angomile.*
6. *Inkomo ayizacile.*
7. *Ihashi alinonile.*

### Exercise 19

*Humusha ngesiNgisi:* (a) *Udadewethu uthenge izicathulo*

*ezinhle esitolo ngesonto eledlule kodwa umfowethu akathenganga ngoba akanamali.* (b) *Abantwana bahambile baye esikoleni; bahambe nezincwadi zabo. Bafake izincwadi zabo ezikhwameni zabo. Bazobuya ntambama ngebhasi. Abantwana bakhipha imali ebhasini.* (c) *Bengifuna ukubona inkosi kodwa inkosi ihambe izolo emini nabantu bayo. Inkosi beyihamba ngezimoto zayo ezinhlanu; beyingahambi ngesitimela.* (d) *Abafana badlalile kodwa amantombazane akadlalanga ngoba izulu belina. Uthisha uthi amantombazane azodlala ngesonto elizayo.* (e) *Sizofunda isiNgisi kusasa; izolo besifunda isiBhunu; asifundanga isiZulu.* (f) *Umakhi ulayishe amapulangwe neminyango namafasitele enqoleni yakhe; unenqola enkulu nezinkabi.* (g) *Umuzi wakhe ushile; ushe izolo ntambama.* (h) *Ekuseni siphuze itiye nekhofi; ntambama sizophuza ubisi nokhokho; sifaka ushukela nobisi etiyeni nasekhofini.* (i) *Ubaba uthenge izimvu eziningi nezinkomo eziningi ezinhle namahashi amaningi endalini* (*indali*—sale—5) *kuthangi.* (j) *Ngonyaka odlule ngakha indlu yami enhle enkulu ePitoli; yabiza imali eningi.* (k) *Ubisi luphelile; abafana abasenganga ekuseni; bazosenga ntambama.* (l) Jane, *amanzi ayabila; yenza itiye noma ikhofi.* (m) *Izolo isikole siphume ntambama ngo-3 ngoba besicula; asiphumanga ngo-2.* (n) *Yesula phansi ngendwangu* (*indwangu*—*cloth*—5); *umntwana uchithe amanzi.* (o) *Udadewethu uthele usawoti nopelepele enyameni kodwa akafakanga uanyanisi notaamatisi.* (p) *Abantwana bayakhala ngoba balambile; umam ulungisa ukudla kwabo.* (q) *Ihashi limile, alidli ngoba liyagula. Kusasa ubaba uzofuna umuthi ekhemesi.* (r) *Amasela ebe izinkukhu zami ezinhlanu kodwa ayaphika.* (s) *Udadewethu akenzi itiye ngoba amanzi ayabanda, futhi ushukela uphelile.* (t) *Kusasa sizobuka umjaho wamahashi; ubaba uthanda umjaho kakhulu.*

# CHAPTER 22

## THE PRONOUN

ALTHOUGH there are four main types of pronouns recognised in Zulu, only three will be discussed in this book.

### THE QUANTITATIVE PRONOUN

These pronouns denote number or quantity and are of three types: (a) "All" is expressed by using the stem *-nke* with pronominal prefixes. The singular forms signify "the whole of".

1st Person

| | Singular | Plural |
|---|---|---|
| | — | *sonke* (all of us) |

2nd Person

| | Singular | Plural |
|---|---|---|
| | — | *nonke* (all of you) |

3rd Person

| | Singular | Plural |
|---|---|---|
| Cl. 1 | *wonke* (whole of him/her) | *bonke* (all of them) |
| Cl. 2 | *wonke* (whole of it) | *yonke* (all of them) |
| Cl. 3 | *lonke* (whole of it) | *onke* (all of them) |
| Cl. 4 | *sonke* (whole of it) | *zonke* (all of them) |
| Cl. 5 | *yonke* (whole of it) | *zonke* (all of them) |
| Cl. 6 | *lonke* (whole of it) | *zonke* (all of them) |
| Cl. 7 | *bonke* (all of it) | |
| Cl. 8 | *konke* (all of it) | |

Examples:—

1. *Abantu bonke bafuna umsebenzi* (All people want work).

2. *Umlilo awushisanga yonke imithi* (The fire did not burn all trees).
3. *Umlimi ulime insimu yonke* (The farmer tilled the whole field).
4. *Ibhubesi liqede imbuzi yonke* (The lion finished the whole goat).
5. *Sizothenga zonke izinkomo* (We shall buy all the cattle).

In word order, the pronoun may precede or follow the related noun without changing the meaning.

(b) "only" or "alone" is expressed by using *-dwa* with pronominal prefixes.

| | Singular | Plural |
|---|---|---|
| 1st Person | | |
| | *ngedwa* (I only/alone) | *sodwa* (we only) |
| 2nd Person | | |
| | *wedwa* (you only/alone) | *nodwa* (you only) |
| 3rd Person | | |
| Cl. 1 | *yedwa* (he/she only/alone) | *bodwa* (they only) |
| Cl. 2 | *wodwa* (it only/alone) | *yodwa* (they only) |
| Cl. 3 | *lodwa* (it only/alone) | *odwa* (they only) |
| Cl. 4 | *sodwa* (it only/alone) | *zodwa* (they only) |
| Cl. 5 | *yodwa* (it only/alone) | *zodwa* (they only) |
| Cl. 6 | *lodwa* (it only/alone) | *zodwa* (they only) |
| Cl. 7 | *bodwa* (it only) | |
| Cl. 8 | *kodwa* (it only) | |

Examples:—

1. *Ngizohamba ngedwa* (I shall go alone).
2. *Umlimi ushaye abafana bodwa* (The farmer beat the boys only).
3. *Letha amazambane odwa* (Bring potatoes only).
4. *Ikati liphuze ubisi lodwa* (The cat drank milk only).
5. *Uhlala vedwa* (He lives alone).

6. *Sizothenga izithombe zodwa* (We shall buy pictures only).

(c) "Both; all three; all four; all five" are expressed by using pronouns formed from the stems *-bili* (two), *-thathu* (three), *-ne* (four), and *-hlanu* (five). Only plural forms are possible; e.g. *sobabili* (both of us), *sobathathu* (all three of us), *sobane* (all four of us), *sobahlanu* (all five of us).

| | | | | | |
|---|---|---|---|---|---|
| 1st p. | | *sobabili* | *sobathathu* | *sobane* | *sobahlanu* |
| 2nd p. | | *nobabili* | *nobathathu* | *nobane* | *nobahlanu* |
| 3rd p. | Cl. 1 | *bobabili* | *bobathathu* | *bobane* | *bobahlanu* |
| | Cl. 2 | *yomibili* | *yomithathu* | *yomine* | *yomihlanu* |
| | Cl. 3 | *omabili* | *omathathu* | *omane* | *omahlanu* |
| | Cl. 4 | *zozimbili* | *zozintathu* | *zozine* | *zozinhlanu* |
| | Cl. 5 | *zozimbili* | *zozintathu* | *zozine* | *zozinhlanu* |
| | Cl. 6 | *zozimbili* | *zozintathu* | *zozine* | *zozinhlanu* |
| | Cl. 7 | *bobubili* | *bobuthathu* | *bobune* | *bobuhlanu* |
| | Cl. 8 | *kokubili* | *kokuthathu* | *kokune* | *kokuhlanu* |

Cl. 4, 5 and 6 forms are generally contracted to: *zombili, zontathu, zone, zonhlanu.*

Examples:—

1. *Umalume uzothuma abafana bobabili* (Uncle will send both boys).
2. *Izinja zami zifile zozine* (All four of my dogs have died).
3. *Izinkukhu zonhlanu ziyazalela* (All five fowls are laying).
4. *Sizohamba sobabili* (Both of us will go).
5. *Ikati lidle amagundane omabili* (The cat ate both mice).

### The Demonstrative Pronoun

There are three positional types of demonstrative pronouns signifying:

(i) this, these, indicating proximity to the speaker;

(ii) that, those, indicating a short distance from the speaker;

(iii) that yonder, those yonder, indicating considerable distance from the speaker but within sight.

TABLE OF DEMONSTRATIVE PRONOUNS

| | This<br>These | That<br>Those | That yonder<br>Those yonder |
|---|---|---|---|
| Class 1 sg. | *lo* | *lowo* | *lowaya* |
| pl. | *laba* | *labo* | *labaya* |
| Class 2 sg. | *lo* | *lowo* | *lowaya* |
| pl. | *le* | *leyo* | *leya* |
| Class 3 sg. | *leli* | *lelo* | *leliya* |
| pl. | *la* | *lawo* | *lawaya* |
| Class 4 sg. | *lesi* | *leso* | *lesiya* |
| pl. | *lezi* | *lezo* | *leziya* |
| Class 5 sg. | *le* | *leyo* | *leya* |
| pl. | *lezi* | *lezo* | *leziya* |
| Class 6 sg. | *lolu* | *lolo* | *loluya* |
| pl. | *lezi* | *lezo* | *leziya* |
| Class 7 | *lobu* | *lobo* | *lobuya* |
| Class 8 | *lokhu* | *lokho* | *lokhuya* |

Examples:—

1. *Abafana laba bashaya amahashi* (These boys beat the horses).
2. *Umntwana lo uyakhala* (This child is crying).
3. *Umlimi ufuna izinkomo lezi* (The farmer wants these cattle).
4. *Umfana lowo uyabaleka* (That boy is running away).
5. *Silanda izimvu leziya* (We are fetching those sheep yonder).
6. *Imifula leyo iyageleza* (Those rivers are flowing).

If, as is more often the case, the demonstrative precede the noun, the initial vowel of the noun drops. In writing the monosyllabic demonstratives form one word group with the noun, whilst those with more than one syllable may remain as separate words, e.g.:

1. *Lomuntu* (*lo-umuntu*) *ufuna umfundisi* (This person wants the parson).
2. *Lezi zinja zibulala izimvu* (These dogs kill sheep).
3. *Lawaya mahashi ayabaleka* (Those horses yonder are running away).
4. *Sibize labo bafana* (We called those boys).
5. *Amadoda azomba lowo mgwaqo* (The men will dig that road).

### The Absolute Pronoun

This pronoun is characterised by the presence of the suffix *-na*.

| | | Singular | Plural |
|---|---|---|---|
| 1st p. | | *mina* (I, me) | *thina* (we, us) |
| 2nd p. | | *wena* (thou, you) | *nina* (you) |
| 3rd p. | Cl. 1 | *yena* (he/she/him/her) | *bona* (they, them) |
| | Cl. 2 | *wona* (it) | *yona* (they, them) |
| | Cl. 3 | *lona* (it) | *wona* (they, them) |
| | Cl. 4 | *sona* (it) | *zona* (they, them) |
| | Cl. 5 | *yona* (it) | *zona* (they, them) |
| | Cl. 6 | *lona* (it) | *zona* (they, them) |
| | Cl. 7 | *bona* (it) | |
| | Cl. 8 | *khona* (it) | |

1. *Mina ngidlala ithenisi* (I play tennis/I am playing tennis).
2. *Umama ubiza thina* (Mother is calling us).
3. *Abalimi batshala yona* (*imithi*) (The farmers are planting them (trees).
4. *Yona* (*inkosi*) *izohamba kusasa* (He (king) will go tomorrow).

5. *Umhloli ufuna wena; akafuni mina* (The Inspector wants you; he does not want me).

### Exercise 20

*Funda; humusha ngesiNgisi:* 1. *Ubaba ubiza thina sonke, thina abantwana bakhe.* 2. *Kusasa umalume akazuya esiteshini; asizuhamba sobabili; ngizohamba ngedwa ngebhayisikili.* 3. *Izolo bengilande imoto yami entsha ePort Elizabeth; bengihambe nomfowethu omncane. Nginelayisense* (licence—3) *yokushayela imoto.* 4. *Gijima kakhulu; isitimela siyahamba manje, uzosala* (*sala*—remain). 5. *John, landani izimpahla zami esitolo noJames ngoba nina ninamajazi; izulu liyana, hambani masinyane* (quickly). 6. *Namuhla umpheki upheka isitshulu ngoba ugogo uthanda isitshulu; ugogo akanamazinyo.* 7. *Ebusika sibona isithwathwa* (frost—4) *phandle ekuseni; thina asithandi ukuvuka ekuseni kakhulu ebusika.* 8. *Mina ngivela ePosini; bengithenga izitembu. Ngithenge izitembu ngamasenti angu*-5. *Esitolo ngizothenga amaphepha okubhala nezimvilophi* (*imvilophi-envelope*—5). 9. *Letha isifutho* (pump—4) *sami leso; shesha; ngifuna ukufutha* (to pump) *ibhayisikili lami. Kusasa ngizothenga amasondo amasha.* 10. *Emadolobheni amakhulu abelungu abaningi banezitezi* (*isitezi*—double storey building—4); *bathanda ukwakha izitezi.* 11. *Onke amaXhosa athanda isitambu kakhulu; amaNdiya athanda irayisi nokhali.* 12. *Thintitha zonke lezo zithombe odongeni; zinothuli.* 13. *Phuza lelo tiye lakho masinyane ngoba lizophola.* 14. *Umfowethu unamathisela* (*namathisela*—stick on, paste on) *izitembu ezimviiophini.* 15. *Ezibhedlela ezikhulu kukhona iziguli eziningi luthi kukhona odokotela abaningi nonesi abaningi. Zonke iziguli zilala emibhedeni.* 16. *Izimpumputhe aziboni emehlweni, izithulu azizwa ezindlebeni, izimungulu azikhulumi* (*impumputhe*—blind person—5; *isithulu*—deaf person—4; *isi-*

*mungulu*—mute—4). 17. *Ngifuna inalithi nokotini; ngifuna ukubekela iyembe lami ngoba lidabukile; linembobo enkulu,* 18. *Uthisha uxoxa indaba yebhubesi negundane; uthisha unezindaba eziningi ezinhle.* 19. *Abelungu bayathanda ukuzingela* (to hunt) *izinyamazane* (*inyamazane*—buck, wild animal—5); *badubula izinyamazane ngezibhamu zabo; abantu bazingela ngemikhonto nangezinja.* 20. *Ubaba ufuna amaphepha okubhala nezimvilophi; ufuna ukuphendula incwadi kababamkhulu.* 21. *Abantwana bazonetha ngoba izulu liyana; abaphathanga amajazi emvula.* 22. *NgoLwesithathu ekuseni sizoya emakethe* (*imakethe*—market—5) *ngelori; sizothenga amawolintshi nobhanana neklabishi notamatisi.* 23. *Sizoya kumfundisi sobabili kusasa ngoba sifuna umsebenzi. Umfundisi wazi abelungu abaningi.* 24. *Lesi salukazi sihlala sodwa ngoba asinabantwana; abantwana baso bafa bonke sasala sodwa.* 25. *Angibizi wena; ngibiza labo bafana bobabili.* 26. *Thina sithanda umalume ngoba unomusa kakhulu; uhleka nialo.*

# CHAPTER 23

## THE RELATIVE

A RELATIVE is another type of word which qualifies a noun or pronoun. In its function, it is like an adjective and a possessive. However, adjectives, possessives and relatives must be classified separately because they employ different concords.

Study the following phrases:

| | Singular | Plural |
|---|---|---|
| 1. | *umfana* **o**-*bomvu* (a red boy) | *abafana* **aba**-*bomvu* |
| 2. | *umuthi* **o**-*bomvu* (red medicine) | *imithi* **e**-*bomvu* |
| 3. | *itshe* **eli**-*bomvu* (a red stone) | *amatshe* **a**-*bomvu* |
| 4. | *isihlalo* **esi**-*bomvu* (a red seat) | *izihlalo* **ezi**-*bomvu* |
| 5. | *indlu* **e**-*bomvu* (a red house) | *izindlu* **ezi**-*bomvu* |
| 6. | *udonga* **olu**-*bomvu* (a red wall) | *izindonga* **ezi**-*bomvu* |
| 7. | *ubuhlalu* **obu**-*bomvu* (red beads) | |
| 8. | *ukukhanya* **oku**-*bomvu* (red light) | |

The stem *-bomvu* is a relative stem, and to it have been prefixed relative concords. It will be seen that the relative concords resemble adjectival concords except that where the adjectival concords have a nasal the relative concords have none.

The following are a few of the more commonly used relative stems:—

*-nzima* (heavy/difficult) *-bukhali* (sharp/greedy)
*-banzi* (wide/broad) *-manzi* (wet/damp)

*-buhlungu* (painful)
*-mbalwa* (few)
*-lula* (light/easy)
*-ngcono* (better)
*-thile, -thize* (a certain)
*-mnyama* (black)
*-mhlophe* (white)
*-mpunga* (grey)
*-mpofu* (dun/poor)
*-luhlaza* (green/raw)
*-nsundu* (brown)
*-nqunu* (naked)
*-munyu* (sour/acid)
*-njeya* (like yonder)
*-makhaza* (cold)
*-ze* (naked)
*-lukhuni* (hard/difficult)
*-duma* (tasteless)
*-mnandi* (nice/pleasant)
*-qotho* (honest)
*-buthuntu* (blunt)
*-ngaka* (as big as this)
*-ngako* (as big as that)
*-ngakaya* (as big as yonder)
*-njani?* (of what sort)?
*-nje* (like this)
*-njalo* (like that)

Examples:—

1. *Umntwana wakhe omhlophe uyagijima* (His white child is running).
2. *Abafana abamnyama basiza umlimi* (The black boys help the farmer).
3. *Umuthi oluhlaza uyakhula* (The green tree is growing).
4. *Sibuka izindlu ezibomvu* (We are looking at the red houses).
5. *Amadada ambalwa aphuza amanzi* (A few ducks are drinking water).
6. *Umama uthanda isihlalo esibanzi* (Mother likes a wide chair).
7. *Angifuni ingubo emanzi* (I do not want a wet dress).
8. *Ubaba ufuna izinkomo ezinjani? Ufuna ezinje* (What sort of cattle does father want? He wants those like this).
9. *Abantwana bahleka umfana onqunu* (The children laugh at the naked boy).

10. *Angifuni indlu engakaya* (I do not want a house as big as that yonder).

From relatives may be formed abstract nouns of Class 7 by prefixing *ubu-* to the relative stem, e.g.:

*ububanzi* (width/breadth) *ubumanzi* (dampness)
*ubumpofu* (poverty) *ubuqotho* (honesty)
*ubuze* (nakedness) *ubumnandi* (pleasantness)
*ubumhlophe* (whiteness/purity)
*ubumnyama* (blackness/darkness).

From adjectives and relatives we may form adverbs by prefixing *ka-*, e.g.

From Adjectives:

| | | |
|---|---|---|
| *-khulu* | > | *kakhulu* (much) |
| *-ncane* | > | *kancane* (softly, slowly, a little) |
| *-ningi* | > | *kaningi* (many times) |
| *-bi* | > | *kabi* (badly) |
| *-fishane* | > | *kafishane* (briefly) |
| *-ngaki* | > | *kangaki?* (how many times?) |
| *-bili* | > | *kabili* (twice) |
| *-thathu* | > | *kathathu* (thrice) |
| *-ne* | > | *kane* (four times) |
| *-hlanu* | > | *kahlanu* (five times) |
| *-hle* | > | *kahle* (nicely, well) |

1. *Ubaba ubize uJames kabili* (Father called James twice).
2. *Udokotela ujove isiguli kathathu* (The doctor injected the patient three times).
3. *Abafana basebenze kahle kakhulu* (The boys worked very well).
4. *Isela likhuluma kabi* (The thief speaks badly).
5. *Sizoya kangaki edolobheni?* (How many times shall we go to town?)

From Relatives:

| | | |
|---|---|---|
| *-buhlungu* | > | *kabuhlungu* (painfully) |
| *-lula* | > | *kalula* (lightly, easily) |
| *-ngcono* | > | *kangcono* (in a better way) |
| *-lukhuni* | > | *kalukhuni* (with difficulty) |
| *-mnandi* | > | *kamnandi* (nicely, pleasantly) |
| *-njani* | > | *kanjani?* (in what way/manner) |
| *-nzima* | > | *kanzima* (with difficulty) |

1. *Izinkabi zilima kalula ngoba izulu belina* (The oxen are ploughing easily because it has been raining).
2. *Abantwana bacule kamnandi esikoleni* (The children sang beautifully at school).
3. *Umalume uhamba kanjani namuhla?* (How is uncle walking today).
4. *Ugogo ukhuluma kalukhuni ngoba uyagula* (Grandmother speaks with difficulty because she is ill).

### Exercise 21

*Humusha ngesiNgisi:* (a) *Amahashi ami amabili amhlophe alahlekile, nezinkabi zami ezibomvu zilahlekile.* (b) *Lezo zicathulo zakhe ezimnyama ezintsha zibiza imali eningi kakhulu; ziyadula.* (c) *Sizohamba sobabili nomfowethu omkhulu ngoMgqibelo; udadewethu omncane akahambi yena. Uzosala nomama ekhaya.* (d) *Umakhi akafuni amatshe anje; ufuna amatshe amakhulu odwa; kodwa ufuna amatshe ambalwa.* (e) *Leli bhantshi likaJames elimnyama livelaphi?* (f) *EVereniging kukhona umfula omkhulu obanzi; izimoto ziwela ebhulohweni, nesitimela sinebhuloho laso. Izimoto azingeni emanzini nesitimela asingeni emanzini.* (g) *Ugogo wesaba umoya omakhaza ngoba uyagula futhi akanajazi.* (h) *Khumula lezi zingubo ezimanzi nezicathulo ezimanzi; uzogula.* (i) *Bengifuna izinkuni ezomile* (dry) *kodwa kukhona izinkuni ezimanzi kuphela.* (j) *Sifuna amanzi asethangeni.*

*Ethangeni sizothola amanzi amnandı apholile* (cool); *amanzi kampompi ayashisa.* (k) *Ngifuna ummese obukhali; angifuni ummese obuthuntu.* (l) *Sibona amafu amaningi amnyama phezulu esibhakabhakeni* (*isibhakabhaka*—sky—4). (m) *Bengifuna amakhandlela; bengingafuni ilambu likaphalafini.* (n) *Udadewethu ubhaka amakhekhe amnandi futhi upheka ukudla okumnandi.* (o) *Umntwana ufuna ukugcoba ibhotela esinkweni sakhe.* (p) *Ubabamkhulu akafuni ukuphuza itiye lakhe ngoba liyabanda.* (q) *Cima izibane; abantwana bafuna ukulala manje; bayozela.* (r) *Ingadi kamalume inezihlahla eziningi zezithelo; ehlobo nasekwindla sithola izithelo ezimnandi engadini kamalume.* (s) *Bonke abantwana bathanda umfundisi ngoba umfundisi unomusa.* (t) *Zonke izihluthulelo zendlu zihambe nobaba ekuseni.* (u) *Izolo iziboshwa* (*isiboshwa* —convict—4) *eziningi bezisebenza emgwaqweni; ezinye bezimba, ezinye bezisusa amatshe. Iziboshwa zihlala ejele* (*ijele*—goal—3). (v) *Sizohola imali yethu ntambama ngoba besisiza umlungu.*

# CHAPTER 24

## RELATIVES USED AS PREDICATIVES

On page 108 we illustrated how an adjective may be used predicatively. Relatives may also be used as predicatives. This is done by dropping the relative concord and using the subjectival concord. e.g.

| | | |
|---|---|---|
| *umfana o-bomvu* (a red boy) | > | *umfana u-bomvu* (the boy is red) |
| *abafana aba-bomvu* (red boys) | > | *abafana ba-bomvu* (the boys are red) |
| *umuthi o-bomvu* | > | *umuthi u-bomvu* |
| *imithi e-bomvu* | > | *imithi i-bomvu* |
| *itshe eli-bomvu* | > | *itshe li-bomvu* |
| *amatshe a-bomvu* | > | *amatshe a-bomvu* |
| *isihlalo esi-bomvu* | > | *isihlalo si-bomvu* |
| *izihlalo ezi-bomvu* | > | *izihlalo zi-bomvu* |
| *indlu e-mnyama* | > | *indlu i-mnyama* |
| *izindlu ezi-mnyama* | > | *izindlu zi-mnyama* |
| *udonga olu-mhlophe* | > | *udonga lu-mhlophe* |
| *izindonga ezimhlophe* | > | *izindonga zi-mhlophe* |
| *ubuhlalu obu-luhlaza* | > | *ubuhlalu bu-luhlaza* |
| *ukukhanya oku-bomvu* | > | *ukukhanya ku-bomvu* |

The negative is formed by prefixing *a-* (*aka-* in Cl. 1 sg. and Cl. 3 pl.):

| | | |
|---|---|---|
| *umuntu ubomvu* | > | *umuntu akabomvu* (The person is not red) |

*abantu babomvu* > *abantu ababomvu*
*umuthi ubomvu* > *umuthi awubomvu*
*imithi ibomvu* > *imithi ayibomvu*
*ihashi libomvu* > *ihashi alibomvu*
*amahashi abomvu* > *amahashi akabomvu* etc.

## Exercise 22

1. *FUNDA: Humusha ngesiNgisi:* (a) *Ihashi lami limhlophe, alimnyama. Izinkabi zami zimnyama, azimhlophe.* (b) *Lezo zicathulo zakho ezintsha zinsundu kodwa izicathulo zami ezintsha zimnyama, azinsundu. Ngithanda izicathulo zami kakhulu.* (c) *Umese kamalume ubukhali kakhulu. Umese kamalume mncane, awumkhulu.* (d) *UThoko uzogula ngoba ugqoka izingubo ezimanzi. Izingubo zimanzi nezicathulo zimanzi. Thoko ugqokelani izingubo ezimanzi nezicathulo ezimanzi?* (e) *Ugogo uyagula kodwa namuhla ungcono. Akakhwehleli kakhulu. Izolo ubekhwehlela kabi.* (f) *Lomuthi uluhlaza kodwa lowo awuluhlaza. Umuthi kagogo awuluhlaza; ubomvu. Ugogo uphuza kangaki umuthi wakhe? Ugogo uphuza umuthi wakhe ekuseni nasemini nasebusuku.* (g) *Ufuna umthwalo onjani? Ngifuna umthwalo olula. Lomthwalo ulula kodwa lowo uyasinda.* )h) *UJabulani ubalekelani? UJabulani ubaleka ngoba unqunu; uyesaba.* (i) *Umalume ulolelani umese wakhe na? Umalume ulola umese wakhe ngoba ubuthuntu.* (j) *Umfowenu akathengi ngani lezi zicathulo? Umfowethu akafuni lezi zicathulo ngoba zimpunga; ufuna izicathulo ezinsundu.* (k) *Lombuzo ulukhuni kakhulu. Phendula wena dadewethu.* (l) *Imigwaqo emadolobheni ibanzi ngoba izimoto ziningi.*

2. Convert the relatives into predicatives:

(a) *Ibhantshi elinje* (b) *Imithi eluhlaza*
(c) *Izinja ezinsundu* (d) *Ilanga elimakhaza*
(e) *Umfana ongaka* (f) *Ukudla okuduma*
(g) *Umthwalo onzima* (h) *Itiye elimnand*

(i) *Iyembe elimanzi*
(j) *Abantu abaqotho*
(k) *Imifula ebanzi*
(l) *Imbazo ebuthuntu*
(m) *Isilonda esibuhlungu*
(n) *Inkabi engakaya*
(o) *Izimvu ezimbalwa*
(p) *Umuzi ongako*
(q) *Amahashi amnyama*
(r) *Isitsha esinjani?*
(s) *Abantu abampofu*
(t) *Umuntu onje*

3. Rewrite the sentences in 2 above with the predicatives in the negative.

4. *FUNDA: Sibona abantu abaningi. Bonke laba bantu baya edolobheni. Bayothenga. Abantu abaningi baya edolobheni ngoMgqibelo. Abanye abantu bahamba ngamabhasi, abanye bahamba ngamabhayisikili, abanye bahamba ngezitimela, abanye bahamba ngezinyawo. Abanye abantu bathenga ukudla, abanye bathenga izingubo, abanye bathenga ezinye izinto. Baningi kakhulu abantu edolobheni ngoMgqibelo.*

*Mina ngizohamba ngedwa. Angizuhamba noJames. Ngifuna ukuya edolobheni. Ngizohamba ngebhasi. Angizuhamba ngebhayisikili ngoba ibhayisikili lihamba kancane. Edolobheni ngifuna ukuthenga ibhantshi elisha nebhulukwe elisha nezicathulo ezintsha. Zonke lezi zinto ziyadula. Izicathulo ziyadula, nebhantshi liyadula nebhulukwe liyadula. Izicathulo zami ezindala zimnyama. Manje ngifuna izicathulo ezibomvu. Ibhantshi lami elidala limpunga. Manje ngifuna ibhantshi elimnyama. Ibhulukwe lami elidala limpunga. Manje ngifuna elimhlophe.*

*Edolobheni ngizothenga futhi upholishi kamama nomuthi kaJames. Umama ufuna upholishi wezicathulo zakhe ezimhlophe. Upholishi kamama uphele ngesonto eledlule. Upholishi ubiza amasenti angu-7. Ngizothenga futhi umuthi kaJames. UJames uyakhwehlela. Izolo ubegqoke izingubo ezimanzi nezicathulo ezimanzi. Manje uyashisa futhi uyakhwehlela. Edolobheni ngizothenga umuthi wokukhwehlela. Mhlawumbe uJames uzoya kudokotela.*

*Ibhasi linejubane. Liya kaningi edolobheni ngelanga. Umshayeli ushayela kahle kakhulu. Abantu abaningi bathanda ukukhwela ibhasi lakhe. Linamasondo amakhulu. Ibhasi lithwala abantu abaningi. Umshayeli mude kodwa akamkhulu. Unamadevu. Ebusweni umhlophe. Ugqoka ijazi elimhlophe. Uthanda ukuthwala ikepisi nokufaka izicathulo ezinsundu.*

# CHAPTER 25

## THE OBJECTIVAL CONCORD

In English there are the object pronouns him, her, it, them, which may be used instead of nouns. Zulu, however, employs objectival concords. In form these concords are the same as the subjectival concords except where the subjectival concord is a vowel only. The following is a list of objectival concords:—

| | | Singular | Plural |
|---|---|---|---|
| 1st Pers. | | *ngi-* | *si-* |
| 2nd Pers. | | *ku-* | *ni-* |
| 3rd Pers. Cl. | 1 | *m-, mu-* | *ba-* |
| | 2 | *wu-* | *yi-* |
| | 3 | *li-* | *wa-* |
| | 4 | *si-* | *zi-* |
| | 5 | *yi-* | *zi-* |
| | 6 | *lu-* | *zi-* |
| | 7 | *bu-* | |
| | 8 | *ku-* | |

In connection with the objectival concords note the following:—

(i) The objectival concord is used when the object is not indicated by using a noun or a pronoun.

(ii) The objectival concord and the substantival object (i.e. noun or pronoun) may both be expressed for definiteness or for emphasis.

(iii) When it is used, the objectival concord must immediately precede the verb stem.

(iv) The use of the objectival concord does not preclude the use of *-ya-*.

(v) In Class 1 sing. the objectival concord is *mu-* when the verb stem is monosyllabic.

Examples:—

1. *Ngiya-m-bona* (I see him/her).
2. *Umlimi uya-ba-biza* (*abantwana*) (The farmer calls them (children)).
3. *Ibhubesi liya-wu-funa* (*umfula*) (The lion wants it (river)).
4. *Indoda i-yi-thengile* (*imibhede*) (The men bought them (beds)).
5. *Umalume u-li-bonile* (*ihashi*) (Uncle saw it (horse)).
6. *Amadoda a-wa-dubulile* (*amabhubesi*) (The men have shot them (lions)).
7. *Abelungu baya-si-thanda* (*isibhedlela*) (The whitemen like it (hospital)).
8. *Umfana u-zi-thengile* (*izinkwa*) (The boy bought them (loaves of bread)).
9. *Ubaba u-yi-landile inkomo* (Father fetched the cow).
10. *Izinsizwa zi-zi-bonile izinyoka* (The young men saw the snakes).
11. *Abantwana ba-lu-phuzile ubisi* (The children drank the milk).
12. *Intombi i-zi-thwalile izinkuni* (The maiden carried the firewood).
13. *Umfana u-bu-shisile utshani* (The boy burnt the grass).
14. *Umfowethu uzo-ngi-shaya* (My brother will hit me).
15. *Umfundisi uzo-si-bona* (The parson will see us).
16. *Umnumzane uya-ku-funa* (The headman wants you).
17. *Abazali baya-ni-biza* (The parents call you).

The objectival concords may also be used with commands. In the singular the final *-a* of the verb becomes *-e*, and in the plural *-ani* becomes *-eni*. Examples:—

1. *bamba ihashi!* (catch the horse!)
   *libambe!* (catch it!)
2. *landa izinkomo!* (fetch the cattle!)
   *zilande!* (fetch them!)
3. *thintitha uthuli!* (remove the dust!)
   *luthintithe!* (remove it!)
4. *biza abantwana*! (call the children!
   *babize!* (call them!)
5. *bambani ihashi!* (catch the horse!)
   *libambeni!* (catch it!)
6. *landani izinkomo!* (fetch the cattle!)
   *zilandeni!* (fetch them!)
7. *thintithani uthuli!* (remove the dust!)
   *luthintitheni!* (remove it!)
8. *bizani abantwana!* (call the children!)
   *babizeni!* (call them!)

## Exercise 23

A. *Humusha ngesiNgisi:* (a) *Abantwana abayiboni inkosi kodwa thina siyayibona.* (b) *Izinja zami ezimnyama ezinkulu azizilumanga izihambi izolo ekuseni.* (c) *Ngibone amadoda amathathu amafishane emgwaqweni izolo kusihlwa kodwa umkami akawabonanga.* (d) *Izinsizwa aziwagibelanga amahashi omlimi ngoba azithandi ukugibela amahashi; ziyawesaba.* (e) *Thina sitshala izimbali ngoba siyazithanda; sitshala izinhlobonhlobo zezimbali; ezinye zibhalasa ehlobo, ezinye zibhalasa ebusika.* (f) *Abantwana bathenga amaswidi zonke izinsuku ngoba bayawathanda; ubaba ubapha imali yokuwathenga.* (g) *Umalume akazuyithenga imoto enkulu ngoba akanamali; uzothenga imoto encane. Imoto enkulu iyadula, ibiza imali eningi.* (h) *Sizibonile izimvu nezimbuzi zikaVan Zyl entabeni izolo ntambama; bezidla entabeni. UVan Zyl uthi izimvu zakhe nezimbuzi zakhe zilahlekile.* (i) *Amasela azithathile izinkukhu zomfazi ebusuku ngoba umfazi akanazinja futhi akanandoda.* (j) *Isiguli siwuphuzile umuthi waso ngoba sifuna ukuphila, kodwa asifuni ukuya esibhedlela; sithi siyesaba.* (k) *Izinja zami zibulala izinkukhu namadada njalo kodwa ngizipha ukudla okuningi.* (l) *Abanumzane abayilolanga imikhonto yabo ngoba amabhubesi bazowadubula ngezibhamu.* (m) *Ngesonto elizayo ubaba uzongithuma eBenoni; kukhona umalume eBenoni.*

B. *Humusha ngesiZulu:* (a) The five little children drank water but the two boys did not drink it; they drank milk. (b) The Inspector did not write the letters in the afternoon; he wrote them in the evening at home. (c) Many animals do not like to live with people because they (animals) fear them. (d) We did not see the three horses at the river but my brother says he saw them. (e) I was going with the strangers; I was showing them the way. (f) Tomorrow the white-man will give us our money; we get our money at the end of the week. (g) Tie (pl.) the horses because they will run away. (h) Call him! I want to send him. (i) Fetch (pl.) them (oxen) because we shall plough in the afternoon. (j) The road has stones; the men are going to the road because they want to dig them out; they want to take them out. (k) The farmer was teaching us (how) to plant potatoes and onions. (l) The girl opened the doors but the children closed them. (m) I shall fetch uncle's books from town; he wants them.

C. *Humusha ngesiNgisi:* (a) *Umfowenu ukhalela izincwadi zakhe zesikole ngoba zilahlekile; zilahleke esitimeleni namuhla ekuseni.* (b) *Thina sithanda ukuthengela abantwana bethu izinto ezinhle ngoKhisimusi.* (c) *Umama akayi edolobheni namuhla ngoba uyathunga; uthungela uThoko noJane.*

(d) *USipho ukhalelani? Ukhala ngoba ufuna amaswidi kaThemba.* (e) *Phekela abantwana ukudla; balambile.* (f) *UNomusa ufundela ugogo incwadi yakhe ngoba ugogo akaboni emehlweni.* (g) *Uhambelani ngebhasi namuhla? Ngihamba ngebhasi ngoba imoto ihambe nobaba izolo.* (h) *Umlimi uyibulalelani injà yakhe? Uyibulala ngoba idla izimvu.* (i) *Maggie, thathela abantwana amajazi abo emvula; izulu liyana.* (j) *Ummeli wethu uzosikhulumela kusasa.* (k) *Laba bafana bagijimelani? Bayabaleka; babona inyoka.* (l) *Abantwana besikole bazoculela inkosi nenkosikazi kusasa ekuseni ngo-*11. (m) *Lethela umama isitulo; umama ufuna ukuhlala.* (n) *Uthisha ufundela abantwana izindaba ezimnandi encwadini yakhe. Incwadi kathisha inezindaba eziningi ezimnandi.* (o) *Thelela umfowenu itiye.* (p) *Ngizokuphathela izimpahla zakho.*

D. *Humusha ngesiZulu*: (a) Collect stones for the builder. (b) The men are ploughing for the parson because the parson has no oxen. (c) Jane is sifting flour for her sister; her sister wants to bake cakes and bread. (d) Mother is lighting up for father; father is writing letters in the house. (e) The boy is playing for his school. (f) Why are the children running away? The children are running away because they see the farmer's dog; they are afraid of it. (g) The parson is praying for the heathen and the Christians. (h) We shall plant for grandfather tomorrow morning or the day after tomorrow. (i) Why is your sister putting on her new shoes and her new dress? My sister is putting on her new shoes and her new dress because she is going to the wedding of her friend. (j) The boy will inflate the bicycle for me. (k) Why do you put out the light? Because the children want to sleep; they are drowsy. (l) Lizzie, take out your brother's clothes for him. (m) I ask for forgiveness on behalf of my cousin. (n) The girl will bring in the chairs for you (pl.). (o) The men are felling trees for the farmer. (p) My sister will iron our shirts for us; mother will patch my trousers for me. (q) The headman is pleading for the men to the chief. (r) In the afternoon I shall chop firewood for my sister. (s) Pick up the handkerchief for mother. (t) The parents are answering for their children. (u) Jesus (*uJesu*-1a) died for sinners.

E. *FUNDA: EZOO*

*Ngiyazi eZoo. EZoo kukhona izilwane eziningi, ezinkulu nezincane. Kukhona nezinyoni eziningi. EGoli iZoo isePark-town. Kukhona futhi iZoo enye ePitoli.*

*EZoo eGoli kukhona imvubu. Imvubu ihlala emanzini. Abantu abaningi, abadala nabantwana bathanda ukubuka imvubu. Ngesinye isikhathi imvubu iyaphuma emanzini, kodwa ngesinye isikhathi ayithandi ukuphuma. Imvubu ine-khanda elikhulu elibi, nomlomo omkhulu, namakhala ama-khulu, nemilenze emikhulu emifishane, nomzimba omkhulu.*

*EZoo kukhona futhi izindlovu. Kukhona izindlovu ezinkulu nezindlovu ezincane. Abantwana abaningi ba-thanda ukugibela izindlovu kodwa abanye abantwana baye-saba. Indlovu inomboko* (trunk—2) *omude, futhi indlovu inamazinyo amakhulu amade. Indlovu ithatha ukudla kwayo ngomboko wayo. Indlovu inomzimba omkhulu namadlebe* (ears of animals—3) *amakhulu nemilenze emikhulu kodwa indlovu inomsila omncane. Inamandla kakhulu. Ehlathini indlovu yephula* (*ephula*—break) *amagatsha* (branches—3) *emithi ngomboko wayo.*

*EZoo sibona futhi amabhubesi. Kukhona amabhubesi amakhulu namancane. Amabhubesi adla inyama kuphela. Amabhubesi anamazinyo amade amakhulu. Ngesinye isi-khathi amabhubesi ayabhonga. Anolaka. Thina siyawesaba kakhulu, nezinye izilwane ziyawesaba kakhulu.*

*Abantwana abaningi nabantu abadala abaningi bathanda ukubuka izimfene nezinkawu eZoo. Izimfene nezinkawu zithanda abantu. Ziyadlala. Abantu bazipha amantongomane* (pea nuts—3) *kodwa umthetho waseZoo awuvumi. Izimfene nezinkawu zithanda amantongomane kakhulu. Abanye abantu bazipha amaswidi. EZoo kukhona izimfene ezinkulu nezincane, nezinkawu ezinkulu nezincane, izinhlobo eziningi.*

*Abantu abanye bathanda ukubuka izinyoka kodwa abanye abantu abathandi ukuzibuka ngoba bayazesaba. Izinyoka zihamba ngezisu. EZoo kukhona izinyoka ezinde nezimfishane, ezinkulu nezincane. Thina sithanda ukubuka izinhlwathi* (pythons—5). *Izinyoka zithanda ukudla amaxoxo.*

*Kukhona futhi eZoo izingwe* (tigers, leopards—5). *Ingwe inolaka kakhulu. Izingwe ezinye zivela eNdiya. Kukhona futhi izinyamazane eziningi nezinyathi* (buffaloes—5) *nengwenya* (crocodile—5) *nezimfudu namakameli* (camels—3) *nezindlulamithi* (giraffes—5). *Kukhona futhi amabhele* (bears —3). *Abantu abanye bathanda ukupha amabhele ukudla.*

*EZoo sibona izinyoni eziningi, izinhlobonhlobo. Kukhona izinkozi* (*ukhozi*—eagle—5) *namanqe* (vultures—3) *nezikhova* (owls—4) *nezinye izinhlobo zezinyoni.*

*Thina siyathanda eZoo. Bonke abantwana bayathanda eZoo. Bathanda ukubuka izilwane; bathanda ukugibela izindlovu; bathanda ukubona izimfene zidlala; bathanda futhi ukudlala eZoo.*

*EZoo ePitoli sikhipha imali esangweni kodwa eGoli asiyikhiphi.*

# CHAPTER 26

## TO INDICATE AN ACTION OR STATE WHICH HAS BEEN GOING ON AND STILL CONTINUES

LET US STUDY the following sentences:

1. *Ngidlala ibhola*—I am playing football.
2. *Ngibhala incwadi*—I am writing a letter (or book).
3. *Umama uyapheka*—Mother is cooking.
4. *Udadewethu uyathunga*—My sister is sewing.
5. *Abantwana bayageza*—The children are washing.

The above sentences will now be altered to convey the meaning that the action taking place has been going on hitherto:

1. *Ngisadlala ibhola*—I am still playing football.
2. *Ngisabhala incwadi*—I am still writing a letter.
3. *Umama usapheka*—Mother is still cooking.
4. *Udadewethu usathunga*—My sister is still sewing.
5. *Abantwana basageza*—The children are still washing.

The difference in meaning is brought about by the introduction of *-sa-* in the verb. *-ya-* is not used with *-sa-*; thus *uyapheka* becomes *usapheka*.

The negative is formed by changing final *-a* to *-i* and prefixing *a-* or *ka-*; e.g.

1. *Angisadlali ibhola*—I no longer play football/I am no longer playing football.
2. *Angisabhali incwadi*—I am no longer writing a letter.
3. *Umama akasapheki*—Mother is no longer cooking.

4. *Udadewethu akasathungi*—My sister is no longer sewing.
5. *Abantwana abasagezi*—The children are no longer washing.

Further examples:

1. *Abantwana basalele* (The children are still asleep).
2. *Izisebenzi azisambi umgodi; zilayisha isihlabathi* (The labourers are no longer digging a hole: they are loading sand).
3. *Udokotela usapopola iziguli* (The doctor is still examining the patients) (*popola*—examine medically).
4. *Unesi akasagezi abantwana; upha iziguli umuthi* (The nurse is no longer washing the children; she is giving the patients medicine).
5. *Ubaba usalima; uzofika ntambama* (Father is still ploughing; he will arrive in the afternoon).
6. *Umama usathunga kodwa udadewethu akasathungi* (Mother is still sewing but my sister is no longer sewing.)
7. *Izinkabi zisaphuza amanzi* (The oxen are still drinking water).
8. *Umfundisi usathandaza* (The minister is still praying).
9. *Amanzi asageleza emfuleni* (The water is still flowing in the river).
10. *Amadoda asalayisha amalahle elorini* (The men are still loading coal on the lorry).

Notice also the following:

*kusekhona amanzi*—there is still water.
*kusekhona imali*—there is still money.
*kusekhona abantu*—there are still people.
(*kukhona* becomes *kusekhona*)

## Exercise 24

*FUNDA* 1. *Mina ngihlala kwaZulu. KwaZulu kusekhona amaxhegu* (*ixhegu*, old man—3). *Kusekhona futhi nezalukazi eziningi. Amaxhegu kwaZulu asathanda ukuphuza utshwala nokudla inyama; futhi asathanda ukuxoxa izindaba zakwaZulu ezindala.*

2. *James, musa ukushiya uJohn; mlinde. UJames usafuna izincwadi zakhe. Akaziboni. UJames uthi ubeke izincwadi zakhe etafuleni kusihlwa kodwa manje akasaziboni. Usafuna endlini.*

3. X: *Uphi umfowenu?* Y: *Usasebenza.*
   X: *Usebenzani?* Y: *Usavala amafasitele.*
   X: *Uwavalelani amafasitele?* Y: *Uvala ngoba kukhona umoya.*

4. *Ugogo usalele, nobabamkhulu usalele. Ugogo akathandi ukuvuka ekuseni kakhulu, nobabamkhulu akathandi ukuvuka ekuseni kakhulu. Ugogo nobabamkhulu bathanda ukuvuka emini.*

5. *Umfowethu omkhulu usekhaya. Ufike ngesonto eledlule. Umfowethu usebenza e-Estcourt. Akasasebenzi eGoli. Akasathandi eGoli. Uthanda ukusebenza eNatali.*

6. *Ngonyaka odlule umhloli wayefika njalo esikoleni sethu kodwa manje akasafiki.*

7. *Angisathandi ukudlala ithenisi* (tennis) *futhi angisathandi ukudlala ibhola. Ngithanda ukudlala icricket.*

# CHAPTER 27

## TO INDICATE THAT THE SUBJECT IS ACTED UPON

STUDY the following sentences:
*Umfana ushaya inja* (The boy beats the dog).
*Inja ishaywa ngumfana* (The dog is beaten by the boy).
*Udadewethu ubasa umlilo* (My sister is making fire).
*Umlilo ubaswa ngudadewethu* (The fire is made by my sister).
*UThemba umba umgodi* (Themba is digging a hole).
*Umgodi umbiwa nguThemba* (The hole is dug by Themba).
*Udadewethu wenza itiye* (My sister is making tea).
*Itiye lenziwa ngudadewethu* (Tea is made by my sister).

The ending of the verb when it expresses that the subject is acted upon is *-wa*; but in the case of monosyllabic verbs and vowel-commencing verbs the ending is *-iwa*.

Examples:

| | | | | | |
|---|---|---|---|---|---|
| *bona* | > | *bonwa* (be seen) | *siza* | > | *sizwa* (be helped) |
| *funda* | > | *fundwa* (be read) | *thenga* | > | *thengwa* (be bought) |
| *dla* | > | *dliwa* (be eaten) | *pha* | > | *phiwa* (be given) |
| *mba* | > | *mbiwa* (be dug) | *zwa* | > | *zwiwa* (be heard) |
| *enza* | > | *enziwa* (be done/ made) | *osa* | > | *osiwa* (be roasted) |
| *eba* | > | *ebiwa* (be stolen) | *alusa* | > | *aluswa* (be herded) |

Let us examine the following verbs:

*thuma* (send) > *thunywa* (be sent)
*bopha* (tie) > *boshwa* (be tied)

*bamba* (catch) > *banjwa* (be caught)
*hlaba* (pierce) > *hlatshwa* (be pierced)

With these verbs we observe that:

(i) they all have a sound produced with the two lips in the final syllable;

(ii) these sounds *m*, *ph*, *mb*, *b* have all been replaced by new sounds viz. *ny*, *sh*, *nj*, *tsh* respectively. (See also pp. 97-98).

These sound changes occur regularly and involve the changing of bilabial sounds into palatal sounds. Vowel commencing verbs of two syllables do not undergo this sound change; e.g.

*eba* (steal) > *ebiwa* (be stolen)
*aba* (divide, portion out) > *abiwa* (be divided)

It will be observed that this type of verb (i.e. ending in -*wa*) implies an agent of the action. If the
indicating the agent is expressed, it also
With all nouns there is a lowering of
vowel. In addition to the lowering of to
ing in *i*- may take *y*- initially, and no
*a*- *o*- *u*- may take *ng*- initially. There
however, which it is not necessary to m

Examples:

| | | | |
|---|---|---|---|
| *inja* | > *yinja* | *isela* | |
| *inkosi* | > *yinkosi* | *inkomo* | |
| *abantu* | > *ngabantu* | *abelungu* | |
| *amadoda* | > *ngamadoda* | *amaguncla* | |
| *odokotela* | > *ngodokotela* | *onesi* | |
| *omalume* | > *ngomalume* | *odadeweth* | |
| *umfana* | > *ngumfana* | *umshayeli* | |
| *umzali* | > *ngumzali* | *umfundisi* | |

Sentence examples:

1. *Abafana balunywa yinja* (The boys are bitten by a dog)
2. *Umlilo ubaswa ngudadewethu* (The fire is kindled by my sister).
3. *Utshani budliwa yizinkomo* (Grass is eaten by cattle).
4. *Izingubo zithungwa ngumama* (The dresses are sewn by mother).
5. *Iziguli zipopolwa ngodokotela* (Patients are examined by doctors).
6. *Ukudla kuphekwa yintombazane* (Food is cooked by the girl).
7. *Abantwana baphiwa ngumfowethu* (Children are given by my brother).
8. *Izimoto zenziwa ngabelungu* (Cars are made by white people).
9. *Imali yebiwa ngamasela* (Money is stolen by thieves).
10. *Ugogo usizwa ngunesi* (Grandmother is helped by a nurse).
11. *Imoto ishayelwa ngumshayeli* (The car is driven by a driver).
12. *Odadewethu babizwa ngomalume* (My sisters are called by the uncles).

In the negative, the final vowel -a of verbs ending in -wa does not change to -i. e.g.

1. *Abafana abalunywa yinja* (The boys are not bitten by a dog).
2. *Umlilo awubaswa ngudadewethu* (Fire is not kindled by my sister).
3. *Utshani abudliwa yizinkomo* (Grass is not eaten by cattle).
4. *Izingubo azithungwa ngumama* (The dresses are not sewn by mother).

5. *Iziguli azipopolwa ngudokotela* (Patients are not examined by the doctor).
6. *Ukudla akuphekwa yintombazana* (Food is not cooked by the girl).
7. *Abantwana abaphiwa ngumfowethu* (Children are not given by my brother).
8. *Izimoto azenziwa ngabelungu* (Cars are not made by white people).
9. *Imali ayebiwa ngamasela* (Money is not stolen by thieves).
10. *Ugogo akasizwa ngunesi* (Grandmother is not helped by a nurse).
11. *Imoto ayishayelwa ngumshayeli* (The car is not driven by a driver).
12. *Odadewethu ababizwa ngomalume* (My sisters are not called by the uncles).

## WHEN THE AGENT IS INDICATED BY PRONOUN

Only the Absolute and Demonstrative pronouns will be illustrated.

### Absolute Pronoun

Singular

| | | | | |
|---|---|---|---|---|
| 1st person | | *mina* | > | *yimina, yimi* |
| 2nd person | | *wena* | > | *nguwena, nguwe* |
| 3rd person Class | 1. | *yena* | > | *nguyena, nguye* |
| | 2. | *wona* | > | *yiwona, yiwo* |
| | 3. | *lona* | > | *yilona, yilo* |
| | 4. | *sona* | > | *yisona, yiso* |
| | 5. | *yona* | > | *yiyona, yiyo* |
| | 6. | *lona* | > | *yilona, yilo* |
| | 7. | *bona* | > | *yibona, yibo* |
| | 8. | *khona* | > | *yikhona, yikho* |

Plural

| | | | | |
|---|---|---|---|---|
| 1st person | | *thina* | > | *yithina, yithi* |
| 2nd person | | *nina* | > | *yinina, yini* |
| 3rd person | Class 1. | *bona* | > | *yibona, yibo* |
| | 2. | *yona* | > | *yiyona, yiyo* |
| | 3. | *wona* | > | *yiwona, yiwo* |
| | 4, 5, 6. | *zona* | > | *yizona, yizo* |
| | 7. | *bona* | > | *yibona, yibo* |
| | 8. | *khona* | > | *yikhona, yikho* |

The use of the long or short forms is optional.

Examples:

Using the sentences above we may substitute the inflected forms of the absolute pronoun as follows:

1. *Abafana balunywa yiyona/yiyo* (The boys are bitten by it).
2. *Umlilo ubaswa nguyena/nguye* (The fire is kindled by her).
3. *Utshani budliwa yizona/yizo* (Grass is eaten by them).
4. *Izingubo zithungwa nguyena/nguye* (The dresses are sewn by her).
5. *Iziguli zipopolwa yibona/yibo* (Patients are examined by them).
6. *Ukudla kuphekwa yiyona/yiyo* (Food is cooked by her).
7. *Abantwana baphiwa nguyena/nguye* (Children are given by him).
8. *Izimoto zenziwa yibona/yibo* (Cars are made by them).
9. *Imali yebiwa yiwona/yiwo* (Money is stolen by them).
10. *Ugogo usizwa nguyena/nguye* (Grandmother is helped by her).
11. *Imoto ishayelwa nguyena/nguye* (The car is driven by him).
12. *Odadewethu babizwa yibona/yibo* (My sisters are called by them).

## Demonstrative Pronoun

(For a table of Demonstrative Pronouns see p. 125.)

Prefix *yi-* to every form of the demonstrative pronoun. Other variants will not be considered at this stage. Again using the sentences above we may substitute the inflected forms of the demonstrative pronoun as follows:

1. *Abafana balunywa yile/yileyo/yileya* (The boys are bitten by this one/that one/that one yonder).
2. *Umlilo ubaswa yilo/yilowo/yilowaya* (Fire is kindled by this one/that one/that one yonder).
3. *Utshani budliwa yilezi/yilezo/yileziya* (Grass is eaten by these/those/those yonder).
4. *Izingubo zithungwa yilo/yilowo/yilowaya* (Dresses are sewn by this one, etc.).
5. *Iziguli zipopolwa yilaba/yilabo/yilabaya* (Patients are examined by these, etc.).
6. *Ukudla kuphekwa yile/yileyo/yileya* (Food is cooked by this one, etc.).
7. *Abantwana baphiwa yilo/yilowo/yilowaya* (Children are given by this one, etc.).
8. *Izimoto zenziwa yilaba/yilabo/yilabaya* (Cars are made by these, etc.).
9. *Imali yebiwa yilawa/yilawo/yilawaya* (Money is stolen by these, etc.).
10. *Ugogo usizwa yilo/yilowo/yilowaya* (Grandmother is helped by this one, etc.).
11. *Imoto ishayelwa yilo/yilowo/yilowaya* (The car is driven by this one, etc.).
12. *Odadewethu babizwa yilaba/yilabo/yilabaya* (My sisters are called by these, etc.).

### Exercise 25

*FUNDA: UFana usakhala. Ukhalelani? Ushaywa ngubani? UFana ukhala ngoba ushaywa ngubaba. UFana ushaywa ngubaba ngenduku. Umshaya ngenduku encane. UFana ushaywa ngoba akafuni ukulanda izimpahla zikababa esiteshini. UFana uyavilapha, akathandi ukuthunywa, akathandi ukusebenza; uthanda ukudlala kuphela. Izimpahla zikababa zisegushede* (*igushede*, goods shed—3). *Zifike izolo kusihlwa. Zifike ngesitimela. Izimpahla eziningi zithwalwa yisitimela. Izimpahla zikababa zivela eGoli. Zizolandwa ngubaba ntambama. Ubaba usasebenza manje, usasebenza umsebenzi omunye. Ubaba uzozilanda izimpahla zakhe ngemoto yakhe. Imoto kababa ishayelwa nguyena ubaba kuphela. Ayishayelwa ngumama futhi ayishayelwa yithina. Ubaba unemoto enhle encane ensundu. Ubaba uthi akathandi imoto enkulu ngoba imoto enkulu ithatha uphethroli omningi. Egaraji ubaba uzothela uphethroli namafutha namanzi. Futhi ubaba uzofaka umoya emasondweni. Uphethroli uyathengwa, ubiza imali; namafutha ayathengwa, abiza imali; kodwa amanzi akathengwa, akabizi imali, nomoya awuthengwa, awubizi imali. Ubaba uzokhipha imali futhi egushede. Uthi uzokhipha ishumi lawosheleni nosheleni abathathu. Kukhona izimpahla eziningi zikababa egushede. Egushede izimpahla zizofakwa ngamadoda emotweni kababa kodwa ekhaya zizokhishwa yimi noFana emotweni.*

*Humusha ngesiNgisi:* (a) *Abanumzane basasizwa ngabafana babo namuhla; kusasa bazosizwa ngamadoda ngoba abafana baya esikoleni.* (b) *Izithelo zithengiswa zonke izinsuku edolobheni kodwa ezinye izinto azithengiswa ngeSonto.* (c) *Udadewethu uhlushwa ngamazinyo akhe kakhulu. Amazinyo kadadewethu azokhishwa ngudokotela wamazinyo ngoLwesithathu ntambama.* (d) *Umfowethu omkhulu akasasebenzi eThekwini; usebenza ePitoli kwaLombard. EPitoli uhola imali eningi.* (e) *Izinja zishaywa ngubani? Zishaywa ngabafana ngamatshe.* (f) *Umfundisi ukhona na? Yebo ukhona kodwa usadla. Uzoqeda masinyane. Mlinde lapha endlini.* (g) *Amathi-*

*kithi esitimela azothengwa yimi kusasa ekuseni kodwa amathikithi ebhasi azothengwa ngumfowethu.* (h) *Sibizwa ngubani? Nibizwa ngumalume. Uphi umalume? Usekhaya.* (i) *Esikoleni sifundiswa ukulondoloza imali. Imali ilondolozwa ebhange.* (j) *Susani ummbila phandle ngoba uzodliwa yizinkukhu; izinkukhu ziyawuthanda kakhulu ummbila.* (k) *Isinkwa sixovwa ngudadewethu; sizobhakwa ntambama noma kusihlwa.* (l) *Izihambi ziyesaba; zikhonkothwa yinja kamalume.* (m) *Umama usageza izingubo zethu kodwa azizuayinwa nguye; zizoayinwa ngumzala.* (n) *Linda lapha; amalahle azolethwa ngumlimi ngelori. Umlimi usalima manje.*

On pages 149-153 it has been shown how nouns and pronouns are inflected when they indicate the agent of an action after a verb ending in *-wa*. These inflected nouns and pronouns are predicatives. The method of forming these predicatives has been shown in the section mentioned above.

Further examples:

*umfana* (boy) > *ngumfana* (he is a boy)
*umuzi* (kraal) > *ngumuzi* (it is a kraal)
*abantu* (people) > *ngabantu* (they are people)
*amahashi* (horses) > *ngamahashi* (they are horses)
*omalume* (uncles) > *ngomalume* (they are uncles)
*omakhelwane* (neighbours) > *ngomakhelwane* (they are neighbours).
*inja* (dog) > *yinja* (it is a dog)
*isela* (thief) > *yisela* (it is a thief)

1. *Umalume ngumlimi* (Uncle is a farmer).
2. *Uyise ngumfundisi* (His father is a minister).
3. *Umfowabo ngudokotela* (His brother is a doctor).
4. *Abakhi ngamaNgisi* (The builders are English).
5. *UJane noMary ngamantombazane* (Jane and Mary are girls).

6. *UFido yin,a* (Fido is a dog).

Subjectival concords may be used with predicatives ormed from nouns; e.g.

| | | |
|---|---|---|
| *ngumuntu* | > | *ngingumuntu* (I am a person) |
| | > | *ungumuntu* (You are a person) |
| | > | *ungumuntu* (He/she is a person) |
| *-ngudokotela* | > | *Yena ungudokotela* (He/she is a doctor) |
| | > | *ngingudokotela* (I am a doctor) |
| *-ngonesi* | > | *singonesi* (we are nurses) |
| | > | *bangonesi* (they are nurses) |
| *-ngamadoda* | > | *bangamadoda* (they are men) |
| | > | *ningamadoda* (you are men) |
| | > | *singamadoda* (we are men) |

These inflected nouns may still govern concord; e.g.

1. *Umlimi ngumuntu omude* (The farmer is a tall person).
2. *Ulunywe yinja ensundu* (He was bitten by a brown dog).
3. *Umfana ubizwe ngudadewethu omkhulu* (The boy has been called by my elder sister).
4. *Lezi yizinkomo ezinhle kakhulu* (These are very fine cattle).
5. *Ibhubesi yisilwane esikhulu* (A lion is a big animal).
6. *Itiye lenziwe ngumama wakho* (Tea was made by your mother).
7. *Umalume wabo uthathwe ngumfula omncane* (Their uncle was taken by a small river, i.e. got drowned in a small river).
8. *Lawa ngamadoda amadala* (These are old men).
9. *Umakhi yindoda emfushane* (The builder is a short man).
10. *Lokhu ngukudla okumnandi* (This is nice food).

# CHAPTER 28

## TO EXPRESS 'ABILITY TO DO'

One of the ways of expressing 'ability to do' or potentiality is to use *-nga-* with the verb; e.g.
*Ngidlala ibhola*—I play football.
*Ngingadlala ibhola*—I can play football.
*Singacula namuhla*—We can sing today.
*Ningambona edolobheni*—You can see him in town.

In Class 1 singular the subjectival concord is *a-* and not *u-*.
Examples:

| | | |
|---|---|---|
| *umuntu uyadlala* | but | *umuntu angadlala* |
| *abantu bayadlala* | but | *abantu bangadlala* |
| *umuthi uyakhula* | | *umuthi ungakhula* |
| *imithi iyakhula* | | *imithi ingakhula* |
| *ihashi liyagijima* | | *ihashi lingagijima* |
| *amahashi ayagijima* | | *amahashi angagijima* |

Notice the negative:
*umuntu angedlale* (The person cannot play).
*abantu bangedlale* (The people cannot play).
*umuthi ungekhule* (The tree cannot grow).

In the negative *-nga-* gives place to *-nge-* and the final *-a* gives place to *-e*.

In Chapter 16 we illustrated the use of the immediate past continuous and the remote past continuous tenses. The same construction is employed with the verbs signifying 'ability to do'.

e.g.

IMMEDIATE PAST

| | |
|---|---|
| 1st pers. | *bengingadlala*—I could play. |
| | *besingadlala*—We could play. |
| 2nd pers. | *bewungadlala*—You could play. |
| | *beningadlala*—You could play (pl.). |
| 3rd pers. Cl. 1. | *Umuntu ubengafunda*—The person could read. |
| | *Abantu bebengafunda*—The people could read. |
| 2. | *Umuthi bewungakhula*—The tree could grow. |
| | *Imithi beyingakhula*—The trees could grow. |
| 3. | *Ihashi belingagijima*—The horse could run. |
| | *Amahashi abengagijima*—The horses could run |

REMOTE PAST

| | | |
|---|---|---|
| 1st pers. | *ngangingadlala* | *sasingadlala* |
| 2nd pers. | *wawungadlala* | *naningadlala* |
| 3rd pers. Cl. 1. | *wayengadlala* | *babengadlala* |
| 2. | *wawungakhula* | *yayingakhula* |
| 3. | *lalingagijima* | *ayengagijima* |

Negative:

| | |
|---|---|
| *bengingedlale* | *besingedlale* |
| *bewungedlale* | *beningedlale* |
| *ngangingedlale* | *sasingedlale* |
| *wawungedlale* | *naningedlale*, etc. |

EXERCISE 26

*Humusha ngesiNgisi:* (a) *Ubaba angagibela ihashi ngoba usathanda ukugibela kodwa umama angegibele ngoba akasathandi ukugibela ihashi; uyesaba.* (b) *Abafowethu bangaya esiteshini kusihlwa ngoba abasebenzi kusihlwa. Mina ngingaya ntambama kuphela; ngingeye kusihlwa.* (c) *Ngisafuna izinkuni namalahle ngoba umlilo uzobaswa yimi. Umama angebase namuhla ngoba uyagula.* (d) *OJohn bangazilanda izinkomo zakho entabeni ntambama kodwa uSipho angehambe ngoba uyaqhuga.* (*qhuga*—limp) (e) *Ngingekutshele igama lakhe ngoba angilazi.* (f) *Umfana wakho angangikhombisa eO.K. Bazaar na? Yebo angakukhombisa ngoba uyazi; usebenza khona.* (g) *Imithi yakhe yezithelo ingekhule kahle ngoba ayitholi amanzi. Imithi yezithelo ifuna amanzi amaningi.* (h) *Landa ihashi lami. Ungalibamba na? Yebo ngingalibamba. Ngizolibopha ngentambo. Kusasa lizolandwa ngumfowethu.* (i) *Iphoyisa lingawababamba amasela.* (j) *Izinkuni zingalandwa kusasa ngenqola kodwa amalahle azolandwa namuhla ngelori.* (k) *Ubabamkhulu angegijime futhi nogogo angegijime.* (l) *Sonke singangena emotweni kababa. Ubaba unemoto enkulu; akasathandi imoto encane.* (m) *Udokotela angebone iziguli manje ngoba uya enkantolo, ufunwa yimantshi. Iziguli uzozibona ngo-12 emini. Iziguli zizogezwa ngubani? Zizogezwa ngonesi.* (n) *Izolo bengingadlala ngoba bengingasebenzi kodwa namuhla ngingedlale ngoba ngiyasebenza.* (o) *Abalimi bebengalima namuhla ekuseni ngoba izulu alini.* (p) *Umnumzane wayengathenga imoto yakhe eThekwini; eGoli izimoto ziyadula.* (q) *Izimpahla zazingalandwa ngabafana ngoMgqibelo ngoba ngoMgqibelo abayi esikoleni.* (r) *Bengingefunde izincwadi kuthangi ngoba bengigula kodwa angisaguli manje.* (s) *Amadoda abengephuze utshwala ngoba utshwala buphelile.* (t) *Besingaya sonke edolobheni.*

# CHAPTER 29

## THE USE OF *uma*, *lapho*, *ngoba*, *mhla*, IN FORMING CERTAIN DEPENDENT CLAUSES

There are a few conjunctives which you will find useful. They are used in dependent clauses. These conjunctives are *uma* (if, when), *lapho* (when), *ngoba* (because), *mhla* (on the day when). e.g.

1. *Umtwana uyajabula uma edlala* (The child is happy when he plays).
2. *Abafowethu basebenza uma bethanda* (My brothers work when they like).
3. *Ubaba ufike lapho ilanga lishona* (My father arrived when the sun was setting, i.e. at sunset).
4. *Sambona mhla eshada* (We saw him/her on the day when he/she was married).
5. *Ucula ngoba ethanda* (He sings because he likes to).

Using the verb *thanda*, the following is a table showing the form the verb will assume after these conjunctives:

| | Singular | Plural |
|---|---|---|
| 1st pers. | *ngithanda* | *sithanda* |
| 2nd pers. | *uthanda* | *nithanda* |
| 3rd pers. Cl. 1. | *ethanda* | *bethanda* |
| 2. | *uthanda* | *ithanda* |
| 3. | *lithanda* | *ethanda* |
| 4. | *sithanda* | *zithanda* |
| 5. | *ithanda* | *zithanda* |

| | Singular | | Plural |
|---|---|---|---|
| 6. | *luthanda* | | *zithanda* |
| 7. | | *buthanda* | |
| 8. | | *kuthanda* | |

Note that in Class 1 the subjectival concords are *e-* and *be-* in the singular and plural respectively. In Class 3 plural it is *e-*. There is, however, a difference also in tone.

Examples:

1. *Umalume angafika uma ethanda* (Uncle can come if he likes).
2. *Abantwana abayi esikoleni uma begula* (Children do not go to school if they are ill).
3. *Izimvu ziyabaleka lapho zibona izinja* (The sheep run away when they see dogs).
4. *Amadoda ayajabula uma ephuza utshwala* (The men are happy when they drink beer).
5. *Ugogo angaphila uma ephuza umuthi kadokotela* (Grandmother can recover if she drinks the doctor's medicine).
6. *Izolo sifike ekhaya kusihlwa lapho udadewethu ekhanyisa izibane* (Yesterday we arrived home in the evening when my sister was lighting the lamps).
7. *Ngisakhumbula mhla inkosi ifika ePitoli* (I still remember the day the king arrived in Pretoria).
8. *Abantwana bayakhala ngoba unina ehamba* (Children are crying because their mother is going away).
9. *Ubumnyama buyaphela lapho ilanga liphuma* (Darkness disappears when the sun rises).
10. *Sizomtshela mhla ebuya* (We shall tell him/her on the day he/she returns).

The negative is formed by inserting *-nga-* and changing final *-a* to *-i*; e.g.

1. *Ubaba uzomshaya umfana uma engasebenzi* (Father will beat the boy if he does not work).
2. *Akaculingoba engathandi* (He does not sing because he does not like to).
3. *Sizonivakashela mhla ningasebenzi* (We shall pay you a visit on the day when you are not working) (*vakashela* —pay a visit).
4. *Umntwana uyakhala ngoba engaboni unina* (The child is crying because she does not see her mother).

### Exercise 27

*FUNDA—*

A. *Kusasa sifuna ukuya emshadweni. Sifuna ukuhamba ekuseni kakhulu. Sifuna ukuhamba lapho ilanga liphuma ngoba sihamba ngekalishi; asihambi ngemoto. Ubaba uzoya emshadweni uma ethanda kodwa uma engathandi akazuya. Bengingafuni mina ukuya emshadweni ngoba sizohamba ngekalishi. Umshado useGrens. Ngiyazi eGrens. Ngabona mhla umama eya kudokotela wamazinyo. Lowo dokotela ukhipha kahle kakhulu. Abantu abaningi bathanda ukuya kudokotela waseGrens. Sizobuya ngoLwesihlanu ntambama.*

B. *Kusasa udadewethu ufuna ukuya ebhayisikobho. Nami ngifuna ukuya ebhayisikobho. Uma udadewethu ehamba mina angizuhamba ngoba ngizobheka umntwana. Uma mina ngihamba udadewethu akazuhamba ngoba uzobheka umntwana. Udadewethu akathandi ukusala nomntwana, nami angithandi ukusala nomntwana. Umntwana uyahlupha kakhulu, uthanda ukukhala. Uma ekhala umntwana simupha ukudla noma ubisi.*

# CHAPTER 30

## THE USE OF THE CONJUNCTIVES
### *ukuba, ukuthi, ukuze, funa, qede, anduba*

Another way of expressing dependent or subordinate ideas is by using a verb which in the present tense positive ends in *-e*; e.g.

*Ngifuna ukuba ngihambe emini* (I want that I go at noon i.e. I want to go at noon).

*Ubaba uthanda ukuba sisebenze ekuseni* (Father likes that we work in the morning i.e. father likes us to work in the morning).
we work in the morning).

Using the verb *bona* the following is a table of this type of verb in the present tense positive:

| | | Singular | Plural |
|---|---|---|---|
| 1st pers. | | *ngibone* | *sibone* |
| 2nd pers. | | *ubone* | *nibone* |
| 3rd pers. Cl. | 1. | *abone* | *babone* |
| | 2. | *ubone* | *ibone* |
| | 3. | *libone* | *abone* |
| | 4. | *sibone* | *zibone* |
| | 5. | *ibone* | *zibone* |
| | 6. | *lubone* | *zibone* |
| | 7. | *bubone* | |
| | 8. | *kubone* | |

Note that the subjectival concord in Class 1a singular is *a-*.

This verb is used after certain conjunctives e.g. *ukuba* (that), *ukuthi* (that), *ukuze* (in order that), *funa* (lest), *qede* (thereafter, as soon as), *anduba* (before). Examples:

1. *Umama ufuna ukuba siye edolobheni* (Mother wants that we go to town i.e. Mother wants us to go to town).
2. *Abantwana bafisa ukuba babone izilwane eZoo* (The children desire to see the animals at the Zoo) (*fisa*—desire).
3. *Sifuna ukuthi ahambe kusasa* (We want that he goes tomorrow i.e. We want him to go tomorrow).
4. *Khanyisa ukuze sibone kahle* (Switch on the light in order that we see well).
5. *Abantwana bazoya esikoleni ukuze bafunde* (The children will go to school in order that they learn).
6. *Bopha ihashi lelo, funa libaleke* (Tie that horse lest it runs away).
7. *Ubaba akazumshaya umfana funa akhale* (Father will not beat the boy lest he cries).
8. *Umlimi uzolima qede atshale* (The farmer will plough and thereafter plant).
9. *Amadoda azosebenza qede ahambe* (The men will work and thereafter go).
10. *Umalume ufuna ukugeza anduba alale* (Uncle wants to wash before he sleeps).
11. *Uthisha ufuna ukuba sisebenze anduba sidlale* (The teacher wants us to work before we play).
12. *Ubaba uzokudla anduba afunde amaphepha* (Father will eat before he reads the papers).

The negative is formed by infixing *-nga-* and changing the final *-a* to *-i.* e.g.

1. *Ubaba ufuna ukuba ngingahambi namuhla* (Father wants that I do not go (should not go) today). Father wants us not to go today.

2. *Ufika qede angasebenzi* (He arrives and does not work).
3. *Sizovala umnyango ukuze zingangeni izinyoka* (We shall close the door in order that the snakes do not come in).
4. *Cima isibane ukuze bangasiboni* (Put out the light in order that they do not see us).
5. *Ngifuna ukuba bangayi edolobheni namuhla* (I want them not to go to town today).

This type of verb is also used in asking permissive questions; e.g.

1. *Sisebenze na?* (Should we work?)
2. *Ngifunde na?* (Should I read?)
3. *Abantwana bageze na?* (Should the children wash?)
4. *Ngenze itiye na?* (Should I make tea?)
5. *Umfana alande iposi na?* (Should the boy fetch the mail?)
6. *Abantu bahlale phansi na?* (Should the people sit down?)
7. *Udadewethu aye kudokotela na?* (Should my sister go to the doctor?)
8. *Singene na?* (Should we come in?)

### EXERCISE 28

*FUNDA: Izingulube ezimbili ziyavakasha, zivakasha ehlathini. Kukhona ingulube enkulu nengulube encane. Izingulube zibona indlu enhle ehlathini. Izingulube ziya endlini leyo. Ingulube enkulu ima phandle nengulube encane ima phandle. Ingulube enkulu ingena endlini kodwa ingulube encane isala phandle, ima phandle ngoba iyesaba ukungena endlini. Ingulube encane ithi engulubeni enkulu: Ngingene na? Ingulube enkulu ithi engulubeni encane: Yebo ngena.*

*Ingulube encane ingena endlini. Ingulube encane ibona ingulube enkulu phakathi endlini. Izingulube ezimbili zibona isibane etafuleni. Isibane siyakhanya. Izingulube ezimbili zibona izihlalo ezimbili ezinhle. Ingulube enkulu ihlala esihlalweni kodwa ingulube encane ayihlali esihlalweni ngoba iyesaba. Ingulube encane iyabuza engulubeni enkulu ithi: Ngihlale na? Ingulube enkulu iphendula ingulube encane ithi: Yebo hlala. Ingulube encane ikhwela esihlalweni, ihlala esihlalweni, iyajabula.*

*Izingulube ezimbili zibona ukudla etafuleni. Ingulube enkulu ibona ukhezo etafuleni, ithatha ukhezo iyadla kodwa ingulube encane ayidli ngoba iyesaba. Ingulube encane iyabuza engulubeni enkulu ithi: Ngidle na? Ingulube enkulu iyaphendula, iphendula ingulube encane ithi: Cha ungadli. Ingulube enkulu iyadla, idla ukudla ngokhezo. Ingulube encane ibuka ukudla etafuleni, ibuka ingulube enkulu, ibona ukuthi ingulube enkulu iyadla, idla ukudla ngokhezo. Ingulube encane iyabuza futhi engulubeni enkulu ithi: Ngidle na? Ingulube enkulu iyaphinda futhi ithi engulubeni encane: Cha ungadli. Ingulube encane ilambile, ifuna ukudla. Ibona ingulube enkulu iyadla. Ingulube enkulu ifuna ukudla konke ukudla. Ingulube encane iyakhala ngoba ilambile, ifuna ukudla. Iyabuza futhi ingulube encane engulubeni enkulu ithi: Ngidle na? Ingulube enkulu iphendula ingulube encane ithi: Yebo yidla. Ingulube encane iyathula, iyeka ukukhala, iyajabula. Ingulube encane ithatha ukhezo etafuleni, iyadla. Izingulube ezimbili ziyadla, zidla ngezinkezo, zidla konke ukudla etafuleni.*

*Izingulube ezimbili ziyaqeda ukudla. Zibona imibhede emibili. Ingulube enkulu ikhwela embhedeni iyalala kodwa ingulube encane ayikhweli embhedeni ngoba iyesaba. Ingulube encane ibona ingulube enkulu embhedeni, iyabuza engulubeni enkulu ithi: Ngilale na? Ingulube enkulu iphendula ingulube encane ithi: Yebo lala kodwa cima isibane leso. Ingulube encane icima isibane, ikhwela embhedeni iyalala.*

## Exercise 29
## ESITOLO

A: *Ufunani?*
B: *Ngizothenga. Ngiphe ushukela kasheleni.*
A: *Ushukela kasheleni?*
B: *Yebo ushukela kasheleni.*
A: *Nani futhi?*
B: *Ngiphe futhi amazambane kazuka nerayisi lawosheleni ababili.*
A: *Irayisi alikho, liphelile kodwa amazambane akhona.*
B: *Irayisi alikho? Sizodlani?*
A: *Nizodla impuphu. Ufunani futhi?*
B: *Lizofika nini irayisi?*
A: *Nami angazi. Mhlawumbe lingafika kusasa noma ngo-Mgqibelo. Iheleyisi awulifuni?*
B: *Likhona?*
A: *Yebo likhona futhi iheleyisi aliduli. Ufuna iheleyisi lamalini?*
B: *Bengingafuni iheleyisi kodwa ngizolithatha. Angifuni iheleyisi eliningi ngoba irayisi lizofika masinyane. Ngiphe iheleyisi losheleni ababili.*
A: *Iheleyisi losheleni ababili. Nani futhi?*
B: *Konje izolo ngithengeni?* (*konje*—by the way?)
A: *Izolo uthenge itiye nekhofi noanyanisi nobhontshisi.*
B: *Ngisalifuna futhi itiye ngoba izolo ngithenge itiye elincane. Kukhona abantu abaningi ekhaya. Bafike namuhla ekuseni. Bonke bathanda itiye kakhulu. Ufuna malini?*
A: *Uthenge ushukela kasheleni namazambane kazuka neheleyisi losheleni ababili netiye losheleni ababili. Ngifuna oshe.eni abahlanu nozuka.*
B: *Nginephepha lerandi.*
A: *Kulungile ngizokunika ushintshi. Awufuni lutho futhi?*
B: *Cha angifuni lutho. Zisonge izimpahla ngephepha elikhulu.*
A: *Kulungile ngizozisonga.*

# CHAPTER 31

## THE INTERROGATIVE

The following are some of the ways in which questions may be expressed in Zulu. Some have already been illustrated but they are referred to again here for easy reference.

1. Any statement may be changed into a question by tonal inflection only; e.g.

| | |
|---|---|
| (a) *Uyahamba* (You are going) | *Uyahamba?* (Are you going?) |
| (b) *Usaphila* (You are still well) | *Usaphila?* (Are you still well?) |
| (c) *Bayabuya* (They are returning) | *Bayabuya?* (Are they returning?) |

In addition *na?* may be added. Any question in Zulu may take *na?* e.g.

(a) *Uyasebenza na?* (Are you working?)
(b) *Abantu bayahleka na?* (Are the people laughing?)
(c) *Umama uyathenga na?* (Is mother buying?)

2. The verb forms on page 163 may be used in asking questions of a permissive nature, or when seeking advice. e.g.

(a) *Sidlale na?* (Are we to play?)
(b) *Umntwana alale na?* (Should the child sleep?)
(c) *Bapheke?* (Are they to cook?)
(d) *Sifunde na?* (Should we read?)

3. *Yini?*—This may be added to any statement which has been inflected to indicate a question, and also to ques-

tions of the type illustrated in 2 above.

(a) *Uyasenga yini na?* (Is he milking?)

(b) *Abantwana abadlali yini?* (Are the children not playing?)

(c) *Ahambe yini umfana?* (Should the boy go?)

4. *-phi?* (where?) This is suffixed to the verb. A verb taking this suffix never employs *-ya-*.

(a) *Uvelaphi?* (Where do you come from? or Where does he/she come from?)

(b) *Umnumzane uhlalaphi?* (Where does the headman stay?)

(c) *Abantwana bagezaphi?* (Where are the children washing?)

*-phi?* may also have subjectival concords prefixed; e.g.

(a) *Baphi abantwana?* (Where are the children?)

(b) *Amahashi aphi namuhla?* (Where are the horses today?)

(c) *Siphi isibhedlela?* (Where is the hospital?)

Possessive concords may also be prefixed to *-phi?* e.g.

(a) *Izinkomo zaphi lezi?* (Where do these cattle belong? lit. They are cattle of where these?)

(b) *Ubaba ufuna indoda yaphi?* (Father wants a man from where?)

(c) *Leli ihashi laphi?* (Where does this horse belong?)

5. *-phi?* (which?) with concords: These are the concords used:

| | Sg. | Pl. | | Sg. | Pl. |
|---|---|---|---|---|---|
| 1. | *mu-* | *ba-* | 5. | *yi-* | *zi-* |
| 2. | *mu-* | *mi-* | 6. | *lu-* | *zi-* |
| 3. | *li-* | *ma-* | 7. | *bu-* | |
| 4. | *si-* | *zi-* | 8. | *ku-* | |

(a) *Nifuna umuntu muphi?* (Which person do you want).

(b) *Inyoka ilume abafana baphi?* (Which boys did the snake bite).

(c) *Umlimi ubulale ihashi liphi?* (Which horse did the farmer kill).

*-phi?* (which?) forms above may be preceded by *yi-*. The part following must employ a relative concord. Verbs taking a relative concord end in *-yo* if there is no adjunct. e.g.

(a) *Yibaphi abantu abaculayo?* (Which people are singing?)

(b) *Yiliphi ihashi elibalekayo?* (Which horse is running away?)

(c) *Iyiphi inja ekhonkothayo?* (Which dog is barking?)

(d) *Yimuphi umfana okhona?* (Which boy is present?)

6. *-ni?* (what?) with concords listed in 5 above:

(a) *Ufuna umuthi muni?* (What kind of tree/medicine do you want?)

(b) *Ihashi lini leli?* (What kind of horse is this?)

(c) *Umuntu muni lo?* (What kind of person is this?)

N.B. It is quite usual to drop the initial vowel of the noun when it is followed by this interrogative form; e.g.

(a) *Ufuna muthi muni?*

(b) *Hashi lini leli?*

(c) *Muntu muni lo?*

These are the forms which are heard more often in speech.

7. *-ni?* (what?) suffixed to verbs. e.g.

(a) *Ubonani?* (What do you see? What does he/she see?)

(b) *Amantombazane adlalani?* (What are the girls playing?)

(c) *Izinja zikhonkothani?* (What are the dogs barking at?)

8. *-ni?* (what?) suffixed to verbs ending in *-ela*. The literal meaning is "to act for what?".

(a) *Ubaba usebenzelani?* (Why is father working?)

(b) *Abafana babalekelani?* (Why are the boys running away?)

(c) *Odadewethu baculelani?* (Why are our sisters singing?)

9. *ngani?* (why?) used with negative verbs:

(a) *Ubaba akasebenzi ngani?* (Why is father not working?)
(b) *Abafana ababaleki ngani?* (Why are the boys not running away?)
(c) *Odadewethu abaculi ngani?* (Why are our sisters not singing?)

10. *ngani?* (by means of what or how?).

(a) *Umlimi ulima ngani*? (What is the farmer ploughing with?)
(b) *Ugogo uzohamba ngani?* (What will grandmother go by? or How will grandmother go?)
(c) *Inyoka uyibulale ngani?* (What did you kill the snake with?)

11. *yini?* (what is it?):

(a) *Umfana ushaywa yini?* (What is hitting the boy?)
(b) *Yini exosha amahashi?* (What is chasing the horses?)
(c) *Inkukhu ibulawe yini?* (What killed the fowl?)

12. *nini?* (when?) requiring specific time:

(a) *Uqale nini ukusebenza?* (At what time did you start work?)
(b) *Ilanga lishona nini?* (When does the sun set?)
(c) *Uya nini eThekwini?* (When are you going to Durban?

13. *-njani* (what sort of?) with relative concords:

(a) *Umzala ufuna ihashi elinjani?* (What sort of horse does the cousin want?)
(b) *Ubaba ubulale inyoka enjani?* (What sort of snake did father kill?)
(c) *Kukhona imithi enjani?* (What sort of trees are there?)

14. *kanjani?* (how? in what manner?):

(a) *Ibhola lidlalwa kanjani?* (How is soccer played?)
(b) *Abantwana bacula kanjani?* (How do the children sing?)

(c) *Umfana uwele kanjani emfuleni?* (How did the boy cross the river?)

15. *-ngaki?* (how many?) with adjectival concords:

(a) *Umama ufuna abafana abangaki?* (How many boys does mother want?)

(b) *Sizothenga izinkomo ezingaki?* (How many cattle shall we buy?)

(c) *Silethe izihlalo ezingaki?* (How many chairs should we bring? or How many chairs did we bring?)

16. *kangaki?* (how often? how many times?):

(a) *Ubaba uye kangaki edolobheni?* (How many times did father go to town?)

(b) *Amahashi angene kangaki ensimini?* (How many times did the horses enter the field?)

(c) *Inkosi ifika kangaki lapha?* (How often does the king come here?)

17. *-ngakanani?* (how much? how big? how great?) with relative concords:

(a) *Nibone ingulube engakanani?* (How big a pig did you see?)

(b) *Uthanda ihashi elingakanani?* (How big a horse do you like?)

(c) *Sizohlaba imvu engakanani?* (How big a sheep shall we slaughter?)

18. *kangakanani?* (how much? how great? how big?):

(a) *Muhle kangakanani udadewabo?* (How very pretty is her sister?)

(b) *Izinyawo zakhe zinkulu kangakanani?* (How big are his feet?)

(c) *Insimu yakhe incane kangakanani?* (How small is his field?)

19. *ubani?* (who?) an interrogative noun of Class 1a:

(a) *Umntwana ufuna ubani?* (Whom does the child want?)
(b) *Umfowenu usebenzela ubani?* (For whom does your brother work?)
(c) *Amantombazane abone ubani?* (Whom did the girls see?)

As a predicative *ubani* > *ubani, ngubani*:

(a) *Ngubani igama lakho?* (What is your name?)
(b) *Ngubani obiza umfana?* (Who is calling the boy?)
(c) *Ngobani abafuna udokotela?* (Who want the doctor?)

Greetings and samples of simple conversation:—

*Sakubona* or *Sawubona*—Greetings!—one person or more greeting ONE person.

*Sanibona*—Greetings!—one person or more greeting MORE THAN ONE.

*Yebo Sakubona* or *Sawubona*—Yes, Greetings!—one person or more replying to greetings by ONE person.

*Yebo, Sanibona*—Yes, Greetings!—one person or more replying to greetings by MORE THAN ONE person.

*Sala kahle*—Remain well, i.e. Good-bye!—one person or more saying good-bye to ONE person.

*Salani kahle*—Remain well!—one person or more saying good-bye to MORE THAN ONE person.

*Hamba kahle*—Go well!—one person or more to ONE person going away.

*Hambani kahle*—Go well!—one person or more to MORE THAN ONE person going away.

*Usaphila na?*—Are you still well?

*Yebo ngisaphila*—Yes, I am still well.

*Nisaphila na?*—Are you (pl.) still well?

*Yebo sisaphila*—Yes, we are still well.

*Cha, angiphili*—No I am not well.

*Cha, asiphili*—No, we are not well.

*Cha, ngiyagula*—No, I am ill.

*Cha*, siyagula—No, we are ill.

*Yini na?*—What is it?

*Ngiphethwe ngumkhuhlane*—I have a cold/fever.

*Ngikhwelwe ngumkhuhlane*—I have a cold/fever.
*Ngikhwelwe/Ngiphethwe yisisu*—I have stomachache.
*Ngikhwelwe/Ngiphethwe yikhanda*—I have headache.
*Ngikhwelwe/Ngiphethwe yindlebe*—I have earache.
*Ngikhwelwe/Ngiphethwe ngamehlo*—I have eye trouble.
*Ngikhwelwe/Ngiphethwe yisifuba*—I have chest trouble.
*Ngikhwelwe/Ngiphethwe ngamazinyo*—I have toothache.
*Ngiyakhwehlela*—I am coughing.
*Ngiyaqhuga*—I am limping.
*Nginenyongo*—I am bilious.
*Nginesilungulela*—I have heartburn or indigestion.
*Ngiyopha*—I am bleeding.
*Ngiyahlanza*—I am vomiting.

*Sawubona Mngane!*—Greetings Friend!
-*Yebo Sawubona*—Yes, Greetings!
-*Usaphila na?*—Are you still in health?
-*Yebo ngisaphila; wena usaphila na?*—Yes, I am still well; and you, are you still well?
-*Nami ngisaphila. Uvelaphi?*—I, too, I am still well. Where do you come from?
-*Ngivela eBenoni*—I come from Benoni.
-*Ufunani lapha?*—What do you want here?
-*Ngifuna umfundisi*—I want the parson.
-*Ufunani kumfundisi?*—What do you want from the parson?
-*Ngizocela umsebenzi*—I have come to ask for work.
-*Ufuna ukusebenzani?*—What work do you want to do?
-*Ngifuna umsebenzi wengadi*—I want to do gardening.
-*Ngifuna ukusebenza ekhishini*—I want to work in the kitchen.
-*Ngena, umfundisi usendlini*—Come in; the parson is in the house.

-*Ngena!*—Come in.

-*Hlala phansi*—Sit down.
-*Hlala lapha*—Sit here.
-*Sondela!*—Come nearer.
- *Yiza lapha!*—Come here.
-*Woza lapha!*—Come here.
-*Sukuma!*—Stand up.
-*Ngiyabonga*—I thank you.
-*Qhela!*—Stand back/Move away.
-*Sikhathi sini?*—What time is it?
-*Isikhathi manje ngu*-10—The time now is 10 o'clock.
-*Igama lakho ngubani?*—What is your name?
-*Igama lami nguJames*—My name is James.
-*Isibongo sakho ngubani?*—What is your surname?
-*Isibongo sami nguHarris*—My surname is Harris.
-*Igama lakhe ngubani?*—What is his/her name?
-*Isibongo sakhe ngubani?*—What is his/her surname?
-*Ikhaya lakho likuphi?*—Where is your home?
-*Ikhaya lami liseGermiston*—My home is at Germiston.
-*Uhlalaphi?*—Where do you stay/live?
-*Ngihlala eMelrose*—I live at Melrose.
-*Uhlala nobani?*—With whom do you stay?
-*Ngihlala nabazali bami*—I live with my parents.
-*Ngihlala nomkami nabantabami*—I live with my wife and my children.
-*Ngihlala nendoda yami*—I live with my husband.
-*Usebenzaphi?*—Where do you work?
-*Ngisebenza eJeppe*—I work at Jeppe.
-*Ngisebenza kwaMarkham*—I work at Markham's.
-*Ngisebenza kwaWoolfson*—I work at Woolfson's.
-*Uqala nini ukusebenza?*—When do you start work?
-*Ntambama uqeda nini?*—When do you finish in the afternoon?
-*Ngiqala ngo*-7 *ekuseni; ntambama ngiqeda ngo*- 4.30—

I start at 7 in the morning; in the afternoon I finish at 4.30.

-*Ntambama uphuma nini?*—When do you come out in the afternoon?

-*Uhola malini ngesonto?*—How much do you earn per week?

-*Uhola malini ngenyanga?*—How much money do you earn per month?

-*Uyasebenza ngoMgqibelo na?*—Do you work on Saturday?

## UJAMES NOFRED

J: *Sawubona Fred.*

F: *Yebo sawubona James. Usaphila na?*

J: *Ngisaphila. Wena usaphila?*

F: *Cha, mina angiphili kahle.*

J: *Awuphili kahle? Yini?*

F: *Ngihlushwa yisisu. Izolo bengiye kudokotela.*

J: *Utheni udokotela?*

F: *Unginike umuthi futhi wangijova (jova*—inject). *Ufunani wena lapha edolobheni?*

J: *Ngifuna ukuya eposini nasebhange.*

F: *Konje wena ubeka imali yakho ebhange?*

J: *Yebo mina ngilondoloza imali yami ebhange. Wena uyilondolozaphi imali yakho?*

F: *Mina ngilondoloza imali yami eposini. Ngithanda ukulondoloza imali yami eposini ngoba amaposi akhona emadolobheni amancane. Amabhange asemadolobheni amakhulu kuphela.*

J: *Cha Fred, amabhange akhona emadolobheni onke. Akhona emadolobheni amakhulu nasemadolobheni amancane.*

F: *Unemali eningi ebhange na?*

J: *Cha, nginamarandi ayishumi kuphela. Wena unemali eningi na eposini?*

F: *Cha, nami nginemali encane. Nginamarandi angu-8 namasenti angu-75.*

J: *Thina esikoleni sifundiswa ukugcina* (*gcina*—keep) *imali. Izingane zonke esikoleni sethu zigcina imali ebhange. Abafowethu abancane uDick noPerry bagcina imali yabo ebhange, nodadewethu omncane uPeggy ugcina imali yakhe ebhange. Niyafundiswa esikoleni senu ukugcina imali na?*

F: *Yebo nathi siyafundiswa esikoleni sethu ukugcina imali. Thina esikoleni sethu sigcina imali yethu eposini. Njalo ngoLwesihlanu ubaba ungipha osheleni ababili. Imali yami ngiyifaka eposini. Nginencwadi yami yaseposini.*

J: *Abazali bami bayajabula kakhulu ngoba esikoleni sifundiswa ukugcina imali. Sala kahle Fred.*

F: *Yebo hamba kahle James. Ngizokuvakashela kusasa ntambama.*

## ESITESHINI

A: *Sawubona mngane wami.*

B: *Yebo sawubona mngane wami.*

A: *Ufunani lapha esiteshini? Awusebenzi namuhla na?*

B: *Ngiyasebenza. Lapha esiteshini ngizothenga ithikithi.*

A: *Uzothenga ithikithi uyahamba na?*

B: *Yebo ngiyahamba.*

A: *Uyahamba? Uhamba uyaphi?*

B: *Ngiyavakasha; ngivakashela udadewethu eThekwini. Ngizodla uKhisimusi eThekwini.* (*ukudla uKhisimusi*—to spend Xmas)

A: *Kukhona udadewenu eThekwini?*

B: *Yebo ukhona. Udadewethu uPearl uhlala eThekwini, eBerea. Uhlala nendoda yakhe nabantwana bakhe eThekwini.*

A: *Konje uPearl unabantwana abangaki?*

B: *Unabantwana abathathu; abafana ababili nentombazana.*

A: *UPearl uyajabula ngoba unabantwana abaningi. Uzohamba namuhla?*

B: *Cha, angihambi namuhla.*

A: *Uhamba nini?*

B: *Ngifuna ukuhamba ngoLwesihlanu ekuseni ngesitimela sika-9. Ngifuna ukuhamba emini ngoba ngithanda ukubuka ilizwe. Ngithanda ukubuka izintaba namathafa amahle aluhlaza.* (*ithafa*, plain—3) *Ngithanda ukubuka nezilwane—izimvu nezinkomo nezinye izilwane.*

A: *Ubhukile na?* (*bhuka*—reserve accommodation)

B: *Yebo ngibhukile; ngibhuke ngesonto eledlule.*

A: *Imali yesitimela malini?*

B: *Angazi kodwa ngicabanga ukuthi ngamarandi ayisikhombisa namasenti angu-*75 *ngoba ngifuna ithikithi lokuya nokubuya. Ngifuna ukuhamba ngosekeni.* (*usekeni*, 2nd class—la)

A: *Uzophatha nezingubo zakho zokulala na?*

B: *Cha izingubo zokulala zikhona esitimeleni nokudla futhi kukhona. Ngizohamba nezingubo zokugqoka nemali kuphela.*

A: *Kodwa uyathanda wena ukuhamba ngesitimela? Mina angithandi ukuhamba ngesitimela. Ngithanda ukuhamba ngemoto ngoba imoto ihamba masinyane.*

B: *Nami ngiyathanda ukuhamba ngemoto kodwa ngithanda kakhulu ukuhamba ngesitimela; Isitimela sihamba kancane; ngibona kahle izindawo eziningi nezinto ezininingi.*

A: *Isitimela sakho sifika nini eThekwini?*

B: *Sisuka lapha ngoLwesihlanu ekuseni ngo-9; sifika eThekwini ngoMgqibelo ekuseni ngo-*10.

A: *Uyazi eThekwini?*

B: *Cha angazi kodwa indoda kaPearl izongihlangabeza esiteshini. Ngithole incwadi yakhe namuhla. Uthi uzongilanda ngemoto. Uzokuza esiteshini noPearl nabantwana bakhe bonke.*

A: *Bazojabula kakhulu oPearl nabantwana.*

B: *Yebo bazojabula. Ngifuna ukuthengela abantwana amaswidi amaningi amnandi. Bonke abantwana bawathanda kakhulu amaswidi.*

A: *Ungikhonzele* (give my regards) *kakhulu kuPearl nasendodeni yakhe.*

B: *Kulungile ngizokukhonzela.*

A: *Sala kahle mngane wami.*

B: *Yebo hamba kahle.*

## Some Useful Expressions

*Ilanga libalele*—The day is clear; the weather is fine.
*Ilanga liyashisa*—The sun is hot.
*Ilanga lipholile*—The day is cool.
*Izulu liguqubele*—The weather is cloudy.
*Izulu liyaduma*—It is thundering.
*Izulu liyabaneka*—It is lightning.
*Izulu liyakhiza*—It is drizzling.
*Izulu liyana/imvula iyana*—It is raining.
*Izulu liyakhithika*—It is snowing.
*Kulele isithwathwa/kunesithwathwa*—There is frost.
*Kuneqhwa*—There is snow.
*Kulele amazolo/kunamazolo*—There is dew.
*Kunenkungu*—There is mist.
*Kuvunguza umoya*—The wind is blowing.
*Kunomoya*—There is wind; it is windy.
*Kunothuli*—There is dust.
*Kunonyezi*—There is moonlight.

# KEY TO EXERCISES

## Exercise 1

(d) 1. *Siza abazali.* 2. *Lethani amatshe.* 3. *Landa amanzi.* 4. *Bulalani inyoka.* 5. *Geza izingubo.* 6. *Khombisani umntwana.* 7. *Gibela ihashi.* 8. *Shanelani indlu.* 9. *Bopha inja.* 10. *Yizwani abazali.* 11. *Yenza itiye.* 12. *Yakhani indlu.* 13. *Yosa inyama.* 14. *Yiphani umntwana.* 15. *Culani iculo.*

(e) 1. *Mary letha amalahle.* 2. *James landa ihashi.* 3. *Jane basa umlilo.* 4. *John bulalani inyoka.* 5. *Annie sebenza.* 6. *Fred cula.* 7. *Jerry gijima.* 8. *Ethel bambani inja.* 9. *Norah gezani izingubo.* 10. *Mary biza umntwana.* 11. *Frank yima.* 12. *Jane yizani.* 13. *Annie phekani ukudla.* 14. *Annie pheka inyama.* 15. *Jerry thatha isibane.* 16. *Norah cula iculo.* 17. *Ethel phumulani.* 18. *Frank hambani.* 19. *Mary shanelani.* 20. *Annie balani izimvu.* 21. *Gertrude thungani izingubo.* 22. *James thatha amatshe.* 23. *James khuluma.*

## Exercise 2

1. Translate into Zulu:

| | | |
|---|---|---|
| *Umuntu/ Abantu* | | *umntwana/ abantwana* |
| *Umfazi/ Abafazi* | *uthanda/ bathanda* | *umngane/ abangane* |
| *Umfundisi/ Abafundisi* | *ushaya/ bashaya* | *umzala/ abazala* |
| *Umlimi/ Abalimi* | *ufuna/ bafuna* | *umhedeni/ abahedeni* |

| | | |
|---|---|---|
| *Umzali/ Abazali* | *ubiza/ babiza* | *umdlali/ abadlali* |
| *Umnumzane/ Abanumzane* | *usiza/ basiza* | *umfana/ abafana* |
| *Umakhi/ Abakhi* | *ukhombisa/ bakhombisa* | *umfowenu/ abafowenu* |
| *Umfowethu/ Abafowethu* | *upha/ bapha* | *umfowethu/ abafowethu* |
| *Umlungu/ Abelungu* | | *umfowabo/ abafowabo* |

2. (f) (a) *Abantwana babona umlungu. Abelungu bagibela ihashi. Abelungu bathanda ihashi. Abelungu bagibela ihashi. Balanda izimvu. Abelungu bapha izimvu amanzi.*

(b) *Abafazi babasa umlilo. Abafazi bafuna ukupheka. Abafazi bafuna ukupheka ukudla futhi bafuna ukupheka inyama. Abantwana balanda amalahle.*

(c) *Abafundisi babiza abantwana. Abantwana babona umlimi. Abantwana balandela umlimi. Abalimi babulala inyoka.*

(d) *Abazala bakha amanzi. Abazala bafuna ukugeza izingubo futhi abazala bafuna ukugeza izitsha.*

(e) *Abafowethu basiza umakhi. Abakhi bafuna amatshe. Abakhi balanda amatshe. Abakhi bafuna ukwakha indlu. Abakhi bakhetha amatshe. Abakhi bafuna futhi amanzi. Abakhi balanda amanzi. Abakhi bathatha inqola, balanda amatshe futhi balanda amanzi. Abakhi bakhombisa umfowabo amatshe. Abakhi bathanda ukusebenza.*

4. (a) *Mngane, letha incwadi.* (b) *Mholi, khetha abantu.* (c) *Mfowethu phumula.* (d) *Mfazi, sheshisa.* (e) *Mshumayeli, cula iculo.* (f) *Mzala pheka inyama.* (g) *Belungu, bulalani inyoka.* (h) *Mfana, khanyisa isibane.* (i) *Bazali, khumbulani abantwana.* (j) *Bahedeni, landelani umfundisi.* (k) *Bafowethu bambani ihashi.* (l) *Msizi, hamba.* (m) *Mngane thatha ukudla.*

(n) *Bafowethu cabangani.* (o) *Mzala, phinda.* (p) *Bantwana hlekani.* (q) *Bantwana yidlani ukudla.* (r) *Bantu yizani.* (s) *Bafana yimani.* (t) *Bafazi phindani iculo.* (u) *Bafundisi fundani incwadi.*

5. (a) *Bangane lethani incwadi.* (b) *Baholi khethani abantu.* (c) *Bafowethu phumulani.* (d) *Bafazi sheshisani.* (e) *Bashumayeli culani iculo.* (f) *Bazala phekani inyama.* (g) *Mlungu bulala inyoka.* (h) *Bafana khanyisani isibane.* (i) *Mzali khumbula abantwana.* (j) *Mhedeni landela umfundisi.* (k) *Mfowethu bamba ihashi* (l) *Basizi hambani.* (m) *Bangane thathani ukudla.* (n) *Mfowethu cabanga.* (o) *Bazala phindani.* (p) *Mntwana hleka.* (q) *Mntwana yidla ukudla.* (r) *Muntu yiza.* (s) *Mfana yima.* (t) *Mfazi phinda iculo.* (u) *Mfundisi funda incwadi.*

### Exercise 3

C. (a) Jane, stir porridge. (b) Scoop sugar. (c) Flavour meat. (d) Sift flour. (e) My sister is throwing out the water. (f) Salt is bitter. (g) The child drinks milk. (h) Cousin, pour out tea. (i) Switch on electric lights. (j) The farmer wants paraffin. (k) My brother likes jam, also he likes cheese. (l) The builder is collecting stones. (m) I like cocoa. (n) The nurse wants the doctor. (o) John, go out; fetch coal. I want to make fire. (p) My sister, look after the children.

D. (a) *Umalume ubhema usikilidi.* (b) *Abantwana baphuza ubisi.* (c) *Umfazi uthenga ubhontshisi nokhokho.* (d) *Chitha amanzi.* (e) *Umfana ulandela umakhelwane.* (f) *Umlungu ugibela ihashi.* (g) *Abantwana bayahleka.* (h) *Udadewethu ushanela indlu.* (i) *Sheshisa; ngifuna itiye.* (j) *Abalimi bayaphumula.* (k) *Umfundisi uzwa iculo.* (l) *Umhloli ufunda incwadi.* (m) *Umfazi unonga inyama.* (n) *Abafana bayalwa.* (o) *Udadewethu upha umntwana ukudla.*

E. (a) *Mngane musa ukuletha incwadi.* (b) *Mholi musa*

*ukukhetha abantu.* (c) *Mfowethu musa ukuphumula.* (d) *Mfazi musa ukusheshisa.* (e) *Mshumayeli musa ukucula iculo.* (f) *Mzala musa ukupheka inyama.* (g) *Belungu musani ukubulala inyoka.* (h) *Mfana musa ukukhanyisa isibane.* (i) *Bazali musani ukukhumbula abantwana.* (j) *Bahedeni musani ukulandela umfundisi.* (k) *Bafowethu musani ukubamba ihashi.* (l) *Msizi musa ukuhamba.* (m) *Mngane musa ukuthatha ukudla.* (n) *Bafowethu musani ukucabanga.* (o) *Mzala musa ukuphinda.* (p) *Bantwana musani ukuhleka.* (q)*Bantwana musani ukudla ukudla.* (r) *Bantu musani ukuza.* (s) *Bafana musani ukuma.* (t) *Bafazi musani ukuphinda iculo.* (u) *Bafundisi musani ukufunda incwadi.*

F. (a) *ba-* (b) *u-* (c) *ba-* (d) *ba-* (e) *u-* (f) *u-* (g) *u-* (h) *ba-* (i) *ba-* (j) *ba-* (k) *u-* (l) *ba-* (m) *u-* (n) *u-* (o) *u-*.

(a) The leaders want to see the farmers. (b) The inspector is calling the boys. (c) The ministers are showing the heathen. (d) The parents want to fetch sugar. (e) The carpenter is counting the keys. (f) His grandfather likes cheese. (His, her, their) (g) Grandmother is resting. (h) The farmers are pulling stones (i.e. dragging). (i) The whitemen want to fetch the windows. (j) My/our sisters are singing. (k) The doctor is washing. (l) The nurses are helping the doctors. (m) The neighbour wants to buy coal. (n) Grandfather is laughing. (o) My wife is cooking porridge.

### EXERCISE 4

2. (a) Mother scoops sugar and salt; she wants to give grandmother. (b) My sister flavours food; she puts in tomatoes, onions, pepper and salt. (c) What do you drink? We drink tea but children drink milk. (d) The children are running; they are playing. (e) The Inspector is smoking. What does he smoke? He smokes cigarettes. (f) What does the builder collect? The builder collects stones; he carries

stones and water. (g) James, bring the lamp and matches. (h) I want to fetch mail and a parcel. (i) The cousin is throwing out the water; she is washing dishes (j) Serve tea my sister. (k) Whom are the boys hitting? The boys are hitting the helper. (l) What work are the preachers doing? The preachers are preaching. (m) What are you fetching? I am fetching coal.

3. (a) *Ubaba ufuna umfowenu nodadewenu.* (b) *Thenga ugwayi nomentshisi.* (c) *Abelungu bathanda uletisi noshizi; abantwana bathanda ujamu.* (d) *Umshumayeli uyacula nabantu bayacula.* (e) *Umakhelwane usebenza nabalimi.* (f) *Umlimi uthengani? Umlimi uthenga izimvu nehashi.* (g) *Umfazi ubasa umlilo kodwa udadewethu ugeza izingubo.* (h) *Ubaba ufunda izincwadi namaphepha kodwa umama uthunga izingubo.* (i) *Abazali banakekela abantwana.* (j) *Sithanda ukuphuza itiye nobisi kodwa udadewethu uthanda ukuphuza ukhokho.* (k) *Udokotela ubiza ubani? Udokotela ubiza unesi.* (l) *Umfana ulandani? Umfana ulanda usikilidi nomentshisi.* (m) *Umakhi ufunani? Umakhi ufuna upende nophalafini.* (n) *UJames ukhuluma nobani? UJames ukhuluma noNorah.*

## Exercise 5

1. (a) *Umakhi uyakha.* (b) *Umdlali uyadlala.* (c) *Umkhandi uyakhanda.* (d) *Umsizi uyasiza.* (e) *Umfundisi uyafundisa.* (f) *Umbazi uyabaza.* (g) *Umpheki uyapheka.* (h) *Umhloli uyahlola.* (i) *Umfundi uyafunda.* (j) *Umholi uyahola.*

3. (a) *UJohn ulanda izinkomo.* (b) *Umama ufuna ubisi.* (c) *Umntwana ukhala ngoba ufuna ubisi.* (d) *Yebo umntwana uthanda ubisi.* (e) *Umntwana uphuza ubisi namanzi.*

4. (a) *Sibona umuzi.* (b) *Abantu babona umlilo nentuthu.* (c) *Abantu bayagijima.* (d) *Abantu bakha amanzi.* (e) *Abantu bafuna ukucima umlilo.*

3. (a) *Umfowethu akalandi iposi.* (b) *Umfazi akagezi izingubo.* (c) *ULizzie akalethi amalahle.* (d) *Abadlali abalandeli umnumzane.* (e) *Odadewethu abashaneli.* (f) *Abakhi abafuni usikilidi.* (g) *Angithengi izimvu.* (h) *Asiboni abakhi.* (i) *Umkhumbi awusizi abantu; awuthwali abantu.* (j) *Imithi ayifuni umlilo.* (k) *Ubaba akagibeli ihashi.* (l) *Abashumayeli abagijimi.* (m) *Udadewenu akathandi umdanso.* (n) *Umnumzane akabizi umhlangano.* (o) *Umakhelwane akathathi umthwalo.* (p) *Umlimi akatshali namuhla.* (q) *Umalume akaloli umese.* (r) *Abafana abavuli iminyango.* (s) *Umama akalungisi ukudla.* (t) *Udokotela akakhulumi nobaba.*

4. (a) *Abafowethu abalandi iposi.* (b) *Abafazi abagezi izingubo.* (c) *OLizzie abalethi amalahle.* (d) *Umdlali akalandeli umnumzane.* (e) *Udadewethu akashaneli.* (f) *Umakhi akafuni usikilidi.* (g) *Asithengi izimvu.* (h) *Angiboni abakhi.* (i) *Imikhumbi ayisizi abantu; ayithwali abantu.* (j) *Umuthi awufuni umlilo.* (k) *Obaba abagibeli ihashi.* (l) *Umshumayeli akagijimi.* (m) *Odadewenu abathandi umdanso.* (n) *Abanumzane ababizi umhlangano.* (o) *Omakhelwane abathathi umthwalo.* (p) *Abalimi abatshali namuhla.* (q) *Omalume abaloli umese.* (r) *Umfana akavuli iminyango.* (s) *Omama abalungisi ukudla.* (t) *Odokotela abakhulumi nobaba.*

5. (a) *Ngithanda ukufunda amaphepha.* (b) *Ngithanda ukufunda kusihlwa.* (c) *Emini ngiyasebenza.* (d) *Umfowethu uthanda ukufunda izincwadi.* (e) *Umfowethu uthanda ukufunda emini.* (f) *Udadewethu akafuni ukufunda amaphepha nezincwadi.* (g) *Udadewethu uthanda ukusebenza.* (h) *Udadewethu ushanela ekuseni.* (i) *Umama uthanda ukusebenza.* (j) *Ekuseni umama ubasa umlilo futhi upheka ukudla.* (k) *Umama uthunga izingubo emini.* (l) *Umama uphumula ntambama. Umama upha abantwana iphalishi nobisi.* (n) *Ubaba uthanda ukubhema nokufunda amaphepha nezincwadi.* (o) *Ubaba*

*uthanda ukugeza imoto.* (p) *Ubaba ushayela imoto.* (q) *Umama akathandi ukushayela.*

6. (a) *Umama akafuni amalahle ngoba umlilo uyavutha.* (b) *Ugogo uvula iminyango ekuseni ngoba uthanda umoya. Udadewethu uvala iminyango kusihlwa.* (c) *Abantu bayagijima ngoba umuzi uyasha.* (d) *Asifuni ukudlala ibhola namuhla ngoba umoya uyavunguza.* (e) *Umfowethu ujikijela amatshe, ushaya izinkomo.* (f) *Ngifuna ukuhluthulela ngoba siyahamba.* (g) *Abafana bamba umgodi; abasiki imithi.* (h) *Umama akathandi ukushayela imoto ngoba umgwaqo uyagwinciza.* (i) *Umakhelwane uyalima; ufuna ukutshala ummbila nobhontshisi. Akafuni ukutshala ubhatata.* (j) *Jane, lungisa itiye; uyihlo ufuna itiye.* (k) *Umalume ulola ummese ngoba ufuna ukusika inyama.* (l) *Umntwana uyadlala; uvala iminyango.* (m) *Abafowethu bathanda umdanso kakhulu kodwa udadewethu akathandi ukudansa.* (n) *Abelungu bathanda umqwayiba.* (o) *Umshumayeli akatshali; ufunda incwadi.* (p) *Ubaba akabizi udokotela; ubiza ubani?* (q) *Imithi ayiboli; iyakhula.* (r) *Uyakhumbula na? Cha, angikhumbuli.* (s) *Abantwana abahleki; bayakhala.*

## Exercise 7

2. (a) In the morning my sisters make a fire, also they cook but father washes the car. During the day my sisters wash windows. (b) The boy fetches the paper and milk in the morning because in the afternoon he fetches cattle and horses. (c) My brother does not like to read papers and books at night; he likes to read in the daytime. (d) At noon the sun is very hot but in the afternoon it is not very hot; it is a little hot. (e) The headmen and the boys sharpen spears; they want to kill the lion. (f) Mother is preparing food; she wants to give it to the children because the children want to sleep; my sister does not help mother

because she is lazy. (g) Father is beating Sipho and Themba because they are fighting. (h) Uncle wants to extract a tooth because it is loose. (i) Father is filling a pipe because he wants to smoke. (j) Jane, bring tea, milk and sugar. (k) The boys chase the thieves because the thieves steal ducks. (l) Maggie, set the table; father wants to eat now. (m) Mother beats the cat because the cat scratches the child. (n) The water is cold. (o) The whiteman wraps butter. (p) Whom is the doctor calling? The doctor is calling the nurse. (q) My sister is cutting onions and what else? My sister is cutting onions and tomatoes.

3. (a) *Umfowethu ufuna ukuwela umfula kodwa ubaba akafuni.* (b) *Abafana bakhahlela ibhola kodwa uJohn akadlali.* (c) *USipho akafuni ukusebenza ngoba uyavilapha.* (d) *Ubaba nomama bayakhuluma kodwa umalume uyasebenza.* (e) *Abantwana bacula amaculo.* (f) *Umhloli ubiza abafana ngoba ufuna ukukhuluma nabafana.* (g) *Ekuseni siyasebenza kodwa emini asisebenzi; siyaphumula.* (h) *Abafowabo batshala imithi kodwa umalume utshala ummbila.* (i) *Khetha iculo; sifuna ukucula; asifuni ukufunda.* (j) *Amasela ayabaleka; abona inja.* (k) *Namuhla angifuni ukugqoka ijazi* (or *ukufaka ijazi*) *ngoba ilanga liyashisa.* (l) *Jane, geza amabhodwe; umama ufuna ukupheka.* (m) *Amanzi ayageleza.* (n) *Vula amafasitele neminyango; sifuna umoya.* (o) *Ubaba uthanda ukufunda nokubhema. Akathandi ukucula.*

### Exercise 8

2. (a) What is the farmer selling? The farmer is selling horses and sheep but he is not selling hides. What is your sister selling? My sister is selling dresses. (b) Sipho, bring a hammer. Why do you want a hammer? I want to hammer the nails. (c) A hen lays eggs but a cock does not lay. (d) John, bring in the chair; father wants to sit. (e) Why are the

boys not ploughing today? The boys are not ploughing because they are chopping trees in the forest. (f) The Christians are singing, also they are praying but heathen do not sing hymns also they do not pray. (g) Why is the parson beating the children? The parson beats the children because the children deceive the parents. (h) The doctor gives mother medicine because mother is ill; she is coughing. (i) What does the builder buy? The builder buys bricks and iron because he wants to build a house; the builder loads (carries) bricks and iron by wagon. (j) The farmer kills the animals with a gun; a gun shoots animals. (k) I want a key; I want to lock the house in the afternoon because we are going away. (l) Grandfather wakes up very early in the morning. (m) Uncle speaks English and Afrikaans and Xhosa but father speaks English only. (n) The child is crying. Why is the child crying? The child is crying because he wants his mother; his mother is working; she sells bread and cakes. (o) The stranger is asking for water; he wants to drink. (p) Why is your brother not working today? My brother is not working because he is ill. My brother removes the coat, shirt, trousers, shoes and socks because he wants to sleep. (q) The builder fetches the wagon; he wants to load sand, bricks, stones and water. (r) My brother likes to work because he gets pay; he does not work on Saturday and on Sunday. (s) A mute cannot speak. (t) The Indian sells hides and fruit. (u) The boys are running away; they are hiding. Why are they running away? They are running away because they are afraid. They are afraid of the headman. (v) My sister is not making tea because the water is not boiling; it is cold. (w) The farmer is buying a plough and bags.

3. (a) *Abafana babalekelani?* (b) *UNorah uphekelani?* (c) *UJames ulandelani iposi?* (d) *Umnumzane ubizelani aba-*

*fana?* (e) *Umbazi uphumulelani?* (f) *Umfazi ulethelani amalahle?* (g) *Umhloli usebenzelani?* (h) *Umshumayeli ushumayelelani?* (i) *Umlimi ulimelani?*

4. (a) *Abafana ababaleki ngani?* (b) *UNorah akapheki ngani?* (c) *UJames akalandi ngani iposi?* (d) *Umnumzane akabizi ngani abafana?* (e) *Umbazi akaphumuli ngani?* (f) *Umfazi akalethi ngani amalahle?* (g) *Umhloli akasebenzi ngani?* (h) *Umshumayeli akashumayeli ngani?* (i) *Umlimi akalimi ngani?*

### Exercise 9

2. (a) Next year I shall be in Std. 6. (b) The boys will play football next week. (c) Mother will return at sunset. (d) We shall not go today; we shall go tomorrow evening. (e) The workers get paid always at the end of the month but they want to get paid at the end of the week. (f) Father will thrash the children. Why will father thrash the children? Father will thrash the children because the children hit windows with stones. (g) The carpenter will make chairs and tables but he will not make doors. (h) Why is uncle not going away now? Uncle is not going away now because the train will arrive at sunset. (i) My sister will not wash windows today; she will wash clothes only. (j) Next year we shall learn Afrikaans; this year we are learning English and Zulu. (k) I shall wear a jersey but I shall not wear an overcoat. An overcoat is heavy. (l) We shall not buy candles because we light electricity (i.e. have electricity.) (m) My sister will marry next week. (n) The Inspector will call a meeting. (o) The boy is happy because he is going to get a reward. (p) My brother anoints the sore with fat (i.e. with an ointment). (q) Cousin will buy pictures; he will not buy buckets. (r) Like whom does your sister work? My sister works like mother. (s) The box is heavy. It is as heavy as stone. (t) Why is the child crying? The child is crying because he wants food.

2 (a) What are the goats eating? The goats are eating trees but the horses are drinking water. (b) The dog is barking. What is it barking at? It sees cattle and donkeys. The dog will chase cattle and donkeys. The cattle and donkeys fear the dog. (c) On Saturday we shall fish because we like fish; we shall not fetch manure. We shall fish with uncle because uncle does not work on Saturday. Uncle, like father, likes to fish. (d) What is the whiteman grinding? The whiteman is grinding mealies. What is the whiteman grinding with? The whiteman is grinding with a machine. Why is he grinding? He is grinding because he wants mealie meal. (e) The sun is hot today; the fat is melting. (f) The whiteman pays the servants at the end of the month; the servants do not get paid at the end of the week. What do the servants earn? They earn money. (g) My sister is kindling a fire. She is making a fire for mother. We see the smoke coming out. Why is grandmother not making a fire? Grandmother is not making a fire because she is ill. (h) The dogs are barking; the sheep are grazing, the cattle are drinking, the birds are flying. (i) Tomorrow afternoon Father will slaughter a beast and a sheep. Father sells meat. He is not going to slaughter for a chief. (j) The hens are sitting; they will hatch next week. (k) Why does the farmer not shear the sheep? The farmer will shear the sheep next month. The farmer sells wool. My brother will help the farmer but my brother is not paid. (l) The child is happy because he sees the mother. The mother will give the child sweets and cakes. (m) What will Mother wash in the morning? Mother will wash clothes in the morning but my sister will iron. My sister irons like Mother. (n) Why does Father plead with the farmer? Father is pleading with the farmer because he wants to buy a horse but the farmer is not selling

(o) Grandmother takes out the children because the children make the house dirty. (p) It is raining; the children will get wet. (q) Uncle is buying sweets for the children. Why is Uncle not buying bread? Uncle is not buying bread because the children do not want bread. They want sweets.

## Exercise 11

2. (a) The builder is looking at the wall; the wall is cracking. The builder will repair the wall because the house will collapse. (b) The children are playing; they are mixing mud. The children will soil their clothes with mud. (c) Uncle will finish ploughing the lands tomorrow. (d) The workers start work at 7 in the morning. (e) What work does the boy do? The boy is chopping wood to-day; to-morrow he will fetch coal with a wagon. (f) Sipho, move away the overcoat, Father wants to sit down. (g) My brother opens the door because he hears someone knocking. (h) Uncle will be angry because the child tears the papers and books. (i) Cousin will not play tennis tomorrow because he is lame. (j) Grandfather is ill but he will recover because he drinks medicine. (k) The girl is dusting the tables and chairs and walls; she is removing the dust. (l) Themba is crying because he sees blood; he is bleeding. (m) Don't pull very hard, the string will break. (n) Move away; I want to sit. (o) Mother throws away the meat because it has a bad smell Meat rots quickly because the sun is hot. (p) In the afternoon I shall cut my hair, also I want to wash my body. (q) People like bees because bees make honey. (r) I shall send a telegram tomorrow morning. (s) The farmer wants to keep/rear cats because mice destroy mealies and kaffir-corn. (t) Whom does the boy speak like? The boy speaks like his father. (u) Why is your sister going? My sister is going because she is lazy.

She does not want to work. She does not want to wash clothes. She does not want to fetch water. (v) Why is his father not returning today? His father is not returning today because he works on Saturday. He will return tomorrow.

3. (a) *bafuna* (b) *aphuza, zidla* (c) *akasebenzi, uyaqhuga, uzosebenza* (d) *ufuna, izobola* (e) *sizotshala* (f) *sithenga, asithengi* (g) *ziyandiza, zifuna* (h) *luyabila* (i) *azolanda, akafuni, ufuna* (j) *iyakhula, ithanda* (k) *iyakhonkotha, ibona* (l) *uxova, uzobhaka* (m) *bathanda.*

4. (a) Father will buy cattle and horses for R400. Cattle are expensive and horses are expensive. (b) How much does a shirt cost? A shirt costs R4.05. (c) Father will buy books for R10.60. (d) Coal costs 45c per bag. Wood costs 25c per bag. Coal is expensive. (e) I shall buy uncle a hat for R4.57. (f) Mother will buy sugar for R1.15. (g) Cars are expensive. The headman is buying a car for R2,800. (h) The child will buy cakes for 7c. He does not want to buy bread.

5. (a) *Umama uthenga ingubo ngamarandi amathathu namasenti angu-*65. (b) *Angizuthenga izicathulo ngamarandi ayisithupha namasenti angu-*75. *Ngizothenga izicathulo ngamarandi amane namasenti-angu-*50. (c) *Isinkwa sibiza malini? Sibiza amasenti angu-*9. (d) *Amalahle ayadula kodwa izinkuni zishibhile. Ngizothenga amalahle ngamasenti angu-*45. (e) *Isigqoko sibiza amarandi ayisithupha namasenti angu-*75. *Ibhulukwe libiza amarandi angu-*12. *Amasokisi abiza amasenti angu-*95. (f) *Umfundisi uzothenga izincwadi ngamarandi angu-*13 *namasenti angu-*65. (g) *Umama ufuna ijazi. Ufuna ukuthenga ijazi ngamarandi angu-*30 *namasenti angu-*87. (h) *Ngizothenga izitembu ngamasenti ayishumi kusasa.*

## Exercise 13

1. (a) The farmer has horses and cattle and sheep and fowls and ploughs, also the farmer has a wagon. (b) A human being has a head and eyes and hands and feet but a human being has no feathers. (c) The Inspector will not arrive tomorrow because he has a cold; he is coughing very much. (d) The builder will not fetch bricks and iron with a wagon because he has a lorry; moreover he has no oxen. (e) Jane is not making tea because she has no sugar; she will buy sugar tomorrow for one rand. (f) The trees are dying because they have no water; the sun is hot; rain does not fall. The people are praying; they ask for rain. (g) The son builds a house because his father has no house; his father has no money because he does not work. (h) An overcoat costs twenty five rand; cousin will buy an overcoat because he has money. (i) A cow has horns and a goat has horns but horses have no horns. (j) The children have shoes and socks/stockings but they have no hats. (k) Sipho is not attending school because he has no books; he will go to school next year. (l) Mother will not make a fire today because she has no coal; the coal will come tomorrow morning by wagon. (m) The king has sons but he has no daughters. The king is not happy because he has no daughters. (n) The farmer will not plant tomorrow because he has no seed. (o) The hen has eggs but the cock has no eggs. (p) Father has a gun; he shoots animals and birds with the gun. (q) The fowls are increasing because they are laying.

2. (a) *Musa ukushaya inja ngoba izobaleka.* (b) *Umuntu uhlafuna ngamazinyo.* (c) *Abantwana bakhalelani? Abantwana bayakhala ngoba bafuna amaswidi namakhekhe.* (d) *Umfana uthini? Uthi ufuna ibhulukwe neyembe. Ubaba uzothengela umfana ibhulukwe neyembe.* (e) *Umalume akazufika kusasa; uzofika ngomhlomunye. Umalume akazufika ngani kusasa?*

*Akazufika kusasa ngoba uyasebenza.* (f) *Umfundisi ufundisa abahedeni iBhayibheli.* (g) *Asithandi amasela ngoba amasela ayeba.* (h) *Umntwana uyakhala ngoba uyesaba. Wesabani?* (i) *Umfana uqhuba izinkomo; zifuna amanzi notshani.* (j) *Umlungu akahambi ngesitimela. Akahambi ngani ngesitimela? Akahambi ngesitimela ngoba unemoto.* (k) *Umbazi uzothenga isando nezipikili.* (l) *Inkosi izodlula ntambama.* (m) *Abantu balinga ukwenza umgwaqo.* (n) *Umhloli ubuza umbuzo; akaphenduli ngani?* (o) *Abafazi baguqelani? Abafazi baguqa ngoba bayathandaza.* (p) *Umuntu uphefumula ngamakhala.* (q) *Intombazane ikhamisa (ivula umlomo) ngoba iphuza umuthi. Intombazane ayithandi umuthi.* (r) *Umlimi uthengisa amahashi nezinkomo nezimvu noboya.* (s) *Abantwana baphuza ubisi, abafazi baphuza amanzi, amadoda aphuza utshwala.* (t) *NgeSonto amakholwa aya esontweni. Abafundisi bayashumayela ngeSonto.* (u) *Amadoda ashayelani isela? Amadoda ashaya isela ngoba akathandi ubusela.* (v) *Umfazi uzoqeda umsebenzi ntambama.* (w) *Umalume ucelelani uxolo? Umalume uyaxolisa/ucela uxolo ngoba uthanda uxolo.* (x) *Musa ukudabula izincwadi.* (y) *Sidla iphalishi ngezinkezo.* (z) *Sizohlakula ngesonto elizayo.*

## EXERCISE 14

1. (a) Yesterday I was working. In the morning I was digging holes because father wanted to plant trees. At noon I was cutting grass because the horses eat grass. In the afternoon I was not working; I was resting. At night I was conversing because I do not read books also I do not read papers. I have no papers and I have no books. (b) What has mother been doing? Mother has been sewing dresses, also she has been cooking. Mother has a machine, also she has a stove. She has not been washing clothes and she has not been ironing. (c) The horses have been eating

grass and mealies, also they have been drinking water but they have not been ploughing; father has been ploughing with cattle. Father has cattle and horses. (d) At night the dogs were barking because they were seeing thieves. The thieves were trying to steal fowls and turkeys. (e) Last year I was at school, I was not working, but this year I am not at school; I am working. (f) My sister was working in Johannesburg but now she is not working; she helps mother. (g) In the morning I was picking up coal because I wanted to make a fire. I wanted to cook food and to bake bread and cakes. (h) Father was killing a snake with a gun. Father has a gun; he does not kill a snake with a stick. Mother is very much afraid of a snake. (i) What was uncle doing on Monday morning? Uncle was showing the strangers the way. (j) What were the oxen pulling on Wednesday? They were pulling a car; they were not pulling a wagon. (k) We were counting sheep and goats yesterday afternoon; father has sheep, goats, cattle and pigs. (l) We were laughing because we were happy; we were eating sweets and cakes. (m) In the evening grandmother was lighting candles; we do not light (i.e. use) electricity. (n) The day before yesterday we were playing tennis but the day after tomorrow we shall play football. (o) The child was following his mother in the morning; he was not following grandmother. (p) Uncle was buying brushes and paint because he is going to paint walls and doors and windows. (q) The boy has not been working but he is denying (i.e. denies it); he says he has been working. (r) The men wipe off perspiration; the men are perspiring because they have been working.

2. (a) *Ekuseni besimba imigodi; ubaba ufuna ukutshala imithi.* (b) *Besibopha amahashi ngoba amahashi abefuna ukubaleka.* (c) *Kusihlwa bengifunda izincwadi namaphepha.* (d) *Izolo umakhi ubelayisha izitini namapulangwe; kusasa*

*uzolanda isihlabathi.* (e) *Izinja bezikhonkotha; bezixosha amasela.* (f) *Ekuseni udadewethu ubegeza izingubo; ntambama uzoayina.* (g) *Intombazane beyenza itiye; beyingashaneli futhi beyingabhaki isinkwa; emini izodeka.* (h) *Izolo umfundisi ubeshumayela.* (i) *Amadoda aphuza utshwala manje; ekuseni abephuza itiye; amadoda akathandi itiye.* (j) *Isela belifihla imali.* (k) *Indoda ishaya abafana ngoba abafana bebejikijela amatshe; bebeshaya amafasitele ngamatshe.* (l) *Abantwana babuka izilwane; abantwana bathanda ukubuka izilwane.* (m) *Ugogo ubegula kodwa manje akaguli.* (n) *Abafana bebeqhuba izinkomo; izinkomo bezifuna amanzi.* (o) *Bengozela kodwa manje angozeli.* (p) *Umntwana ukhotha ukhezo ngoba uthanda uju kakhulu; umama ubepha umntwana uju.* (q) *Uyaxubha ngoba ubedla.* (r) *USipho uzobheka izimvu nezimbuzi ngoba uMandla uyahamba.* (s) *Bengigeza amazinyo.*

## Exercise 17

1. (a) Father is going to town. It is a big town, and there are many houses. (b) In Johannesburg and in Pretoria there are many people, many cars and many beautiful roads. (c) My brother is big but your brother is not big; he is small. My brother wears big trousers whereas your brother wears small trousers. (d) Mother does not want water as water is not short; water is plentiful. (e)Why is Father buying coal? Father is buying coal because coal is short. Why does he not buy wood? He does not buy wood because it is plentiful. (f) Why isn't James wearing a jacket? James is not wearing a jacket because it is too big for him. (g) John works like James but he is smaller; James is bigger. (h) Are there four or five boys outside? There are four boys but five girls. (i) Is your sister tall or short? My sister is not short; she is tall. (j) Are there two or three white men at the store? There are three white men at the store, not two.

(k) There are many doctors, (many) nurses and (many) patients at the hospital. There are many beds at the hospital. (l) Uncle was buying a small horse but Father did not want a small horse. He wanted a big one. It cost R45.

2. (a) *Umfowenu mude na? Yebo umfowethu mude kodwa udadewethu mfishane.* (b) *Ehlathini elikhulu imithi miningi nezinyoni ziningi. Kukhona imithi emide nemithi emifishane.* (c) *Esikoleni abafana baningi namantombazane maningi. Abafana abanye bakhulu, abanye bancane. Amantombazane amanye made kodwa amanye mafishane.* (d) *Abafana bane noma bahlanu phandle? Bane; ababahlanu.* (e) *Udadewethu muhle kodwa udadewenu mubi.* (f) *Inkabi inkulu kodwa inja incane.* (g) *Ibhantshi lisha kodwa ibhulukwe lidala. Ubaba uthengeleni ibhulukwe elidala? Angazi.* (h) *Sibona imithi notshani. Imithi mide kodwa utshani bufishane.* (i) *Zingaki izitolo? Izitolo zine.* (j) *Izimoto ziningi kodwa umgwaqo mude.*

## Exercise 18

A. 1. Fetch my old shoes from the repairer in town. 2. The headman is selling his two horses; he has many fine horses but he has no donkeys. 3. I have many fine dogs. I shall sell some of my dogs. 4. I wanted my trousers; I did not want a jacket. 5. The preacher sees his children in the street; they come from church. The preacher has two children, a boy and a girl. 6. I shall buy a dog chain because my dog bites people. I like my dog because it drives away thieves in the daytime and at night. A dog chain does not cost much money; it is cheap. 7. Children love their parents, and parents love their children. 8. I was taking my hat and my stick into the house; I have a fine hat but it costs much money. 9. My brother will extract two of his teeth (i.e. have two of his teeth extracted) because they are loose; he will go to a dentist at Brakpan. 10. The farmer will fetch his horse cart from the repairer tomorrow. The farmer will pull the cart with his horses. The repairer was repairing its wheels. 11. The dogs come because they sense (i.e. get) the scent of meat. Dogs like meat very much. 12. We were polishing our shoes. We have nice new shoes. Our shoes are expensive. 13. I want to buy a bottle of medicine from the chemist because I am coughing; at night I perspire. 14. The builder will carry a load of sand and a load of planks with his wagon; he has a big wagon. 15. In the mines the white-men take out much gold. 16. In the morning I was buying a railway ticket; in the afternoon I shall be going to Durban. 17. Mother likes tap water but father likes tank water. 18. Buses carry workers in the morning and in the afternoon. In Johannesburg there are big buses. 19. Father is arranging his books; he has many books, big ones and small ones. He has English books and Afrikaans books. 20. Grandfather is tying his sheep and his goats; grandfather does not like pigs. 21. The boys are putting the cattle into the kraal. 22. The doctor gives the patient medicine for headache and fever. The patient will drink the medicine in the morning, at noon and in the evening. 23. My sister wants cotton; she wants to sew her dress. She will buy cotton at a drapery shop. 24. Always in the evening Father smokes his pipe but during the day he smokes cigarettes. 25. Good parents take care of their children; good children respect their parents. 26. I shall plant flowers in my garden tomorrow. I want to plant many varieties; the flowers will bloom in summer. 27. The cattle and the sheep want to enter the cattle kraal but there is a dog at the gate of the kraal. 28. Drink your tea; it will get cold. 29. Throw away the bad water. 30. Collect your belongings. 31. I was loading tables and chairs on to a lorry. 32. The girl is making up her bed.

33. In summer we see many varieties of very pretty flowers; at home we have a fine flower garden. 34. Tomorrow we are going to my sister's wedding in Pretoria; my sister is going to marry a Pretoria young man. 35. It was raining at night; the water is flowing in the river. 36. In summer lightning kills many people and many animals; moreover lightning burns houses.

## EXERCISE 19

(a) My sister bought pretty shoes at the shop last week but my brother did not buy because he has no money. (b) The children have gone away to school; they went with their books. They put their books in their bags. They will return in the afternoon by bus. Children pay money in the bus. (c) I wanted to see the king but the king went away yesterday at noon with his people. The king was travelling with five of his cars; he was not going by train. (d) The boys played but the girls did not play because it was raining. The teacher says that the girls will play next week. (e) We shall learn English tomorrow; yesterday we were learning Afrikaans; we did not learn Zulu. (f) The builder loaded planks, doors, and windows in his wagon; he has a big wagon and oxen. (g) His kraal/home was burnt down; it was burnt down yesterday afternoon. (h) In the morning we drank tea and coffee; in the afternoon we shall drink milk and cocoa; we add sugar and milk to tea and to coffee. (i) Father bought many sheep and many fine cattle and many horses at the sale the day before yesterday. (j) Last year I built my fine big house in Pretoria; it cost a lot of money. (k) Milk is finished; the boys did not milk in the morning; they will milk in the afternoon. (l) Jane, the water is boiling; make tea or coffee. (m) Yesterday school came out in the afternoon at 3 o'clock because we were singing; it did not come out at 2 o'clock. (n) Wipe the floor (down) with a cloth; the child spilt water. (o) My sister added salt and pepper to the meat but she did not put in onions and tomatoes. (p) The children are crying because they are hungry; mother is preparing their food. (q) The horse is standing; it is not grazing because it is ill. Tomorrow father will get medicine from the chemist. (r) The thieves stole five fowls of mine but they are denying it. (s) My sister is not making tea because the water is cold; moreover sugar is finished. (t) Tomorrow we shall watch a horse race; father likes racing very much.

## Exercise 20

1. Father is calling all of us, us his children. 2. Tomorrow uncle will not go to the station; we shall not go together; I shall go alone by bicycle. 3. Yesterday I had gone to fetch my new car from Port Elizabeth; I had gone with my younger brother. I have a driving licence. 4. Run fast; the train is pulling out now, you will remain (i.e. be left behind.) 5. John, fetch (pl.) my parcels from the store with James because you have overcoats: it is raining; go quickly. 6. Today the cook cooks stew because grandmother likes stew. Grandmother has no teeth. 7. In winter we see frost outside in the morning; we do not like to get up early in winter. 8. I come from the Post Office; I was buying stamps. I bought five cents worth of stamps. At the shop I shall buy a writing pad and envelopes. 9. Bring that pump of mine; be quick; I want to pump my bicycle. Tomorrow I shall buy new wheels. 10. In big towns many white people have double storey buildings; they like to build double storey buildings. 11. All Xhosa people like stamped mealies very much. Indians like rice and curry. 12. Dust all those pictures on the wall; they have dust. 13. Drink that tea of yours quickly

because it will get cold. 14. My brother is sticking the stamps onto the envelopes. 15. In big hospitals there are many patients and there are many doctors and many nurses. All patients sleep on beds. 16. The blind cannot see (with their eyes), the deaf cannot hear (with their ears), the mute cannot speak. 17. I want a needle and cotton; I want to patch my shirt because it is torn; it has a big hole. 18. The teacher is telling the story of a lion and a mouse; the teacher has many fine stories. 19. Whitemen like to hunt wild animals; they shoot the wild animals with their guns; black people hunt with spears and dogs. 20. Father wants a writing pad and envelopes; he wants to reply to Grandfather's letter. 21. The children will get wet because it is raining; they did not carry rain coats. 22. On Wednesday morning we shall go to market by lorry; we shall buy oranges, bananas, cabbage and tomatoes. 23. We shall both of us go to the parson tomorrow because we want work. The parson knows many white people. 24. This old woman lives by herself because she has no children. Her children all died and she remained by herself. 25. I am not calling you; I am calling both those boys. 26. We like uncle because he is very kind; he laughs always.

### EXERCISE 21

(a) My two white horses are lost, and my red oxen are lost. (b) Those new black shoes of his cost a lot of money. They are expensive. (c) We shall go with my elder brother, the two of us, on Saturday; my younger sister is not going. She will remain with mother at home. (d) The builder does not want such stones; he wants big stones only. But he wants few stones. (e) Where does this black jacket of James come from? (f) At Vereniging there is a big wide river; the cars cross at the bridge, the train has also its bridge. The cars do not get into the water and the train does not get into the water. (g) Grandmother fears cold air because she is ill, also she has no overcoat. (h) Take off these wet clothes and wet shoes; you will get ill. (i) I wanted dry firewood but there is wet firewood only. (j) We want water in (i.e. from) the tank. From the tank we shall get nice cool water; tap water is warm. (k) I want a sharp knife; I do not want a blunt knife. (l) We see many black clouds up in the sky. (m) I wanted candles; I did not want a paraffin lamp. (n) My sister bakes nice cakes also she cooks nice food. (o) The child wants to spread butter onto his bread. (p) Grandfather does not want to drink his tea because it is cold. (q) Put out the lights; the children want to sleep now; they are drowsy. (r) Uncle's garden has many fruit trees; in summer and in autumn we get nice fruit from uncle's garden. (s) All children like the parson because the parson is kind. (t) All the house keys went away with father in the morning. (u) Yesterday many convicts were working on the road; some were digging, others removing stones. Convicts live in gaol. (v) We shall get our money (we shall be paid) in the afternoon because we have been helping the whiteman.

## Exercise 22

1. (a) My horse is white; it is not black. My oxen are black; they are not white. (b) Those new shoes of yours are brown but my new shoes are black. They are not brown. I like my shoes very much. (c) Uncle's knife is very sharp. Uncle's knife is small; it is not big. (d) Thoko will get ill because she wears wet clothes. The clothes are wet and the shoes are wet. Thoko why do you put on wet clothes and wet shoes? (e) Grandmother is ill but she is better today. She does not cough very much. Yesterday she was coughing badly. (f) This medicine is green; but that one is not green. Grandmother's medicine is not green; it is red. How many times does Grandmother drink her medicine? Grandmother drinks her medicine in the morning, at noon and at night.

(g) What sort of load do you want? I want a light load. This load is light but that one is heavy. (h) Why is Jabulani running away? Jabulani is running away because he is naked; he is afraid. (i) Why is uncle sharpening his knife? Uncle is sharpening his knife because it is blunt. (j) Why does your brother not buy these shoes? My brother does not want these shoes because they are grey; he wants brown shoes. (k) This question is very difficult. You answer it my sister. (l) The roads in towns are wide because cars are many. (i.e. there are many cars).

2. (a) *Ibhantshi linje.* (b) *Imithi iluhlaza.* (c) *Izinja zinsundu.* (d) *Ilanga limakhaza.* (e) *Umfana ungaka.* (f) *Ukudla kuduma.* (g) *Umthwalo unzima.* (h) *Itiye limnandi.* (i) *Iyembe limanzi.* (j) *Abantu baqotho.* (k) *Imifula ibanzi.* (l) *Imbazo ibuthuntu.* (m) *Isilonda sibuhlungu.* (n) *Inkabi ingakaya.* (o) *Izimvu zimbalwa.* (p) *Umuzi ungako.* (q) *Amahashi amnyama.* (r) *Isitsha sinjani?* (s) *Abantu bampofu.* t) *Umuntu unje.*

3. (a) *Ibhantshi alinje.* (b) *Imithi ayiluhlaza.* (c) *Izinja azinsundu.* (d) *Ilanga alimakhaza.* (e) *Umfana akangaka.* (f) *Ukudla akuduma.* (g) *Umthwalo awunzima.* (h) *Itiye alimnandi.* (i) *Iyembe alimanzi.* (j) *Abantu abaqotho.* (k) *Imifula ayibanzi.* (l) *Imbazo ayibuthuntu.* (m) *Isilonda asibuhlungu.* (n) *Inkabi ayingakaya.* (o) *Izimvu azimbalwa.* (p) *Umuzi awungako.* (q) *Amahashi akamnyama.* (r) *Isitsha asinjani?* (s) *Abantu abampofu.* (t) *Umuntu akanje.*

### Exercise 23

A. (a) The children do not see the king but we see him. (b) My big black dogs did not bite the travellers yesterday morning. (c) I saw three short men in the street yesterday evening but my wife did not see them. (d) The young men did not ride the farmer's horses because they do not like to ride horses; they fear them. (e) We plant flowers because we like them; we plant many varieties of flowers; some bloom in summer others bloom in winter. (f) Children buy sweets everyday because they like them; father gives them money to buy them. (g) Uncle will not buy a big car because he has no money; he will buy a small car. A big car is expensive, it costs much money. (h) We saw Van Zyl's sheep and goats on the mountain yesterday afternoon; they were grazing on the mountain. Van Zyl says his sheep and goats are lost. (i) The thieves took the woman's fowls at night because the woman has no dogs, moreover she has no husband. (j) The patient drank his medicine because he wants to recover, but he does not want to go to hospital; he says he is afraid. (k) My dogs always kill fowls and ducks but I give them a lot of food. (l) The headmen did not sharpen their spears because they are going to shoot the lions (with guns.) (m) Next week father will send me to Benoni; there is my uncle at Benoni.

B. (a) *Abantwana abahlanu abancane baphuze amanzi kodwa abafana ababili abawaphuzanga; baphuze ubisi.* (b) *Umhloli akazibhalanga izincwadi ntambama; uzibhale kusihlwa ekhaya.* (c) *Izilwane eziningi azithandi ukuhlala nabantu ngoba ziyabesaba.* (*d*) *Asiwabonanga amahashi amathathu emfuleni kodwa umfowethu uthi uwabonile.* (e) *Bengihamba nezihambi; bengizikhombisa indlela.* (f) *Kusasa umlungu uzosinika imali yethu; sithola imali yethu ekupheleni kwesonto.* (g) *Bophani amahashi ngoba azobaleka.* (h) *Mbize! Ngifuna ukumthuma.* (i) *Zilandeni ngoba sizolima ntambama.* (j) *Umgwaqo unamatshe; amadoda aya emgwaqweni ngoba afuna ukuwamba; afuna ukuwakhipha.* (k) *Umlimi ubesifundisa ukutshala amazambane noanyanisi.* (1) *Intombazane ivule iminyango kodwa abantwana bayivalile.* (m) *Ngizolanda izincwadi zikamalume edolobheni; uyazifuna.*

C. (a) Your brother is crying for his school books because they are lost; they got lost in the train this morning. (b) We like to buy nice things for our children at Christmas. (c) Mother is not going to town today because she is sewing; she is sewing for Thoko and Jane. (d) Why is Sipho crying? He is crying because he wants Themba's sweets. (e) Cook food for the children; they are hungry. (f) Nomusa is reading Grandmother's letter for her because Grandmother is blind. (g) Why are you going by bus today? I am going by bus because the car went away with Father yesterday. (h) Why is the farmer killing his dog? He kills it because it eats sheep. (i) Maggie, take the raincoats for the children; it is raining. (j) Our lawyer will speak for us tomorrow. (k) Why are these boys running? They are running away; they see a snake. (l) The school children are going to sing for the king and queen tomorrow morning at 11. (m) Bring a chair for Mother; Mother wants to sit down. (n) The teacher reads interesting stories to the children from his book. The teacher's book has many interesting stories. (o) Pour out tea for your brother. (p) I shall carry your parcels for you.

D. (a) *Qoqela umakhi amatshe.* (b) *Amadoda alimela umfundisi ngoba umfundisi akanazinkabi.* (c) *UJune usefela udadewabo ufulawa; udadewabo ufuna ukubhaka amakhekhe nesinkwa.* (d) *Umama ukhanyisela ubaba; ubaba ubhala izincwadi endlini.* (e) *Umfana udlalela isikole sakhe.* (f) *Abantwana babalekelani? Abantwana babaleka ngoba babona inja yomlimi; bayayesaba.* (g) *Umfundisi uthandazela abahedeni namakholwa.* (h) *Sizotshalela ubabamkhulu kusasa ekuseni noma ngomhlomunye.* (i) *Udadewenu uzigqokelani izicathulo zakhe ezintsha nengubo yakhe entsha? Udadewethu ugqoka izicathulo zakhe ezintsha nengubo yakhe entsha ngoba uya emshadweni womngane wakhe.* (j) *Umfana uzongifuthela ibhayisikili.* (k) *Usicimelani isibane? Ngoba abantwana bafuna ukulala; bayozela.* (l) *Lizzie, khiphela umfowenu izingubo zakhe.* (m) *Ngicelela umzala uxolo* (or *Ngixolisela umzala*). (n) *Intombazane izoningenisela izihlalo.* (o) *Amadoda agawulela umlimi imithi.* (p) *Udadewethu uzosiayinela amayembe ethu; umama uzongibekelela ibhulukwe lami.* (q) *Umnumzane uncengela amadoda enkosini.* (*r*) *Ntambama ngizocandela udadewethu izinkuni.* (s) *Coshela umama iduku.* (t) *Abazali baphendulela abantwana babo.* (u) *UJesu wafela izoni.*

### EXERCISE 25

(a) The headmen are still helped by their boys today; tomorrow they will be helped by the men because the boys are going to school. (b) Fruit is sold every day in town but other things are not sold on Sunday. (c) My sister is troubled by her teeth very much. My sister's teeth will be extracted by a dentist on Wednesday afternoon. (d) My elder brother no longer works in Durban; he works in Pretoria at Lombard's. In Pretoria he earns much money. (e) Who is striking the dogs? They are being struck by boys with stones. (f) Is the minister present? Yes he is present but he is still eating. He will finish quickly. Wait for him here in the house. (g) The railway tickets will be bought by me tomorrow morning but the bus tickets will be bought by my brother. (h) Who is calling us? You are called by uncle. Where is uncle? He is at home. (i) At school we are taught to save money. Money is kept in the bank. (j) Remove (i.e. take) the mealies outside because they will be eaten by the fowls; fowls like mealies very much. (k) Bread is kneaded by my sister; it will be baked in the afternoon or in the evening. (l) The strangers are afraid; they are barked at by uncle's dog. (m) Mother is still washing our clothes but they will not be ironed by her; they will be ironed by my cousin. (n) Wait here; the coal will be brought by the farmer by lorry. The farmer is still ploughing.

### Exercise 26

(a) Father can ride a horse because he still likes to ride but Mother cannot ride because she no longer likes to ride a horse; she is afraid. (b) My brothers can go to the station in the evening because they do not work in the evening. I can go in the afternoon only; I cannot go in the evening. (c) I still want wood and coal because the fire will be kindled by me. Mother cannot kindle fire today because she is ill. (d) John and the others can fetch your cattle from the mountain in the afternoon but Sipho cannot go because he is limping. (e) I cannot tell you his name because I do not know it. (f) Can your boy show me the O.K. Bazaar? Yes he can show you because he knows the place; he works there. (g) His fruit trees cannot grow well because they do not get water. Fruit trees need plenty of water. (h) Fetch my horse. Can you catch it? Yes I can catch it. I shall tie it with a rope. Tomorrow it will be fetched by my brother. (i) The policeman can catch the thieves. (j) The wood can be fetched tomorrow by wagon but the coal will be fetched today by lorry. (k) Grandfather cannot run and Grandmother cannot run. (l) All of us can go into Father's car. Father has a big car; he no longer likes a small car. (m) The doctor cannot see the patients now because he is going to court; he is wanted by the magistrate. He will see the patients at 12 noon. Who will wash the patients? They will be washed by the nurses. (n) Yesterday I could play because I was not working but today I cannot play because I am working. (o) The farmers could plough this morning because it is not raining. (p) The headman could buy his car in Durban; in Johannesburg cars are expensive. (q) The parcels could be fetched by the boys on Saturday because on Saturday they do not go to school. (r) I could not read books the day before yesterday because I was ill but I am no longer ill now. (s) The men could not drink beer because the beer is finished. (t) We could all go to town.

# ADDITIONAL READING EXERCISES

## 1. IKATI LAMI

*Mina nginekati. Nginekati elihle elincane. Ikati lami limnyama. Igama lekati lami nguPussy. UPussy mncane; akamkhulu.*

*UPussy unoboya obuhle. UPussy unoboya obuthambile. Unamehlo amabili. Unamehlo aluhlaza. Unamadlebe amabili. UPussy unamazinyo futhi. Unamazinyo acijile. UPussy unolimi olubomvu. Unemilenze emine. Unamazipho acijile. Unamadevu. Unomsila omude.*

*UPussy uthanda ubisi kakhulu. Uthanda ukuphuza ubisi. Ekuseni mina ngipha uPussy ubisi lwakhe. UPussy unesitsha sakhe esincane. Umama uthenge isitsha sikaPussy esitolo edolobheni. UPussy uthanda isitsha sakhe kakhulu. Isitsha sikaPussy sihlala ekhishini. Mina ngithela ubisi lukaPussy esitshensi akhe.*

*UPussy uthanda futhi inyama. UPussy udla inyama emini nasebusuku. Umama akapheki inyama kaPussy. UPussy uthanda inyama eluhlaza. UPussy uthanda ukuzingela. Uthanda ukuzingela ebusuku. Uzingela amagundane. UPussy uthanda amagundane kakhulu. Udla amagundane. UPussy uyagxuma uma ebona igundane. Ubamba amagundane ngamazipho akhe acijile. Amagundane esaba uPussy kakhulu. Amagundane ayabaleka uma ebona uPussy. Angena emigodini yawo. Acasha emigodini yawo.*

*UPussy uthanda futhi ukubamba izinyoni. UPussy udla izinyoni. Izinyoni ziyandiza uma zibona uPussy. Izinyoni zesaba uPussy njegamagnundane. UPussy akazidli izinkukhu zikamama. Eduze kwasekhaya kukhona ihlathi. UPussy uyathanda ukuya ehlathini. Uthanda ukuzingela izinyoni ehlathini.*

*UPussy uthanda kakhulu ukudlala. Uthanda ukudlala ngoboya. Uthanda futhi ukudlala ngebhola.*

*UPussy uthanda ukulala eceleni kwesitofu. Uthanda futhi ukulala ezitulweni nasembhedeni. UPussy ukhwela phezu kwesitulo noma phezu kombhede. Ngesinye isikhathi uPussy ulala ngaphansi kwetafula.*

*UPussy wesaba izinja kakhulu. Uma ebona izinja uyabaleka.*

| | |
|---|---|
| *khwela* (climb) | *cijile* (sharp, pointed) |
| *gxuma* (jump) | *amazipho* (claws—3) |
| *thambile* (tame, soft) | *amadlebe* (ears of animals—3) |

## 2. INJA YAKITHI

*Ekhaya kukhona inja. Inja yakithi inkulu. Igama lenja yakithi nguBull. Ubaba wathenga uBull edolobheni. Ubaba wathenga uBull ngonyaka odlule. Ubaba wakhipha amarandi ayisikhombisa.*

*Bonke abantu besaba uBull ngoba uBull unolaka. UBull uyakhonkotha emini. Uyakhonkotha futhi nasebusuku. UBull unezwi elikhulu. Ubheka ekhaya emini nasebusuku. Uxosha amasela emini nasebusuku.*

*UBull unombala omuhle. Umbala kaBull unsundu. Ubaba uthanda izinja ezinsundu. Akathandi izinja ezimnyama. Izinja ezinsundu zinhle.*

*UBull unekhanda elikhulu. Unamadlebe amabili. Uname-hlo amabili. UBull unekhala. Ikhala likaBull liyabanda njalo.*

*Unomlomo omkhulu. Umlomo wakhe umnyama. Emlonyeni kaBulll kukhona amazinyo. Amazinyo akhe made futhi makhulu. Abantu besaba amazinyo kaBull. Besaba ilizwi lakhe elikhulu. Besaba umlomo wakhe omkhulu omnyama. UBull unemilenze emine. Unomsila owodwa. UBull unomsila omude. Ubaba akathandi ukunquma umsila wenja. UBull unoboya. Uboya bakhe abufani noboya bekati. Uboya bekati buthambile. Uboya bukaBull abuthambile. UBull unezidladla ezinkulu. Unamazipho njengekati kodwa amazipho kaBull akafani namazipho ekati. Amazipho ekati acijile kakhulu. Amazipho kaBull akacijile kakhulu.*

*UBull akathandi ukuhamba kancane. Uthanda ukugijima. Uma ilanga lishisa uBull uthanda ukukhipha ulimi. UBull uthanda kakhulu ukuphuza amanzi.*

*UBull unendlu yakhe. Unendlu yamapulangwe. Phakathi endlini kaBull kukhona isaka. UBull uthanda indlu yakhe kakhulu. Uthanda isaka lakhe kakhulu. Ulala phezu kwesaka lakhe. UBull akesabi imvula ngoba unendlu yakhe. Akesabi amakhaza ebusika ngoba ulala endlini yakhe.*

*UBull uthanda kakhulu inyama namathambo. UBull udla inyama zonke izinsuku. UBull uthanda kakhulu ukuqhoba amathambo.*

*UBull uthanda ukukhwela emotweni kababa. Uhlala phakathi nobaba. UBull uthanda imoto kodwa akathandi ukukhwela enqoleni.*

*izidladla* (paws—4) *qhoba* (chew bone)

**Notes:**

| | | |
|---|---|---|
| *thina* (we, us) | > | *kithina* or *kithi*—to, from, etc. us. |
| *nina* (you—pl.) | > | *kinina* or *kini*—to, from, etc. you. |
| *bona* (they) | > | *kubona* or *kubo*—to, from, etc. them. |

*kithi* also means my/our home, country
*kini* also means your home, country

*kubo* also means his/her/their home, country.

These may have formatives prefixed; e.g.

*Inja yakithi* (*ya* + *kithi*) The dog of my home.

*Ubaba uzoya kini nakubo*—Father will go to your home and to his home.

*Kumakhaza njengakithi*—It is cold like in my country.

## 3. IZINKUKHU

*Abantu abaningi bathanda ukufuya izinkukhu. Izinkukhu yizinyoni zasekhaya. Kukhona izinhlobo eziningi zezinkukhu. Ezinye izinkukhu zimhlophe, ezinye izinkukhu zimnyama, ezinye izinkukhu zibomvu. Zikhona futhi nezinye izinhlobo. Abanye abantu bathanda ukufuya izinkukhu ezimhlophe. Abanye abantu bathanda ukufuya izinkukhu ezibomvu. Abanye abantu bathanda ukufuya izinkukhu ezimnyama.*

*Kukhona amaqhude nezikhukhukazi. Izikhukhukazi zizalela amaqanda. Amaqhude akazaleli amaqanda. Abanye abantu bafuya izinkukhu ngoba bafuna ukuzithengisa. Bafuya izinkukhu eziningi. Abanye abantu bafuya izinkukhu ngoba bafuna ukuthengisa amaqanda. Abanye abantu bafuya izinkukhu ngoba bafuna ukudla inyama yenkukhu. Abantu abaningi bathanda inyama yenkukhu. Abantu abaningi bathanda ukudla amaqanda. Amakhosikazi abhaka amakhekhe ngamaqanda. Izinkukhu ezimhlophe zizalela amaqanda amaningi. Zona azifukami. Ziyazalela kuphela. Izinkukhu ezibomvu nezinkukhu ezimnyama zinenyama eningi.*

*Izinkukhu zizalela amaqanda. Zizalela amaqanda ezidlekeni. Isikhukhukazi senza isidleke. Sizalela amaqanda esidlekeni saso. Isikhukhukazi siyaqeda ukuzalela bese siyafukama. Uma sifukama sihlala phezu kwamaqanda aso. Sihlala emaqandeni emini nasebusuku. Emini siyaphuma emaqandeni isikhathi esifishane. Ebusuku asiphumi. Sihlala phezu kwamaqanda njalo. Isikhukhukazi sifudumeza amaqanda ngomzimba waso. Umzimba waso uyashisa. Isikhukhukazi sifukama amasonto amathathu bese kuvela amachwane. Amachwane ngabantwana benkukhu. Umntwana oyedwa sithi ichwane. Amachwane aphuma emaqandeni.*

*Izinkukhu zidla ummbila namabele nokunye ukudla. Ziphuza amanzi amaningi. Inkukhu icosha ukudla ngomlomo wayo. Inkukhu ayinamazinyo; ayihlafuni.*

*Inkukhu inemilenze emibili. Ayinazandla. Inezinsiba njengenyoni. Inkukhu ayikwazi ukundiza.*

*Izinkukhu ziyahlupha engadini. Zilimaza izimbali. Zidla iklabishi nezinye izilimo. Izinkukhu zifuna indlu yazo. Azihluphi uma zinendlu.*

| | |
|---|---|
| *fuya* (rear animals) | *isidleke* (nest—4) |
| *fudumeza* (make warm) | *bese* (and then) |

## 4. INGADI YASEKHAYA

*Thina sithanda izimbali kakhulu. Sonke ekhaya sithanda izimbali kakhulu. Umama uthanda izimbali kakhulu. Nobaba unjengomama; uthanda izimbali kakhulu. Nami ngithanda izimbali kakhulu. Nabafowethu nawodadewethu bathanda izimbali kakhulu. Sonke sithanda izimbali ngoba izimbali zinhle. Zihlobisa ikhaya.*

*Umama uthenga imbewu yezimbali edolobheni. Ehlobo umama utshala izimbali zasehlobo. Ebusika umama utshala izimbali zasebusika. Ingadi yakithi ayinkulu. Umama ufaka umquba engadini yezimbali. Umama uthenga umquba kumlimi. Izimbali ezinye zifuna umquba omningi kodwa izimbali ezinye azifuni umquba omningi. Izimbali ezinye zifuna amanzi amaningi kodwa izimbali ezinye azifuni amanzi amaningi. Izimbali ezinye zifuna ilanga kodwa ezinye zifuna umthunzi. Ilanga lishisa kakhulu ehlobo kodwa ebusika alishisi kakhulu.*

*USipho usebenza ekhaya. Ulima ingadi kamama. USipho uqala ukusebenza ngo-8 ekuseni. Uyaphumula emini ngo-1. Uqala futhi ukusebenza ngo-2. Ntambama uSipho uyeka ukusebenza ngo-5.*

*USipho usebenza kahle kakhulu. USipho ngumfana omncane. Umama uthanda uSipho ngoba uSipho ukhuthele, akavilaphi. Umama akathandi umfana ovilaphayo. USipho ulima ingadi ngehalavu noma ngemfologo. Ekhaya kukhona ihalavu nemfologo. Kukhona futhi ihala. USipho uhala engadini ngehala. USipho uyakwazi manje ukutshala izimbali. Ufundiswa ngumama. USipho muhle ngoba uyathanda ukufunda.*

*Umama akafuni ukhula engadini yakhe. NoSipho unjengomama. Naye akafuni ukhula engadini yakhe. USipho ususa ukhula engadini. Uhlakula ingadi. Ususa ukhula ngezandla noma ngemfologo. Uhlakula ngezandla noma ngemfologo. Kukhona imfologo encane yokuhlakula.*

*Ehlobo asihlupheki ngoba kukhona imvula eningi. Imvula iningi endaweni yakithi. USipho akaniseli zonke izinsuku ehlobo. Ebusika imvula ayikho. USipho unisela zonke izinsuku ngoba izimbali zifuna amanzi. Izimbali ziyafa uma zingatholi amanzi. USipho unisela ngethumbu. Kukhona ithumbu lokunisela ekhaya. Ithumbu lide. Lifika kahle engadini. USipho ufaka ithumbu empompini. Kukhona futhi ekhaya ikani lokunisela. Ngesinye isikhathi uSipho unisela ngekani.*

*Izimbali zikamama ziqhakaza ehlobo kodwa ezinye ziqhakaza ebusika. Izimbali zasehlobo ziqhakaza ehlobo. Izimbali zasebusika ziqhakaza ebusika. Izimbali ezinye zibomvu, ezinye zimhlophe, ezinye zineminye imibala eminingi emihle kakhulu. Ingadi kamama inhle ehlobo nasebusika.*

*Umama uthanda ukuhlobisa endlini ngezimbali zakhe. Umama ukha izimbali engadini yakhe. Ufaka izimbali ezitsheni zezimbali. Umama akafuni ukuthenga izimbali edolobheni. Izimbali ziyadula edolobheni. Zibiza imali eningi.*

*nami* (*na* + *mina:* Absolute pronouns lose suffix *-na* when preceded by formatives; e.g. *na* + *thina* > *nathi*—and we; *njenga* + *thina* > *njengathi*—like us; etc.)

*khuthele* (diligent)
*ihalavu* (spade—3)
*ihala* (rake—3)
*nisela* (to water garden)
*ikani* (watering can—3)
*hlobisa* (decorate)

## 5. AMANZI

*Zonke izinto eziphilayo zifuna amanzi. Abantu bafuna amanzi. Izilwane zifuna amanzi. Utshani bufuna amanzi. Imithi ifuna amanzi. Izinyoni zifuna amanzi. Izilwane ezinye zihlala emanzini. Ziphila emanzini.*

*Ulwandle lunamanzi amaningi. Amanzi olwandle ayababa ngoba anosawoti omningi. Amanzi emifula aya olwandle. Kukhona imifula emikhulu; kukhona nemifula emincane. Imikhumbi iyahamba emifuleni eminye.*

*Amanzi sigeza ngawo. Sigeza imizimba yethu. Sigeza nezingubo zethu. Nezindlu zethu sizigeza ngamanzi. Amanzi sipheka ngawo ukudla kwethu. Sigeza ngawo izitsha ezingcolile namabhodwe angcolile. Sinisela ngawo izingadi zethu. Amanzi sakha ngawo izindlu zethu. Sixova ngawo udaka.*

*Isitimela samalahle siphuza amanzi amaningi. Sisebenzisa amanzi amaningi. Isitimela sikagesi asiphuzi amanzi. Izimoto eziningi ziphuza amanzi kodwa izithuthuthu azisebenzisi amanzi.*

*Ezindaweni ezinye amanzi enza ugesi. Kukhona izindlu ezinemishini yokwenza ugesi. Kwezinye izindawo kukhona izimpophoma. Amanzi adilika phezulu. Awela kude phansi. Abanga umsindo omkhulu. Abantu abaningi bayathanda ukubuka izimpophoma. Bayathanda ukubuka amanzi edilika phezulu. Bayathanda ukuthatha izithombe zempophoma.*

*Abanye abantu bayathanda ukuhlamba emanzini. Bathanda ukuhlamba emfuleni. Abanye bathanda ukuhlamba elwandle. Ngesinye isikhathi izulu liyana kakhulu. Imifula iyagcwala. Umfula ogcwele uyingozi enkulu. Ungabulala abantu nezilwane. Ngesinye isikhathi amabhuloho ayalimala, nemigwaqo yezimoto iyalimala nojantshi wesitimela uyalimala.*

*Emadolobheni amakhulu kukhona amadamu amakhulu. Lamadamu anamanzi amaningi. Amadamu akhiwa ngaphandle kwedolobha. Amanzi asuka emadamini ngamaphayiphi amakhulu. Amanzi ahamba ngamaphayiphi aye phakathi emadolobheni. Abantu emadolobheni baphuza lamanzi; basebenzisa lamanzi. Emadamini amanzi afakwa imithi. Imithi ibulala konke okubi emanzini.*

*ujantshi* (railway line—1a)
*ngcolile* (be dirty)
*ukuthatha isithombe* (to take a picture)
*gcwala* (become full)
*impophoma* (water-fall—5)

## 6. ESIKOLENI

*Thina siyafunda. Sifunda esikoleni. Isikole sethu sikhulu. Esikoleni sethu kukhona abafana namantombazana. Esikoleni sethu kufunda abafana namantombazana. Kukhona abafana abaningi. Kukhona amantombazana amaningi. Esikoleni sethu kukhona futhi othisha abaningi.*

*Umama uyasivusa ekuseni. Thina asithandi ukuvuka ekuseni kakhulu. Sithanda ukulala. Sithanda ubuthongo.*

*Thina sigeza ngamanzi ashisayo. Siyesaba ukugeza ngamanzi abandayo. Ubaba akathandi ukugeza ngamanzi ashisayo. Uthanda ukugeza ngamanzi abandayo. Ebusika asithandi ukuvuka.*

*Zonke izinsuku sigeza imizimba yethu. Sigeza ngamanzi nangensipho. Zonke izinsuku sigqoka izingubo ezihlanzekile. Asigqoki izingubo ezingcolile. Ekuseni sidla iphalishi nobisi. Ngesinye isikhathi sidla iCorn Flakes noma iJungle Oats. Sidla futhi amaqanda nesinkwa ekuseni.*

*Siya esikoleni ngoMsombuluko nangoLwesibili nangoLwesithathu nangoLwesine nangoLwesihlanu. Asiyi esikoleni ngoMgqibelo. Asiyi futhi esikoleni ngeSonto.*

*Uma siya esikoleni sihamba ngamabhayisikili. Sonke sinamabhayisikili. Sifaka izincwadi zethu ezikhwameni. Sonke sinezikhwama zezincwadi. Uma izulu lina sigqoka amajazi emvula. Sonke sinamajazi emvula. Ngesinye isikhathi ubaba usihambisa ngemoto yakhe. Ubaba unemoto enhle. Ubaba ushayela imoto yakhe. Nomama uyakwazi ukushayela.*

*Esikoleni sethu abantwana abaningi bagibela amabhayisikili. Abafana bagibela amabhayisikili, namantombazana agibela amabhayisikili. Abanye abantwana abagibeli amabhayisikili. Bahamba ngamabhasi. Abanye baya esikoleni ngezimoto. Balethwa ngabazali babo.*

*Isikole sethu singena ngo-*8.30 *ekuseni; Siphuma ngo-*3 *ntambama. Esikoleni sifunda izifundo eziningi. Siyathanda esikoleni sethu ngoba sidlala imidlalo eminingi. Sidlala i*basket ball *ne*tennis *ne*cricket *ne*rugby *ne*soccer. *Ngesinye isikhathi sidlala nezinye izikole.*

*Esikoleni sethu kukhona izingadi ezinhle zezimbali. Izingadi zihlobisa isikole sethu. Izimbali zinemibala eminingi emihle. Kukhona futhi imithi emihle eluhlaza notshani obuhle obuluhlaza.*

*ezihlanzekile* (clean) *amajazi emvula* (raincoats)

## 7. IMIDLALO

Abantu abaningi bathanda imidlalo. Nathi sithanda imidlalo kakhulu. Abanye abantu bathanda ukudlala imidlalo. Abanye abantu bathanda ukubuka imidlalo. Kukhona imidlalo eminingi. Kukhona imidlalo yabesilisa. Kukhona futhi imidlalo yabesifazane. Abafana abancane bathanda kakhulu ukudlala ibhola. Bathanda ukukhahlela ibhola. Nezinsizwa zithanda kakhulu ukudlala ibhola. Ibhola balikhahlela ngezicathulo zebhola. Abantu besifazane abathandi ukukhahlela ibhola.

Abanye abantu besilisa bathanda ukudlala irugby. Ibhola lerugby alifani nebhola lesoccer. Ibhola lerugby libanjwa nangezandla. Ibhola lezinyawo alibanjwa ngezandla. Likhahlelwa ngezinyawo. Abantu besilisa badlala irugby kodwa abantu besifazane abathandi ukudlala irugby.

Abanye abantu bathanda ukudlala icricket. Abantu besilisa nabantu besifazane badlala icricket. Abantu besilisa badlala bodwa nabantu besifazane badlala bodwa. Abantu abadala abadlali icricket. Abakwazi ukugijima futhi badinwa masinyane.

Abantu abaningi bathanda itennis. Abantu besilisa nabantu besifazane bathanda kakhulu itennis. Abantu abadala abaningi bathanda ukudlala itennis. Labo abadlala itennis bagqoka izicathulo ezimhlophe zetennis. Bagqoka amasokisi amhlophe. Bagqoka izingubo ezimhlophe. Bathwala izigqoko ezimhlophe. Ibhola letennis alifani nebhola lezinyawo. Alifani futhi nebhola lerugby. Alifani nebhola lecricket. Ibhola letennis lincane futhi lilula. Ibhola letennis lishaywa ngeracquet.

Abelungu abaningi bathanda ukudlala igolf. Igolf idlalwa endaweni enkulu ebanzi. Igolf idlalwa ngabantu besilisa nabantu besifazane. Ibhola legolf alifani nebhola letennis. Ibhola legolf lincane kunebhola letennis. Ibhola legolf lilu-

*khuni. Lishaywa ngezinduku ze*golf.

*Abanye abantu abadala abathandi ukudlala* itennis *futhi abathandi ukudlala* igolf. *Bathanda ukudlala ama*bowls. *Abantu abadlala ama*bowls *bagqoka izingubo ezimhlophe.*

*Kukhona futhi imidlalo edlalwa endlini. Mina ngithanda ukudlala* icricket *ne*tennis.

| | |
|---|---|
| *abantu besilisa* (male persons) | *abantu besifazane* (female persons) |
| *imidlalo yabesilisa* (games for males) | *imidlalo yabesifazane* (games for females) |

*kunebhola* (*kuna* + *ibhola*) *kuna-* used for purposes of comparison; e.g.

*Umfowethu mkhulu kunami*—My brother is bigger than me.
*Itshe liyasinda kunephepha*—A stone is heavier than a paper.
*Ibhola letennis likhulu kunebhola legolf*—A tennis ball is bigger than a golf ball.
*banjwa* (be caught)

## 8. ISIBHEDLELA

*Emadolobheni amaningi kukhona izibhedlela. Kukhona izibhedlela ezinkulu. Kukhona nezibhedlela ezincane. Izibhedlela izindlu zabantu abagulayo. Kukhona iziguli zesilisa. Kukhona futhi iziguli zesifazane. Kukhona abantu abadala. Kukhona futhi nabantwana.*

*Esibhedlela kukhona odokotela abaningi. Kukhona odokotela besilisa. Kukhona futhi odokotela besifazane. Kukhona onesi abaningi. Kukhona izindlu eziningi ezinemibhede. Iziguli zilala emibhedeni. Kukhona izindlu zabantu besilisa. Kukhona izindlu zabantu besifazane. Iziguli zabantu besilisa zilala zodwa. Iziguli zabantu besifazane zilala zodwa ezindlini zazo. Iziguli zibhekwa ngonesi.*

*Esibhedlela kukhona indawo yokupopola. Odokotela bapopola umuntu ogulayo kuqala. Umuntu ogula kancane akalali esibhedlela. Uphindela ekhaya. Uthola umuthi kuphela. Umuntu ogula kakhulu akaphindeli ekhaya. Ulala esibhedlela. Ukhumula izingubo zakhe. Ugqoka izingubo zasesibhedlela. Umuntu wesilisa ulala endlini yabesilisa. Umuntu wesifazane ulala endlini yabesifazane. Abantu abalimele balala bodwa. Abantu abanezifo balala bodwa. Abantu besifazane ababelethayo balala bodwa.*

*Kukhona izibhedlela zabantu abaphethwe yisifuba, iT.B. Abantu abaphethwe yiT.B. bahlala bodwa. Abahlali nezinye iziguli. Banezibhedlela zabo bodwa. Kukhona futhi izibhedlela zabantu abaphethwe yisilephero. Abantu abanesilephero nabo bahlala bodwa. Abahlali nezinye iziguli.*

*Esibhedlela kukhona izisebenzi eziningi. Kukhona abantu abapheka ukudla. Kukhona abantu abaletha ukudla kweziguli. Kukhona abantu abageza izitsha. Kukhona abantu abashanela izindlu. Kukhona abantu abageza izingubo. Kukhona abantu abasebenza phandle. Abantu abasebenza phandle bayashanela futhi balungisa izingadi.*

*Abantu abaningi bayasinda ezibhedlela kodwa abanye bayafa. Ezindaweni ezinye izibhedlela azikho. Kukhona amaclinic kuphela. Abantu abalali eclinic. Ayikho imibhede eclinic. Eclinic basebenza emini kuphela. Abasebenzi ebusuku. Eclinic abantu bathola umuthi. Abantu abalimele bayaboshwa izingozi zabo. Abanye abantu besifazane baletha izingane zabo eclinic. Iclinic iyasiza kakhulu.*

*phindela* (return to)
*beletha* (give birth—of person)
*ingozi* (severe wound, accident—5)
*isilephero* (leprosy—4)

## 9. AMASILAHA

*Ezindaweni eziningi kukhona amasilaha. Amasilaha yizindawo zomsebenzi. Kukhona amasilaha abelungu namasilaha abantu abansundu namasilaha amaNdiya. Esilaheni kuthengiswa inyama. Esilaheni kuthengiswa inyama yenkomo. Kuthengiswa inyama yemvu. Kuthengiswa inyama yengulube. Kuthengiswa izinkukhu. Kuthengiswa amaqanda. Kuthengiswa nenhlanzi. Emasilaheni sithola futhi upoloni namasositshi.*

*Inyama yengulube iyadula kakhulu. Nenyama yemvu iyadula kakhulu. Inyama yenkomo ayiduli kakhulu. Izinkukhu ziyadula kakhulu. Ngesinye isikhathi emasilaheni bathengisa amadada namagalikuni.*

*Esilaheni inyama iyakalwa. Ikalwa esikalini. Onke amasilaha anezikali. Isikali silinganisa isisindo. Inyama iyasikwa bese ibekwa esikalini. Esilaheni banamatafula amade amakhulu. Esilaheni kukhona imimese emide ebukhali. Basebenzisa futhi izimbazo ezibukhali. Basebenzisa amasaha abukhali. Amanye amasilaha anomshini kagesi osika inyama. Umshini kagesi ubukhali kakhulu. Usika inyama namathambo.*

*Amasilaha avula ekuseni kakhulu. Amanye amasilaha avula ngo-*4 *ekuseni. Amasilaha amaningi avala emini ngo-*1 *noma ngo-*2. *Amanye avala ntambama kakhulu.*

*Izimpukane azifuneki emasilaheni. Izimpukane zingcolile. Zithwala ukungcola nokufa. Amatafula emasilaheni ayagezwa zonke izinsuku. Agezwa ngamanzi nangensipho. Abantu abathandi ukuthenga inyama emasilaheni angcolile anezimpukane eziningi. Bafuna amasilaha ahlanzekile.*

*Emasilaheni amanye kukhona ama*fridge *amakhulu. Ama*fridge *ayabanda. Agcina kahle inyama ingaboli. Ama*fridge *ayadula. Abiza imali eningi kodwa anosizo olukhulu. Ama*fridge *asebenza ngogesi.*

*Izinkomo azibulawa esilaheni. Izimvu azibulawa esilaheni nezingulube azibulawa esilaheni. Izinkomo zibulawa emadeleni, nezimvu zibulawa emadeleni nezingulube zibulawa emadeleni. Kukhona amalori amakhulu enyama. Inyama ilandwa emadeleni ngamalori.*

| | |
|---|---|
| *kala* (weigh) | *isikali* (scale) |
| *isisindo* (weight) | *emadeleni* (at the abattoir) |

## 10. IZINYONI

*Izinyoni zikhona ezindaweni eziningi. Zikhona emahlathini. Zikhona ezintabeni. Zikhona emifuleni. Zikhona olwandle. Zikhona nasemakhaya.*

*Kukhona izinhlobo eziningi zezinyoni. Kukhona izinyoni ezinkulu nezinyoni ezincane. Izinyoni zinemibala eminingi. Ezinye zinemibala emihle kakhulu. Zinezimpaphe ezinhle. Ezinye izinyoni ziyacula. Zicula kamnandi. Ezinye aziculi kamnandi.*

*Izinyoni zakha izidleke. Ezinye izinyoni zenza izidleke ezimbi. Ijuba lenza isidleke esibi. Ezinye izinyoni zakha izidleke ezinhle kakhulu. Inkonjane yakha isidleke ngodaka. Ithatha udaka ngomlomo wayo. Inkonjane yakha isidleke esihle kakhulu. Ezinye izinyoni zakha izidleke zazo emithini. Ezinye zakha izidleke phansi etshanini. Ezinye zakha emakhaya ethu. Inkonjane iyathanda ukwakha isidleke sayo kuvulande.*

*Izinyoni zizalela amaqanda ezidlekeni zazo. Izinyoni ziyafukama njengezinkukhu. Emaqandeni kuphuma abantwana benyoni. Abantwana benyoni sithi amaphuphu. Umntwana wenyoni oyedwa sithi iphuphu. Abantwana benkukhu sithi amachwane. Umntwana wenkukhu oyedwa sithi ichwane.*

*Izinyoni ziyalala ebusuku kodwa isikhova asilali. Isikhova sona silala emini. Ebusuku siyavuka. Siyazingela.*

*Sifuna ukudla. Isikhova siyathanda ukudla amagundane.*

*Izinyoni ezinye ziyahlupha kakhulu. Amajuba adla amabele emasimini. Uheshane udla amachwane. Amagwababa alimaza amazinyane ezimvu. Amagwababa ayahlupha nasemasimini. Akhipha imbewu yommbila emasimini. Abalimi abawathandi amagwababa. Izinyoni ezinye ziyasiza. Zinosizo olukhulu. Izikhova zidla amagundane. Amanqe adla izinto ezifile. Udoye udla izinyoka. Amalanda adla imikhaza.*

*Izinyoni ziyandiza. Zindiza ngamaphiko azo. Zinamehlo abukhali. Amehlo azo abona kude. Izinyoni ezinye zesaba amakhaza. Ebusika ziyahamba. Ziya emazweni amanye. Zibuya ehlobo. Izinkonjane asiziboni ebusika ngoba ziyahamba. Zesaba amakhaza asebusika. Zibuya ehlobo. Amalanda nawo esaba amakhaza. Ebusika asiwaboni.*

*Emadolobheni amakhulu kukhona indawo yezilwane nezinyoni. Umuntu ubona izinyoni eziningi khona. Umuntu ubona izinyoni zezinhlobo ngezinhlobo.*

*amajuba* (doves—3)
*uheshane* (hawk—1a)
*inkonjane* (swallow—5)
*iphuphu* (fledgling—3)
*igwababa* (crow)
*udoye* (secretary bird—1a)
*ichwane* (chicken—3)
*imikhaza* (ticks—2)

## 11. IBHANOYI

*Thina sinenhlanhla. Ezikhathini zethu sekukhona izinto eziningi zokuhamba. Sesihamba kalula. Kukhona izimoto. Kukhona izitimela. Kukhona imikhumbi. Kukhona namabhanoyi. Emadolobheni kukhona izimoto eziningi. Izimoto zihamba emigwaqweni. Izitimela zihamba kujantshi. Imikhumbi ihamba elwandle emanzini. Amabhanoyi ahamba phezulu emoyeni. Amabhanoyi ayaphapha, ayandiza. Emoyeni ibha-*

*noyi lifana nenyoni.*

*Amabhanoyi anejubane elikhulu. Ahamba amabanga amade ngesikhathi esifishane. Izimoto zihamba ngophethroli. Namabhanoyi ahamba ngophethroli. Amabhanoyi anabashayeli bawo. Kukhona izihlalo zokuhlala abantu. Phakathi ibhanoyi lifana nendlu enhle.*

*Abantu baphiwa ukudla phezulu emoyeni. Bafunda izincwadi zabo phezulu emoyeni. Bafunda amaphepha abo phezulu emoyeni. Bayabhema phezulu emoyeni. Babuka phandle ngamafasitele. Amabhanoyi andiza ngaphezulu kwamafu. Abantu bayalala phezulu emoyeni.*

*Kukhona amabhanoyi amancane namabhanoyi amakhulu. Amabhanoyi amakhulu athwala abantu abaningi. Amabhanoyi asuka ezweni lakithi aye emazweni amanye. Kukhona amabhanoyi athwala abantu. Ibhanoyi lithwala abantu nezimpahla zabo. Abantu abahamba ngebhanoyi abaphathi impahla esinda kakhulu. Kukhona futhi amabhanoyi empi. Amabhanoyi empi anejubane elikhulu kakhulu.*

*Abanye abantu bathanda ukuhamba ngebhanoyi ngoba linejubane. Bathanda ukuphapha phezulu njengenyoni. Bathanda ukuhamba masinyane. Phezulu emoyeni bathanda ukubuka phansi. Bathanda ukubuka ulwandle kude phansi. Bathanda ukubuka imifula kude phansi. Bathanda ukubuka amahlathi kude phansi. Bathanda ukubuka amadolobha amakhulu namadolobha amancane kude phansi. Bathanda ukubuka izintaba kude phansi. Bathanda ukubuka amafu ngaphansi kwabo. Amafu afana noboya bemvu.*

*Abanye abantu abathandi ukuhamba ngebhanoyi. Bayesaba. Besaba ukuwa. Besaba ukufa. Besaba ukudilika phezulu emoyeni. Bafuna ukuhamba ngezimoto noma ngezitimela noma ngemikhumbi.*

*Ukuhamba ngebhanoyi kuyadula. Ithikithi lebhanoyi libiza imali eningi.*

*inhlanhla* (good fortune—5) *phapha* (fly)
*ibanga* (distance—3) *impi* (war, battle—5)
*sekukhona* (there is now)

*se-* is used to indicate something which now takes place but has not been taking place hitherto; e.g.
*sengibona* (I now see)
*sengiyafunda* (I now read or I now attend school)
*sengiyasebenza* (I am now working)

The negative is expressed by using *-ka-*; e.g.
*angikaboni* (I do not yet see)
*angikafundi* (I do not yet read/go to school)
*angikasebenzi* (I do not yet work)

## 12. EPULAZINI

*Ubabamkhulu uhlala epulazini. Epulazini akufani nasedolobheni. Epulazini azikho izimoto eziningi. Epulazini azikho izithuthuthu eziningi. Epulazini abekho abantu abaningi njengasedolobheni. Epulazini azikho izitolo eziningi njengasedolobheni. Epulazini awekho amasilaha amaningi njengasedolobheni. Izimoto azizininingi, nezithuthuthu azizininingi nabantu ababaningi nezitolo azizininingi namasilaha akamaningi.*

*Emzini kababamkhulu kukhona izinkomo eziningi. Ufuye izinkomo zobisi. Izinkomo zikababamkhulu zinobisi oluningi. Izinkomo zakhe zisengwa ekuseni nantambama. Kukhona isibaya sezinkomo. Izinkomo zikababamkhulu zinamabele amakhulu. Zinemibele emide emikhulu.*

*Ubisi luthelwa emakanini obisi. Ubabamkhulu unamakani amaningi. Kukhona amakani amakhulu namakani amancane. Ubabamkhulu unabantu abaningi epulazini lakhe. Abanye abantu bayasenga. Abanye abantu bayalima. Abanye abantu bayapheka. Abanye abantu balungisa endlini. Abanye abantu benza eminye imisebenzi.*

*Ubabamkhulu ufuye amahashi nezingulube nezimvu. Ubabamkhulu akafuyile izimbuzi. Akazithandi izimbuzi. Ubabamkhulu uthi izimbuzi ziyahlupha. Thina sithanda ukugibela amahashi kababamkhulu. Amahashi kababamkhulu athambile. Asesabi ukuwa. Siyakwazi ukubophela. Sifaka itomu kuqala bese sibeka isihlalo emhlane wehashi. Siya emasimini noma emfuleni noma ehlathini ngamahashi.*

*Amahashi adla utshani nommbila nomgqakazo. Amahashi kababamkhulu akhuluphele.*

*Ubabamkhulu unenqola enkulu. Uthwala amasaka ngenqola yakhe. Ubabamkhulu udonsa inqola yakhe ngezinkabi. Unezinkabi ezinhle ezibomvu. Ubabamkhulu akalimi amasimu akhe ngezinkabi. Ulima ngogandaganda. Sekukhona ogandaganda epulazini likababamkhulu. Ugandaganda ulima masinyane kunezinkabi. Awufani nezinkabi. Ogandaganda bakababamkhulu bayakhanyisa ebusuku. Ubabamkhulu uthanda ukusebenza nasebusuku.*

*Emasimini ubabamkhulu utshala ummbila namabele nokolo namazambane nobhontshisi. Uthanda futhi ukutshala amantongomane.*

*Ubabamkhulu ufuye izinkukhu eziningi. Ufuye izinkukhu ezimhlophe nezinkukhu ezibomvu nezinkukhu ezimnyama. Ubabamkhulu uthengisa amaqanda. Uthumela amaqanda emakethe. Uthumela amanye amaqanda emahotela. Ubabamkhulu uthumela izinkukhu eziphilayo emakethe. Izinkukhu ezinye eziphilayo uzithumela emahotela. Ubabamkhulu uthumela futhi emakethe nasemahotela izinkukhu ezihlatshiwe. Ubabamkhulu uthola imali eningi ngezinkukhu zakhe.*

*Ubabamkhulu ufuye futhi izingulube. Ufuye izingulube ezimhlophe. Uthanda izingulube ezimhlophe kakhulu. Ubabamkhulu uthengisa izingulube zakhe edolobheni. Uthola imali eningi ngezingulube zakhe. Abantu abaningi bathanda inyama yengulube. Ubabamkhulu ufuye izimvu zoboya. Ugunda uvolo. Uvolo unemali eningi.*

*Emzini kababamkhulu kukhona imithi eminingi yezithelo. Kukhona izinhlobo zezithelo eziningi. Ehlobo sidla izithelo eziningi kwababamkhulu. Ubabamkhulu uthengisa ezinye izithelo zakhe emakethe.*

*imibele* (teats—2)
*thumela* (send to)
*isihlalo* (saddle—4)
*umgqakazo* (crushed mealies—2)
*ugandaganda* (tractor—1a)
*ezihlatshiwe* (which are slaughtered)
*bophela* (inspan, saddle)
*itomu* (bridle—3)
*khuluphele* (stout, fat)
*amantongomane* (pea-nuts—3)

## 13. IZINYOKA

*Ezweni lakithi kukhona izinyoka eziningi. Kukhona izinyoka ezinkulu nezinyoka ezincane. Kukhona izinyoka ezinde nezinyoka ezimfishane. Izinyoka azinazo izinyawo. Zihamba ngezisu zazo. Zonke izinyoka zihamba ngezisu.*

*Inyoka inomlomo. Inamehlo. Inolimi. Inomsila. Ulimi lwenyoka alufani nolimi lwezinye izilwane. Ulimi lwenyoka lunezimbaxa ezimbili. Inyoka ayicwayizi.*

*Izinyoka ezinye zihlala emigodini. Izinyoka ezinye zihlala ematsheni. Izinyoka ezinye zihlala emithini emahlathini. Izinyoka ezinye zithanda otshanini.*

*Izinyoka ezinye zinesihlungu. Abantu besaba izinyoka ezinesihlungu. Ngesinye isikhathi izinyoka zibulala abantu. Ngesinye isikhathi izinyoka zibulala izilwane. Izinyoka eziningi zithanda ukudla amaxoxo namagundane. Isihlungu siphuma ngembobo emazinyweni enyoka.*

*Ezweni lakithi kukhona izimamba. Kukhona izimamba ezimnyama nezimamba eziluhlaza. Bonke abantu besaba imamba kakhulu. Imamba inolaka kakhulu. Ibulala abantu nezilwane. Imamba inesihlungu esibi. Umuntu uyashesha ukufa, nezilwane ziyashesha ukufa. Ezindaweni ezinye izimamba zivala izindlela. Zivimbela abantu ezindleleni.*

*Endaweni ethile kwakukhona imamba enolaka. Lemamba yayibulala abantu nezilwane. Bonke abantu babesaba ukuyibulala. Yabulawa yinkosikazi enesibindi. Inkosikazi yapheka isijingi. Yathwala isijingi esishisayo ekhanda. Yahamba yaya lapho imamba ihlala khona. Imamba yabona inkosikazi. Yashaya inkosikazi ekhanda kanti ifaka ikhanda layo esijingini esishisayo. Yafa khona lapho imamba. Abantu bajabula kakhulu. Babonga inkosikazi leyo.*

*Ezweni lakithi kukhona futhi izinhlwathi. Inhlwathi yinyoka enkulu. Inhlwathi inamazinyo amakhulu. Inhlwathi ayinaso isihlungu. Ayibulali abantu nezilwane ngesihlungu. Inhlwathi igwinya abantu nezilwane. Umlomo wenyoka uyanwebeka.*

*Izinyoka zesaba amakhaza ebusika. Ebusika ziyacasha ngoba kuyabanda. Ziphuma ehlobo. Ziphuma zilambile kakhulu sezinolaka. Izinyoka ziyebuza yonke iminyaka. Zilahla isikhumba esidala.*

*izimbaxa* (forks—5)
*isijingi* (pumpkin porridge —4)
*vimbela* (obstruct)
*isihlungu* (snake poison—4)
*nwebeka* (be elastic)
*ebuza* (cast off skin)

## 14. UBUSIKA

*Abantu abaningi bathanda ihlobo. Abathandi ubusika. Besaba amakhaza obusika. Abanye abantu bathanda ubusika.*

*Abathandi ihlobo. Besaba ukushisa ehlobo. Ebusika ilanga alishisi kakhulu. Ezindaweni ezinye kulala isithwathwa. Utshani bembatha ingubo emhlophe. Ngesinye isikhathi ompompi abavuleki ekuseni. Amanzi empompini aphenduka iqhwa.*

*Ezindaweni ezinye izulu liyakhithika ebusika. Ezintabeni kulala iqhwa elinengi. Imithi ezintabeni yembatha ingubo emhlophe namatshe embatha ingubo emhlophe. Iqhwa lilala phezu kwezintaba naphezu kwemithi naphezu kwamatshe. Izilwane eziningi nezinyoni ziyafa. Ngesinye isikhathi abantu nabo bayafa.*

*Abantu bathanda umlilo ebusika. Bathanda ukotha. Bathanda futhi ukudla okushisayo ngoba bayagodola. Ebusika abantu bathanda ukugqoka izingubo ezifudumalayo. Bagqoka amajezi namajazi. Bagqoka namasokisi afudumalayo.*

*Abantu abaningi bayagula ebusika. Baphathwa ngumkhuhlane. Izingane ziyakhwehlela namaxhegu ayakhwehlela nezalukazi ziyakhwehlela. Odokotela basebenza kanzima ebusika nezibhedlela ziyagcwala.*

*Ezindaweni ezinye abalimi bayahlupheka ebusika. Bayahlupheka ngoba abukho utshani bezilwane zabo. Izinkomo zabo nezimvu zabo ziyalamba. Ziyazaca. Abalimi bayahlupheka futhi ngoba amanzi akakho. Abanye abalimi bakha amadamu amanzi. Ehlobo ngesikhathi sezimvula amanzi ayangena emadamini. Kungena amanzi amaningi. Bathola amanzi amaningi. Ebusika abahlupheki ngoba amanzi akhona, maningi. Eminye imifula iyasha ebusika.*

*Ebusika ingozi yomlilo inkulu ngoba utshani bomile. Ngesinye isikhathi amadlelo ayasha. Ngesinye isikhathi amahlathi ayasha. Nemizi yabantu iyasha ebusika. Umlilo ugijima kalula ngoba kukhona umoya omningi ebusika. Umoya uyavunguza nezintuli ziningi ebusika.*

*Imithi eminingi ayibukeki kahle ebusika. Mibi. Ayibukeki*

*kahle ngoba amahlamvu ayo ayawohloka. Amahlamvu awela phansi. Notshani buyaphenduka umbala ebusika. Buyoma bube mhlophe. Kodwa ezindaweni ezinye imithi iluhlaza ebusika. Amahlamvu akawohloki. Notshani abuphenduki umbala ebusika.*

*embatha* (to be covered)
*ukotha* (to warm oneself)
*omile* (be dry, be thirsty)
*hlupheka* (suffer)
*amadlelo* (pastures—3)
*ayibukeki kahle* (do not look attractive)
*zaca* (become thin)
*godola* (be cold)
*wohloka* (fall down)
*lamba* (become hungry)
*amahlamvu* (leaves—3)

## 15. BESIYE EBHAYISIKOBHO

*Kuthangi besiye ebhayisikobho. Besihambe nomfowethu omkhulu nodadewethu omncane nomama nobaba. Sonke ekhaya sithanda ukuya ebhayisikobho. Indlu yebhayisikobho isedolobheni. Sihamba ngemoto uma siya ebhayisikobho. Sihlala kude nedolobha.*

*Ebhayisikobho bekukhona abantu abaningi. Bekukhona amadoda namakhosikazi. Bekukhona izinsizwa nezintombi. Izingane eziningi aziyi ebhayisikobho ebusuku. Siya ebhayisikobho kusihlwa ngoba emini siyasebenza. Sonke siyasebenza. Ubaba usebenza edolobheni, nomama usebenza edolobheni nomfowethu usebenza edolobheni nami ngisebenza edolobheni. Udadewethu omncane naye usebenza edolobheni.*

*Ebhayisikobho sibona izithombe ezikhulumayo. Ngesinye isikhathi sibona izithombe ezinhle kakhulu. Abanye abantu bathanda ukuya ebhayisikobho zonke izinsuku. Abakhethi izithombe. Thina asiyi zonke izinsuku. Sikhetha izithombe. Sibuka izithombe ezinhle kuphela. Abantwana bathanda izithombe zezilwane ezikhulumayo nezithombe zabantu abadubulayo. Abafana bathanda izibhamu namahashi.*

*Abanye abantu bayahlupha ebhayisikobho. Bathanda ukukhuluma. Babanga umsindo. Kubi lokhu ngoba asizwa ukuthi izithombe zikhuluma zithini. Abanye abantu babhema ugwayi. Kugcwala ugwayi endlini. Thina asiyithandi intuthu kagwayi. Siyakhwehlela uma kukhona intuthu kagwayi.*

*Ebhayisikobho singena ngemali. Ubaba uthanda ukuthenga amaswidi kodwa umama akawathandi amaswidi. Umama uthanda ukuphuza unamanedi.*

*Ibhayisikobho iqala ngo-*8 *kusihlwa. Ngesinye isikhathi iphuma ngo-*10 *ebusuku. Ezinye izithombe zinde. Zithatha isikhathi eside. Kuthangi ibhayisikobho iphume ngo-*10.45 *ebusuku ngoba besibuka isithombe eside. Sibuye nomalume. Umalume ubehambe ngebhasi. Umalume akanamoto.*

*unamanedi* (lemonade, cold drink—1a)

## 16. KUSASA NGIYAHAMBA

*Kusasa ngiyahamba. Ngiya eJohannesburg. Ngiyavakasha. Ngizohamba ngesitimela. Ngizohamba ngesitimela sikagesi. Isitimela sikagesi sinejubane. Mina angisithandi isitimela samalahle. Ngizonda intuthu yaso. Ngizohamba ngedwa. Angizuhamba nobaba nomama nodadewethu. Ubaba uyasebenza. Umama uyasebenza. Udadewethu usafunda esikoleni. Mina ngiyasebenza kodwa yisikhathi sami sokuphumula lesi.*

*Umfowethu omkhulu uhlala eJohannesburg. Uhlala khona nenkosikazi yakhe nabantwana bakhe. Umfowethu unabantwana abathathu. Umfana munye kodwa amantomba-*

*zana mabili. Umfowethu unendlu yakhe eGoli. Indlu yakhe inhle futhi inkulu. Inamakamelo amaningi.*

*Isitimela sisuka esiteshini sakithi ngo-*5 *ntambama. Sifika eJohannesburg ngo-*8 *ekuseni. Ngizolala khona esitimeleni. Thina sihlala enhla kwesiteshi. Isiteshi siseduze. Esiteshini ngizoya ngezinyawo. Angizuhamba nge*taxi *futhi angizuhamba ngebhasi.*

*Ithikithi sengilithengile. Ngilithenge namuhla ekuseni. Ngilithenge esiteshini. Ngithenge ithikithi lika-*2*nd Class. Ithikithi lika-*1*st Class liyadula. Libiza imali eningi. Ithikithi lami libize amarandi ayisikhombisa namasenti angu-*80. *Ngikhiphe amarandi ayisikhombisa namasenti angu-*80.

*Ngizohlala eJohannesburg inyanga eyodwa. Ngizohlala kwamfowethu omkhulu. Angizuhlala ehotela. Amahotela aseGoli ayadula. Umuntu ukhipha imali eningi. Umfowethu usebenza eGoli. Usebenza esitolo sezicathulo. Uthengisa izicathulo.*

*Esitimeleni kukhona imibhede. KuFirst Class kukhona imibhede emine kuphela. KuSecond Class kukhona imibhede eyisithupha. Esitimeleni kukhona futhi izingubo zokulala. Uma ufuna izingubo zokulala ukhipha amasenti angu-*65.

*Esitimeleni kuthengiswa nokudla. Ukudla esitimeleni kuyadula. Kubiza imali eningi. Mina angizuthenga ukudla esitimeleni. Ngizothenga itiye kuphela. Angithandi ukudla esitimeleni.*

*Esitimeleni kukhona ugadi. Ugadi ugqoka izingubo ezimnyama. Uthwala ikepisi elimnyama. Ufaka izicathulo ezimnyama. Ugadi ubheka amathikithi esitimeleni.*

*ugadi* (ticket examiner, guard—1a)

## 17. UYEZA UBABAMKHULU

*Umama uyalungisa ekhaya. Uyalungisa ngoba kusasa kuzofika ubabamkhulu. Ubabamkhulu uzofika emini ngemoto yakhe. Ubabamkhulu uhlala epulazini lakhe. Unepulazi elikhulu. Ubabamkhulu uzohlala isonto elilodwa kuphela bese ephindela epulazini. Ubabamkhulu uzothenga izimpahla zepulazi lakhe. Uzothenga amageja. Ufuna ukuthenga nogandaganda. Ubabamkhulu akazuthenga imoto ngoba unemoto entsha. Ubabamkhulu uthenge imoto entsha ngonyaka odlule.*

*Ubabamkhulu uzofika nogogo. Ugogo uyathanda ukuza edolobheni. Ugogo uthanda ukusibona. Ugogo uthanda futhi ukubuka izingubo nezigqoko nezicathulo ezitolo. Ugogo akazuhlala isonto elilodwa njengobabamkhulu. Uzohlala inyanga yonke. Ubabamkhulu uzophindela epulazini kodwa ugogo uzosala. Ubabamkhulu uzohamba yedwa. Ubabamkhulu uzobuya futhi ngenyanga ezayo. Uzolanda ugogo.*

*Ugogo ufuna ukuhamba nathi ngenyanga ezayo. Ufuna ukuba siyogibela amahashi epulazini. Ufuna ukuba siyophuza ubisi oluningi epulazini. Ufuna ukuba siyodla izithelo eziningi epulazini. Ufuna ukuba siyobona izinkomo zikababamkhulu namahashi kababamkhulu. Thina asizuhamba nogogo ngoba siyafunda esikoleni. Siyovakashela ugogo nobabamkhulu ebusika ngoJuly.*

*Kusasa ngoLwesibili. NgoLwesithathu ubabamkhulu uzobona ogandaganda namageja. NgoLwesine uzothenga imbewu. Ufuna imbewu eningi ngoba ipulazi lakhe likhulu. Amasimu akhe makhulu. NgoLwesihlanu ubabamkhulu uzobona udokotela wamehlo. Amehlo kababamkhulu abuhlungu. Ufuna umuthi kudokotela nezibuko. Ubabamkhulu akanazo izibuko. Uzoqala ukusebenzisa izibuko. Ugogo akafaki izibuko. Amehlo akhe akahluphi.*

*NgoMgqibelo ubabamkhulu ufuna ukubuka ibhola. Ubabamkhulu uthanda imidlalo kakhulu. Epulazini ayikho imidlalo eminingi. NgoMgqibelo kusihlwa uzohlala ekhaya. Akazukuya ebhayisikobho. Ubabamkhulu akathandi ukuya ebhayisikobho. Akathandi ebhayisikobho ngoba wesaba intuthu kagwayi.*

*NgeSonto sizoya esontweni nobabamkhulu. Sizohamba ngemoto yakhe entsha. Siyajabula thina ngoba sizohamba ngemoto kababamkhulu entsha. Asizuhamba ngemoto kababa endala.*

*NgoMsombuluko ubabamkhulu uzophindela ekhaya epulazini. Siyombona futhi ngenyanga ezayo.*

*sebenzisa* (use)

## 18. IZOLO

*Izolo bengiye edolobheni. Bengihambe ngehashi. Mina ngiyathanda ukugibela. Nodadewethu uyathanda ukugibela. Ubaba unamahashi amane. Amahashi kababa mahle kakhulu. Ekhaya kukhona amahashi amabili ansundu namahashi amabili amnyama. Amahashi kababa athambile.*

*Edolobheni ngibone abantu abaningi. Ngibone abantu besilisa nabantu besifazane. Ngibone abantu abadala nezingane. Abantu abanye bebehamba emgwaqweni. Abantu abanye bebephakathi ezitolo. Abantu bebethenga ezitolo. Bebethenga izingubo zokulala. Besaba amakhaza obusika. Abanye bebethenga amabhulukwe. Abanye bebethenga amayembe. Abanye bebethenga izicathulo. Abanye bebethenga izigqoko. Abanye bebethenga ukudla. Mina ngithenge amayembe amabili namasokisi. Ngithenge amayembe ngamarandi angu-7. Ngithenge amasokisi ngerandi elilodwa.*

*Ngiye futhi esilaheni. Esilaheni ngithenge inyama yengulube. Ngithenge futhi inyama yemvu nenhlanzi namasositshi. Ubaba akayithandi inyama yengulube. Akayithandi futhi inyama yemvu. Uthanda inhlanzi. Umama uthanda inyama yengulube kakhulu.*

*Esilaheni bekukhona omunye umuntu ngaphambi kwami. Naye ubethenga inyama. Yena uthenge inyama yengulube kuphela. Akathenganga inyama yemvu. Akathenganga inhlanzi. Akathenganga amasositshi. Mina ngithenge emuva kwakhe. Bekukhona futhi abanye abantu emuva kwami.*

*Eposini ngipose izincwadi zikababa nezincwadi zikamama. Izincwadi zikababa beziya ePretoria. Izincwadi zikamama beziya eDurban. Eposini ngithenge futhi izitembu. Ngithenge izitembu ezingu-24. Ngikhiphe amasenti angu-24. Ngithenge futhi ama*postal orders *amabili. Ngithenge i*postal order *yamarandi angu-*3 *ne*postal order *yamasenti angu-*85. *Eposini bekukhona abantu abaningi ngaphambi kwami nangemuva kwami.*

*Angiyanga esiteshini. Bengingafuni lutho esiteshini. Bengingafuni ukuthenga ithikithi. Angiyanga futhi ebhange. Bengingafuni ukufaka imali ebhange. Bengingafuni ukukhipha imali ebhange.*

*Edolobheni ngiye ekuseni ngo-9. Ngibuye ntambama ngo-2. Bengihamba ngedwa. Udadewethu akahambanga. Usale ekhaya. Ubesiza umama.*

## 19. NGANGIHLALA EDURBAN

*Mina ngangihlala eDurban. Ngangivuka ekuseni kakhulu. Ekuseni ngangigeza. Ngangigeza ngamanzi abandayo kodwa ebusika ngangigeza ngamanzi ashisayo. Ngangiya esikoleni ngebhayisikili. Ngangingayi ngemoto futhi ngangingayi ngebhasi. Ngangifaka izincwadi zami esikhwameni sami sezincwadi. Nganginesikhwama esihle kakhulu. Ngangibuya esikoleni ntambama. Nganginejazi lemvula. Uma* izulu lina ngangigqoka ijazi lami lemvula.

Umzala naye wayefunda. Wayefunda esikoleni eDurban. Wayevuka ekuseni kakhulu. Wayegeza ngamanzi abandayo kodwa ebusika wayegeza ngamanzi ashisayo. Umzala wayeya esikoleni ngebhayisikili. Wayengayi ngemoto futhi wayengayi ngebhasi. Umzala naye wayefaka izincwadi zakhe esikhwameni sakhe sezincwadi. Wayenesikhwama esihle sokufaka izincwadi.

Sobabili sasihlala kwababamkhulu. Ubabamkhulu wayenendlu enkulu eDurban. Ubabamkhulu wayehlala nogogo eDurban. Ngangithanda kakhulu eDurban. Umzala naye wayethanda kakhulu eDurban. Sasithanda ukubuka izimpahla emafasiteleni ezitolo. Sasibuka amabhulukwe namayembe nezigqoko nezicathulo. Sasithanda futhi ukubuka izicathulo zebhola nezicathulo zecricket namaracquet. Esikoleni sasithanda kakhulu ukudlala. Sobabili sasidlala itennis necricket kodwa sasingathandi ukudlala irugby.

EDurban sasithanda ukuhamba ngoricksha. Oricksha babegqoka kahle. Ekhanda babefaka izimpondo. Sasithanda ukuhamba ngoricksha uma siya elwandle. Njalo ngeSonto sasithanda ukuya elwandle. Sasithanda ukubuka abanye behlamba. Nathi sasithanda ukubhukuda. Sasiphatha izingubo zethu zokubhukuda. Sasithanda futhi ukulala esihlabathini.

EDurban kukhona izindlu eziningi zamabhayisikobho. Sasiya njalo ebhayisikobho. Ubabamkhulu wayesipha imali yokungena ebhayisikobho. Ebhayisikobho sasiya ntambama. Sasingayi ebusuku. Ebusuku sasesaba. Sasesaba izigebengu. Zikhona izigebengu eDurban.

Manje mina angisafundi eDurban. Angisahlali nobabamkhulu nogogo eDurban. Sengihlala nabazali bami eJohannesburg. Sengifunda esikoleni esikhulu eGoli.

Ngasuka eDurban ngonyaka odlule ngoba umama wayegula. Umama wayesesibhedlela. Esibhedlela odokotela babe-

*nika umama umuthi. Babemnika umuthi ekuseni nasemini nasebusuku. Wayelala embhedeni sonke isikhathi, emini nasebusuku. Onesi babenika umama ukudla embhedeni. Umama wayedla ukudla ngokhezo. Wayengadli ngomese nemfologo. Umama wayethanda ukulala esibhedlela ngoba wayefuna ukuphila. Umama wahlala esibhedlela izinyanga ezine. Usekhaya manje. Usephilile.*

*bhukuda* (swim)

## 20. NGANGISEBENZA EGOLI

*Mina ngangisebenza eGoli. Ngangisebenza efekthri· Efekthri sasiqala umsebenzi ekuseni kakhulu. Sasiqala ngo-7· Sasisebenza ngoMsombuluko nangoLwesibili nangoLwesithathu nangoLwesine nangoLwesihlanu. Sasingasebenzi ngoMgqibelo. Sasingasebenzi futhi ngeSonto.*

*NgoMgqibelo sasiphumula. Sasigeza izingubo zethu. Sasiya futhi edolobheni ezitolo. Sasithenga ngoMgqibelo kuphela. Ngezinsuku ezinye sasingathengi. NgoMgqibelo sasivakasha futhi. Sasivakashela izihlobo zethu.*

*Ngangiya emsebenzini ngesitimela. Ngangithenga ithikithi lenyanga. Ithikithi lenyanga lalibiza amarandi amabili. Ngangihlala kude nendawo yomsebenzi.*

*NgeSonto ngangithanda ukuya esontweni. Abazali bami babengifundisile ukuthanda isonto. Esontweni ngangingayi ngesitimela. Ngangihamba ngezinyawo. NgeSonto ngangingagqoki izingubo zomsebenzi. Ngangigqoka ezinye izingubo. Ngangingagqoki izicathulo zomsebenzi. Ngangigqoka ezinye izicathulo.*

*Indlu yeSonto yayinezindonga ezinde. Yayinamafasitele amakhulu amaningi. Esontweni kwakukhona izihlalo eziningi. Lapha esontweni kwakuza abantu abaningi. Bonke abantu babehlala ezihlalweni. Babebheka phambili. Babebheka umfundisi. Umfundisi wayema ngaphambili. Wayebheka abantu. Umfundisi wayegqoka izingubo ezinde ezimhlophe noma ezimnyama.*

*Sonke sasiphatha amaculo ethu. Sasivula amaculo ethu sicule. Uma sicula sasisukuma. Sasima ngezinyawo. Uma singaculi sasihlala phansi. Uma sithandaza sasiguqa ngamadolo. Umfundisi wayevula iBhayibheli. Wayefunda amazwi eBhayibhelini. Umfundisi wayeshumayela. Wayesitshela ngoNkulunkulu nangoJesu. Isonto lalingena ngo*-11 *ekuseni. Laliphuma ngo*-12.15.

*Angisasebenzi manje eGoli. Sengihlala ekhaya.*

*efekthri* (at a factory)

## 1. MY CAT

I have a cat. I have a pretty little cat. My cat is black. My cat's name is Pussy. Pussy is small; she is not big.

Pussy has lovely hair. Pussy has soft hair. She has two eyes. She has green/blue eyes. She has two ears. Moreover Pussy has teeth. She has sharp teeth. Pussy has a red tongue. She has four legs. She has sharp claws. She has whiskers. She has a long tail.

Pussy likes milk very much. She likes to drink milk. In the morning I give Pussy her milk. Pussy has her own small dish. Mother bought Pussy's dish in town. Pussy likes her dish very much. Pussy's dish is kept in the kitchen. I pour Pussy's milk into her dish.

Pussy also likes meat. Pussy eats meat during the day and at night. Mother does not cook Pussy's meat. Pussy likes raw meat. Pussy likes hunting. She likes to hunt at night. She hunts mice. Pussy likes mice very much. She eats mice. Pussy springs when she sees a mouse. She catches the mice with her sharp claws. Mice fear Pussy very much. Mice run away when they see Pussy. They go into their holes. They hide in their holes.

Pussy also likes to catch birds. Pussy eats birds. Birds fly away when they see Pussy. Birds, like mice, fear Pussy. Pussy does not eat mother's chickens. Close to our home there is a forest. Pussy likes to go into the forest. She likes to hunt birds in the forest.

Pussy likes to play very much. She likes to play with wool. She also likes to play with a ball.

Pussy likes to lie down near a stove. She also likes to sleep on a chair and on a bed. Pussy climbs onto a chair or a bed. Sometimes Pussy lies down under a table.

Pussy fears dogs very much. When she sees dogs she runs away.

## 2. OUR DOG

At home there is a dog. Our dog is big. Our dog's name is Bull. Father bought Bull in town. Father bought Bull last year. Father paid R7,00.

All the people fear Bull because he is vicious. Bull barks during the day. He also barks at night. Bull has a big voice. He guards the home day and night. He drives the thieves away day and night.

Bull has a pretty colour. Bull is brown. Father likes brown dogs. He does not like black dogs. Brown dogs look nice.

Bull has a big head. He has two ears. He has two eyes. Bull has a nose. Bull's nose is always cold. He has a big mouth. His mouth is black. Inside Bull's mouth there are teeth. His teeth are long and big. People fear Bull's teeth. They fear his big voice. They fear his big black mouth. Bull has four legs. He has one tail. Bull has a long tail. Father does not like to shorten a dog's tail. Bull has hair. His hair is not like that of a cat. A cat's hair is soft. Bull's hair is not soft. Bull has large paws. Like a cat he has claws but Bull's claws are not like those of a cat. A cat's claws are much sharper. Bull's claws are not so sharp.

Bull does not like to move slowly. He likes to run. When the sun is hot Bull likes to hang out his tongue. Bull likes to drink water very much.

Bull has his own kennel. He has a wooden kennel. Inside Bull's kennel there is a sack. Bull likes his kennel very much. He likes his sack very much. He lies on his sack. Bull is not afraid of rain because he has a kennel. He is not afraid of cold in winter because he sleeps in his kennel.

Bull likes meat and bones very much. Bull eats meat daily. Bull likes to crunch bones very much.

Bull likes to ride in Father's car. He sits inside with Father. Bull likes a car but he does not like to ride on a wagon.

## 3. FOWLS

Many people like to keep fowls. Fowls are domestic birds. There are many breeds of fowls. There are white fowls, black fowls and red fowls. There are other breeds as well. Some people like to keep white fowls. Other people like to keep red fowls and yet others like to keep black fowls.

There are cocks and hens. Hens lay eggs. Cocks do not lay eggs. Some people keep fowls in order to sell them. They keep many fowls. Other people keep fowls because they want to sell eggs. Some people keep fowls for their meat. Many people like chicken. Many people like eggs. Women use eggs for baking. White fowls lay many eggs. They do not go broody. They lay eggs only. Red fowls and black fowls have more meat.

Fowls lay eggs. They lay eggs in nests. A hen makes a nest. It lays eggs in its nest. When a hen stops laying, it sits on its eggs. It sits on the eggs day and night. During the day it leaves its nest for a short while. At night it does not leave the nest. It sits on the eggs all the time. The hen warms the eggs with its body. Its body is warm. The hen sits on the eggs for three weeks and then chicks appear. Chicks are the babies of a fowl. We call one baby a chick. Chicks come out of the eggs.

Fowls eat mealies, corn and other food. They drink a lot of water. A fowl picks up food with its beak. A fowl has no teeth. It does not chew.

A fowl has two legs. It has no hands. It has feathers like a bird. A fowl cannot fly.

Fowls are troublesome in the garden. They damage flowers. They destroy cabbages and other vegetables. Fowls require a fowl house (run). They give no trouble if they are kept in their house.

## 4. OUR GARDEN

We like flowers very much. All of us at home like flowers. Mother likes flowers very much. Father also is like Mother; he likes flowers very much. I also like flowers very much. My brothers and sisters also like flowers very much. We all like flowers because they are pretty. They decorate the home.

Mother buys flower seed in town. In summer Mother plants summer flowers. In winter Mother plants winter flowers. Our garden is not big. Mother adds manure in the flower garden. Mother buys manure from the farmer. Some flowers require a good application of manure but others do not require very much. Some flowers require much water but others do not want a lot of water. Some flowers like sunshine but others like the shade. The sun is very hot in summer but in winter it is not so hot.

Sipho works at my home. He digs Mother's garden. Sipho commences work at 8 a.m. He rests at midday at 1.00. He starts work again at 2 p.m. In the afternoon Sipho stops work at 5 p.m.

Sipho is a very good worker. Sipho is a young boy. Mother likes Sipho because he is diligent; he is not lazy. Mother does not like a lazy boy. Sipho digs the garden with a spade or with a garden fork. At home there is a spade and a garden fork. There is also a rake. Sipho rakes the garden with a rake. Sipho is now able to plant flowers. Mother shows him how to do it. Sipho is good because he likes to learn.

Mother does not like weeds in the garden. Sipho is like Mother in that respect. He too does not want weeds in his garden. Sipho removes the weeds from the garden. He weeds the garden. He removes the weeds with his hands or with a garden fork. There is a small garden fork for removing weeds.

In summer we do not experience difficulty because rain is plentiful. Rain is plentiful in our area. In summer Sipho does not water the garden every day. In winter there is no rain. Sipho waters the garden daily because flowers need water. Flowers perish if they do not get water. Sipho uses a hosepipe for watering. There is a hosepipe at home.

It is a long hosepipe. It reaches the garden easily. Sipho attaches the hosepipe to the tap. At home there is also a watering can. Sometimes Sipho uses a can for watering.

Mother's flowers bloom in summer but others bloom in winter. Summer flowers bloom in summer. Winter flowers bloom in winter. Some flowers are red, others white, and others have various pretty colours. Mother's garden is pretty in summer and winter. Mother likes to decorate the house with her flowers. Mother picks flowers from her garden. She arranges the flowers in the vases. Mother does not like to buy flowers in town. Flowers are expensive in town. They cost a lot of money.

## 5. WATER

All living things need water. People need water. Animals need water. Grass needs water. Trees need water. Birds need water. Some animals live in the water.

The sea has a lot of water. Sea water is salty because it contains much salt. River water flows into the sea. There are big rivers and small rivers. Some rivers are navigable.

We wash with water. We wash our bodies. We also wash our clothes. We scrub our homes with water. We use water for cooking our food. We use it for washing dirty dishes and dirty pots. We use it for watering our gardens. We use water for building our houses. We use it for mixing mortar.

A steam engine takes in a lot of water. It uses a lot of water. An electric engine does not use water. Many motor cars use water but motor cycles do not use water.

In some areas water is used for making electricity. There are buildings which house engines for making electricity.

In some areas there are waterfalls. Water descends from above. It falls to a great depth. It makes a lot of noise as it falls. Many people like to watch waterfalls. They like to see water falling from above. They like to take photographs of waterfalls.

Many people like to swim in the water. They like to swim in rivers. Others like to swim at sea. Sometimes it rains heavily. The rivers become flooded. A river in flood is very dangerous. It is likely to kill people and animals. Sometimes bridges are damaged, roads are damaged, and railway lines are damaged.

In big towns there are large dams. These dams contain a lot of water. The dams are built out of town. The water is led from the dams in large pipes. The water flows through the pipes into the town. People in town drink this water; they use this water. Chemicals are added to the water in the dams. The chemicals destroy all that may be dangerous in the water.

## 6. AT SCHOOL

We are learners. We learn at school. Our school is big. At our school there are boys and girls. Our school is a co-educational school. There are many boys and there are many girls. Our school has many teachers.

Mother wakes us up in the morning. We do not like to get up very early in the morning. We like to sleep. We like sleep. We wash with warm water. We are afraid of washing with cold water. Father does not like to wash with hot water. He likes to wash with cold water.

Everyday we wash our bodies. We wash with water and soap. Everyday we put on clean clothes. We do not wear dirty clothes. In the morning we eat porridge with milk. Sometimes we eat Corn Flakes or Jungle Oats. Moreover we eat eggs and bread in the morning.

We go to school on Mondays, Tuesdays, Wednesdays, Thursdays and Fridays. We do not go to school on Saturdays and on Sundays. When we go to school we cycle. We all have bicycles. We put our books into bags. We all have bags for books. When it is raining we put on raincoats. We all have raincoats. Sometimes Father takes us to school in his car. Father has a beautiful car. Father drives his car. Mother can also drive.

At our school many children cycle. Boys cycle and girls cycle. Some children do not cycle. They go by bus. Others go to school by car. They are brought by their parents.

Our school starts at 8.30 a.m. It stops at 3.00 p.m. At school we learn many subjects. We like our school because we play many games. We play basket ball, tennis, cricket, rugby and soccer. Sometimes we play against other schools.

At our school there are pretty flower gardens. The gardens decorate our school. The flowers have many pretty colours. Also there are pretty green trees and beautiful green grass.

## 7. SPORT

Many people like sport. We also like sport very much. Some people like to play sport. Others like to watch sport. There are many kinds of games. There are games for men and games for women. Young boys like to play soccer very much. They like to kick a football. Young men also like to play soccer very much. They use football boots for kicking the ball. Women do not like to play football.

Some men like to play rugby. A rugby ball is not like a soccer ball. A rugby ball is handled but a soccer ball is not handled. It is kicked. Men play rugby but women do not like to play rugby.

Other people like to play cricket. Men and women play cricket. Men play by themselves and women play by themselves. Aged people do not play cricket. They are unable to run. Moreover they tire easily.

Many people like to play tennis. Men and women like to play tennis very much. Many old people also like to play tennis. Those who play tennis wear white shoes. They put on white socks. They put on white clothes. They wear white caps. A tennis ball is not like a soccer ball. Moreover it is not like a rugby ball. It is not like a cricket ball. A tennis ball is small and light. It is played with a racquet.

Many white people like to play golf. Golf is played in a big, wide area. It is played by men and women. A golf ball is not like a tennis ball. A golf ball is smaller than a tennis ball. A golf ball is hard. It is played with golf sticks.

Some aged people do not like to play tennis, moreover they do not like to play golf. They like to play bowls. People who play bowls put on white clothes.

There are also games which are played indoors. I like to play cricket and tennis.

## 8. HOSPITAL

In many towns there are hospitals. There are big and small hospitals. Hospitals are places for sick people. There are male and female patients. There are old people and children.

In a hospital there are many doctors. There are male and female doctors. There are many nurses. There are many wards with beds. Patients lie on beds. There are male wards. There are also female wards. Male patients are by themselves. Female patients are by themselves in their wards. Patients are attended to by nurses.

In a hospital there is a place for examining patients. Doctors first examine a patient. A person who is not very ill is not admitted to hospital. He goes back home. He is only given medicine. A person who is very ill does not go back home. He is admitted. He removes his clothes and puts on hospital clothes. A male patient goes to the male ward and a female patient goes to the female ward. Surgical cases are kept by themselves and medical cases are kept by themselves. Maternity cases have their own place.

There are hospitals for T.B. patients. People suffering from T.B. are kept away from others. They do not mix with other patients. They have their own hospitals. There are also hospitals for lepers. Lepers are also kept by themselves. They do not mix with other patients.

There are many workers in hospital. There are cooks, there are those who bring food to the patients, there are those who wash dishes. There are sweepers and those who do laundry. There are others who attend to the premises. Those who attend to the premises sweep and prepare the gardens.

Many people recover in hospital but others die. In some places there are no hospitals. There are clinics only. There are no inpatients at clinics. There are no beds at a clinic. Clinics work only during the day. They do not work at night. At a clinic people receive medicine. Those who are injured are bandaged. Some women bring their children to the clinic. A clinic helps very much.

## 9. BUTCHERIES

There are butcheries in many areas. Butcheries are places of work. There are European, African and Indian owned butcheries. Meat is sold at a butchery. At a butchery they sell beef, mutton, pork, chicken, eggs and fish. Moreover we get polony and sausages.

Pork is very expensive. Mutton is also very expensive. Beef is not so expensive. Chicken is very expensive. Sometimes butcheries sell ducks and turkeys.

At a butchery meat is weighed on a scale. All butcheries have scales. A scale determines weight. Meat is cut and placed on a scale. There are long big tables at a butchery. There are long sharp butcher's knives. Moreover they use sharp choppers. They use sharp saws. Some butcheries have electric saws for cutting meat. An electric saw is very sharp. It cuts flesh and bone.

Butcheries open very early in the morning. Some butcheries open at 4 a.m. Many butcheries close at 1 p.m. or 2 p.m. Others close much later.

Flies are not wanted at a butchery. Flies are dirty. They carry dirt and disease germs. Tables at a butchery are cleaned everyday. They are washed with soap and water. People do not like to buy meat at dirty butcheries with many flies. They want clean butcheries.

At some butcheries there are big refrigerators. Refrigerators are cold. They stop meat from going bad. Refrigerators are expensive. They cost a lot of money but they are very useful. Refrigerators work with electricity.

Cattle are not slaughtered at the butchery. Sheep and pigs are not slaughtered at the butchery. Cattle, sheep and pigs are all slaughtered at the abattoir. There are large meat vans (lorries). Meat is fetched from the abattoir in vans.

## 10. BIRDS

Birds are found in many places. They are found in forests, mountains, rivers, at sea and even at our homes.

There are many varieties of birds. There are big and small birds. Birds have a variety of colours. Some have very pretty colours. They have pretty plumes. Some birds sing sweetly. Others do not sing sweetly.

Birds build nests. Some birds make ugly looking nests. A dove makes an ugly nest. Other birds make pretty nests. A swallow uses mud for making a nest. It carries the mud with its beak. A swallow builds a very pretty nest. Some birds build their nests on trees. Others make their nests in the grass on the ground. Others make their nests at our homes. A swallow likes to build its nest in the verandah.

Birds lay eggs in their nests. Birds sit on eggs like fowls. From the eggs emerge the young ones. We call the young ones of a bird fledglings. One young one is called a fledgling. The young of fowls are called chickens. One young one of a fowl is a chicken.

Birds sleep at night, but the owl does not. The owl sleeps during the day. It wakes up at night and hunts. It searches for food. An owl likes to eat mice.

Some birds are very troublesome. Doves destroy grain in the fields. The hawk eats chickens. Crows do damage to young lambs. Crows also give trouble in the fields. They dig up mealies planted in the fields. Farmers do not like crows. Other birds are very useful. Owls eat mice. Vultures are scavengers. The secretary bird devours snakes. Cattle egrets eat ticks.

Birds fly. They fly with their wings. They have sharp eyes. Their eyes can see a long way off. Some birds are afraid of cold. In winter they migrate to other countries.

They return in summer. We do not see swallows in winter because they migrate. They are afraid of the cold in winter. They return in summer. Cattle egrets are also afraid of cold. We do not see them in winter.

In big towns there is a place for animals and birds. One sees many birds there. One observes many varieties of birds.

## 11. AN AEROPLANE

We are very fortunate. In our time there are many forms of transport. We travel easily. There are motor cars. There are trains. There are ships. There are also aeroplanes. In towns there are numerous cars. Cars travel on roads. Trains run on rails. Ships sail at sea in the water. Aeroplanes move high up in the sky. Aeroplanes fly. In the air an aeroplane looks like a bird.

Aeroplanes are very fast. They cover long distances in a short time. Cars use petrol. Aeroplanes also use petrol. Aeroplanes have pilots. There are seats for passengers. Inside an aeroplane looks like a pretty room.

Passengers are served with meals in the air. They read their books in the air. They read their newspapers in the air. They smoke up in the air. They look out through the windows. Aeroplanes fly above the clouds. People sleep up in the air.

There are small and large aeroplanes. Large aircraft carry many passengers. Aeroplanes go from our country to other countries. There are aeroplanes which carry passengers. An aeroplane carries passengers and their luggage. People travelling by air do not carry very heavy luggage. There are also war planes. War planes are very fast.

Some people like to travel by aeroplane because it is fast. They like to fly in the air like a bird. They like to travel quickly. Up in the air they like to look below. They like to watch forests far below. They like to watch big towns and small towns far below. They like to watch the mountains far below. They like to look at the clouds under them. Clouds look like wool.

Other people do not like to go by plane. They are afraid. They are afraid of crashing. They are afraid of death. They are afraid of falling from the sky above. They like to travel by car or by train or by boat.

Travelling by air is expensive. An air ticket costs a lot of money.

## 12. ON THE FARM

Grandfather lives on a farm. A farm is not like a town. There are not many cars on the farm. There are not many motor cycles on the farm. There are not many people on the farm as in town. On the farm there are not many butcheries as in town. Cars are not many, (and) motor cycles are not many (and) people are not many (and) shops are not many (and) butcheries are not many.

At my grandfather's place there are many cattle. He keeps dairy cattle. Grandfather's cattle have much milk. His cows are milked in the morning and in the afternoon. There is a cattle kraal. Grandfather's cows have big udders. They have long teats.

Milk is poured into milk cans. Grandfather has many cans. There are big cans and small cans. Grandfather has many people on his farm. Some people milk, others plough. Some cook, others prepare the house. Yet others do other chores. Grandfather also keeps horses, pigs and sheep. Grandfather does not keep goats. He does not like goats. Grandfather says goats are troublesome. We like to ride Grandfather's horses. Grandfather's horses are tame. We do not fear falling down. We know how to saddle a horse. We take the bridle first and then place the saddle on the back of the horse. We go on horseback to the fields or to the river or to the forest.

Horses eat grass, maize and crushed mealies. Grandfather's horses are fat.

Grandfather has a big wagon. He carries bags with his wagon. Grandfather pulls his wagon with oxen. He has fine looking brown oxen. Grandfather does not cultivate his lands with oxen. He ploughs with a tractor. There are now tractors at Grandfather's farm. A tractor ploughs quicker than oxen. It is not like oxen. Grandfather's tractors put on lights at night. Grandfather likes to work even at night.

In the fields Grandfather plants maize, kaffir corn, wheat, potatoes and beans. He also likes to plant peanuts.

Grandfather keeps many fowls. He rears white, red and black fowls. Grandfather sells eggs. He sends eggs to market. Some of the eggs he sends to hotels. Grandfather sends live fowls to market. Other live fowls he sends to hotels. Grandfather also sends dressed fowls to market and to hotels. Grandfather gets a lot of money from his fowls.

Grandfather also keeps pigs. He keeps white pigs. He likes white pigs very much. Grandfather sells his pigs in town. He gets a lot of money from his pigs. Many people like pork. Grandfather rears sheep for wool. He shears wool. Wool fetches a lot of money.

At grandfather's place there are many fruit trees.

There are many varieties of fruit. In summer we eat a lot of fruit at grandfather's place. Grandfather sells some of his fruit at market.

## 13. SNAKES

In our country there are many snakes. There are big snakes and small snakes. There are long and short snakes. Snakes have no legs. They crawl on their bellies. All snakes crawl on their bellies.

A snake has a mouth. It has eyes. It has a tongue. It has a tail. The tongue of a snake is not like that of other animals. It is forked. A snake does not blink.

Some snakes live in holes. Other snakes live among stones. Some snakes live in trees in the forests. Other snakes like grass.

Some snakes are poisonous. People fear poisonous snakes. Sometimes snakes kill people. At other times snakes kill animals. Many snakes like eating frogs and mice. Poison comes out through an opening in the fangs.

In our country there are mambas. There are black and green mambas. All people fear mambas very much. A mamba is vicious. It kills people and animals. A mamba is very poisonous. A person dies quickly and animals also die quickly. In some areas mambas close paths (i.e. frighten people away). They stop people from using those paths.

In a certain area there was a vicious mamba. This mamba killed people and animals. All the people were afraid to kill it. It was killed by a brave woman. She cooked pumpkin porridge. She carried the hot porridge on her head. She walked to the place where the mamba was. The mamba saw the woman. It struck the woman on the head thereby plunging its head into the hot porridge. The mamba died there. People were very happy. They thanked that woman.

In our country there are also pythons. A python is a big snake. It has large teeth. A python is not poisonous. It does not poison people and animals. It swallows people and animals. The jaws of a snake can be extended.

Snakes fear cold in winter. In winter they hibernate because of the cold. They come out in summer. They come out very hungry and very vicious. Snakes cast off the skin every year. They cast off the old skin.

## 14. WINTER

Many people like summer. They do not like winter. They fear the cold in winter. Other people like winter. They do not like summer. They fear the heat in summer. In winter the sun is not very hot. In some places there is frost. Grass wears a white blanket (of frost). Sometimes the taps do not open in the mornings. The water in the taps turns into ice.

In some places it snows in winter. On the mountains there lies a lot of snow. The trees on the mountains wear a white dress and the stones wear a white dress. Snow falls on mountains, and on trees and on stones. Many animals and birds die. Sometimes even people die.

People like fire in winter. They like to bask in the fire. Also they like hot food because they feel cold. In winter people like to wear warm clothes. They put on jerseys and overcoats. They also wear warm stockings.

Many people fall ill in winter. They suffer from colds. Children, old men and old women cough. Doctors work hard in winter and hospitals become full.

In some places farmers suffer hardship in winter. They suffer because there is no grass for their stock. Their cattle and their sheep starve. They become emaciated. Farmers also suffer because water is scarce. Some farmers build dams. In summer when there are rains, water runs into the dams. A lot of water enters the dams. They (farmers) get a lot of water. In winter they suffer no hardship because there is a lot of water. Some rivers dry up in winter.

In winter the danger of fire is considerable because grass is dry. Sometimes pastures get burnt. At other times forests get burnt. Even homes of people get burnt in winter. Fire spreads easily because there is a lot of wind in winter. The wind blows and there is also a lot of dust in winter.

Many trees do not look attractive in winter. They look ugly. They do not look attractive because the leaves fall. The leaves fall onto the ground. Even the grass changes its colour in winter. It dries up and looks parched. But in some areas trees remain green in winter. Leaves do not fall off. Even the grass does not get parched.

## 15. WE HAD GONE TO THE CINEMA

Day before yesterday we had gone to the cinema. We had gone with my elder brother, my younger sister, my mother and my father. All of us at home like to go to the cinema. The cinema is in town. We go by car to the cinema. We live far from town.

At the cinema there were many people. There were married men and married women. There were young men and young girls. Many children do not go to the cinema at night. We go to the cinema at night because we work during the day. All of us are working. Father works in town, (and) mother works in town, (and) my brother works in town and I also work in town. My younger sister also works in town.

At the cinema we see pictures which speak. Sometimes we see very good films. Some people like to go to the cinema daily. They are not selective. We do not go daily. We choose the pictures we see. We only watch good pictures. Children like pictures of animals which speak and pictures of people with guns. Boys like guns and horses.

Some people are a nuisance at the cinema. They like to chat. They make noise. This is bad because we do not hear the dialogue of the film. Other people smoke. The hall becomes full of tobacco smoke. We do not like tobacco smoke. We cough when there is tobacco smoke.

We pay an admission fee at the cinema. Father likes to buy sweets but mother does not like sweets. Mother likes a cool drink.

The show starts at 8.00 p.m. Sometimes it stops at 10.00 p.m. Some pictures are long. They take a long time. Day before yesterday the show stopped at 10.45 p.m. because we were watching a long film. We came back with uncle. Uncle had gone by bus. Uncle has no car.

## 16. TOMORROW I AM GOING AWAY

Tomorrow I am going away. I am going to Johannesburg. I am on a visit. I shall go by train. I shall travel in an electric train. An electric train is fast. I do not like a train pulled by a steam engine. I hate its smoke. I shall travel by myself. I shall not go with Father or Mother or my sister. Father is working. Mother is working. My sister is still at school. I am a worker but this is my period of rest.

My elder brother lives in Johannesburg. He lives there with his wife and children. My brother has three children. There is one boy and two girls. My brother has his own house in Johannesburg. His house is big and beautiful. It has many rooms.

The train departs from our station at 5.00 p.m. It gets to Johannesburg at 8.00 a.m. I shall sleep on the train. We live above the railway station. The railway station is near. I shall walk to the station. I shall not go by taxi nor by bus.

I have already purchased the ticket. I bought it this morning. I bought it at the station. I bought a second class ticket. A first class ticket is expensive. It costs a lot of money. My ticket cost R7,80. I paid R7,80.

I shall stay one month in Johannesburg. I shall stay at my elder brother's place. I shall not stay at a hotel. Johannesburg hotels are expensive. One pays a lot of money. My brother works in Johannesburg. He works at a shoe shop. He sells shoes.

In the train there are sleeping berths. In a first class compartment there are four sleeping berths only. In a second class compartment there are six berths. On the train one also gets bedding. If one wants bedding one pays 65c.

Meals are also served on the train. Meals are expensive on the train. They cost a lot of money. I shall not buy food on the train. I shall buy tea only. I do not like to eat on the train.

On the train there is a ticket examiner (guard). A ticket examiner wears black clothes. He puts on a black cap. He wears black shoes. The ticket examiner checks tickets on the train.

## 17. GRANDFATHER IS COMING

Mother is preparing the home. She is preparing it because Grandfather will be coming tomorrow. Grandfather will arrive at noon in his car. Grandfather lives on his farm. He has a big farm. Grandfather will stay one week only and then return to the farm. Grandfather has come to buy stuff for his farm. He will buy ploughs. He also wants to buy a tractor. Grandfather will not buy a car bacause he has a new car. Grandfather bought a new car last year.

Grandfather will come with Grandmother. Grandmother likes to come to town. Grandmother likes to see us. Grandmother also likes to look at dresses, hats and shoes at the shops. Grandmother will not stay one week like Grandfather. She will stay a whole month. Grandfather will return to the farm but Grandmother will remain. Grandfather will go back by himself. Grandfather will come again next month. He will fetch Grandmother.

Grandmother wants to go with us next month. She wants us to ride horses on the farm. She wants us to drink a lot of milk on the farm. She wants us to eat a lot of fruit on the farm. She wants us to see Grandfather's cattle and horses. We shall not go with Grandmother because we are at school. We shall visit Grandmother and Grandfather in winter in July.

Tomorrow is Tuesday. On Wednesday Grandfather will see the tractors and the ploughs. On Thursday he will buy seed. He wants a lot of seed because his farm is big. His fields are big. On Friday Grandfather will visit an eye specialist. Grandfather's eyes are sore. He wants medicine and spectacles from the doctor. Grandfather has no spectacles. He will be using spectacles for the first time. Grandmother does not use spectacles. Her eyes do not give trouble.

On Saturday Grandfather wants to watch soccer. Grandfather likes sport very much. On the farm there are not many games. On Saturday evening he will stay at home. He will not go to the cinema. Grandfather does not like to go to the cinema. He does not like going to the cinema because he fears tobacco smoke.

On Sunday we shall go to Church with Grandfather. We shall go in his new car. We are happy because we shall go in Grandfather's new car. We shall not go in Father's old car.

On Monday Grandfather will return home on the farm. We shall see him again next month.

## 18. YESTERDAY

Yesterday I had gone to town. I had gone on horseback. I like riding. My sister also likes riding. Father has four horses. Father's horses are very pretty. At home there are two brown horses and two black horses. Father's horses are tame.

I saw many people in town. I saw men and women. I saw old people and young people. Some people were walking in the street. Other people were inside the shops. People were making purchases at the shops. They were buying blankets. They are afraid of the cold in winter. Others were buying trousers, shirts, shoes and hats. Yet others were buying food. I bought two shirts and socks. I bought the shirts for R7,00. I bought socks for one rand.

I also went to the butchery. At the butchery I bought pork, mutton, fish and sausages. Father does not like pork. He does not like mutton either. He likes fish. Mother likes pork very much.

At the butchery there was someone in front of me. He too was buying meat. He bought pork only. He did not buy mutton. He did not buy fish. He did not buy sausages. I bought after him. There were other people behind me.

At the Post Office I posted Father's letters and Mother's letters. Father's letters were going to Pretoria. Mother's letters were going to Durban. At the Post Office I also purchased stamps. I bought twenty four stamps. I paid 24c. I also bought two postal orders. I bought a postal order for R3 and another for 85c. At the Post Office there were many people in front of me and behind.

I did not go to the Railway Station. I did not want anything at the Ststion. I did not want to purchase a ticket. I did not go to the bank either. I did not want to bank any money. I did not want to withdraw money from the bank.

I went to town in the morning at 9.00 a.m. I returned in the afternoon at 2.00 p.m. I was by myself. My sister did not go with me. She remained at home. She was helping Mother.

## 19. I WAS LIVING IN DURBAN

I was living in Durban. I used to get up very early in the morning. In the morning I washed. I washed with cold water but in winter I washed with hot water. I went to school by bicycle. I did not go by car nor did I go by bus. I put my books in my book case. I had a very fine case for carrying books. I returned from school in the afternoon. I had a rain coat. When it was raining I put on my rain coat.

My cousin also attended school. He went to school in Durban. He got up very early in the morning. He washed with cold water but in winter he washed with hot water. My cousin went to school by bicycle. He did not go by car nor did he go by bus. My cousin also carried his books in a case. He had a pretty case for carrying his books.

Both of us lived at Grandfather's home. Grandfather had a big house in Durban. Grandfather lived with Grandmother in Durban. I liked Durban very much. My cousin also liked Durban very much. We liked looking at articles at the show windows. We looked at trousers, shirts, hats and shoes. We also liked to look at football boots and cricket boots and at tennis racquets. At school we liked to play sport. Both of us played tennis and cricket but we did not like to play rugby.

In Durban we liked to go by ricksha. The ricksha pullers dressed smartly. On their heads they wore horns. We liked going by ricksha to the seaside. We liked to watch others swimming. We also liked to swim. We carried our bathing costumes. We also liked to lie down on the sand.

In Durban there are many cinemas. We went to the cinema regularly. Grandfather gave us money to pay at the cinema. We went to the cinema in the afternoon. We did not go at night. We were afraid to go at night. We were afraid of gangsters. There are gangsters in Durban.

I no longer attend school in Durban. I no longer live with Grandfather and Grandmother in Durban. I now live with my parents in Johannesburg. I now go to a big school in Johannesburg.

I left Durban last year because Mother was ill. Mother was in hospital. In hospital the doctors gave mother medicine. They gave her medicine in the morning, at noon and at night. She kept in bed all the time day and night. Nurses gave mother food in bed. Mother used a spoon for eating. She did not use a knife and fork. Mother liked to stay in hospital because she wanted to get well. Mother remained in hospital for four months. She is at home now. She has now recovered.

## 20. I USED TO WORK IN JOHANNESBURG

I used to work in Johannesburg. I used to work at a factory. At the factory we used to commence work very early. We used to start at 7 o'clock. We worked on Monday and on Tuesday and on Wednesday and on Thursday and on Friday. We did not work on Saturday and on Sunday.

On Saturday we rested. We washed our clothes. We also went to the shops in town. We made our purchases on Saturday only. We made no purchases on other days. On Saturday we also visited. We visited our friends.

I went to work by train. I used to buy a monthly ticket. A monthly ticket cost R2,00. I lived far from the place of work.

On Sunday I liked to go to Church. My parents had taught me love for worship. I did not go to Church by train. I used to walk there. On Sunday I did not put on my working clothes. I put on other clothes. I did not wear working shoes. I put on other shoes.

The Church house had high walls. It had many big windows. In Church there were many pews. Many people came to Church. All people sat on the pews. They faced to the front. They faced the Priest. The Priest stood in front. He faced the congregation. The Priest wore long white or black robes.

We all carried our hymn books. We opened our hymn books and sang. We stood up when we were singing. We stood on our feet. When we were not singing we sat down.

We knelt on our knees when we were praying. The Priest opened the Bible. He read texts from the Bible. The Priest preached. He told us about God and about Jesus Christ. The service started at 11.00 a.m. and came out at 12.15 p.m.

I no longer work in Johannesburg. I now stay at home.